D1466786

# FEAGLER'S
# CLEVELAND

# FEAGLER'S CLEVELAND

*Dick Feagler*

*Richard J. Osborne*
*Edward J. Walsh*
Editors

GRAY & COMPANY, PUBLISHERS
CLEVELAND

GRAY & COMPANY, PUBLISHERS
1588 E. 40th Street
Cleveland, Ohio 44103-2302
info@grayco.com

Library of Congress Cataloging-in-Publication Data

Feagler, Dick, 1938–
Feagler's Cleveland / by Dick Feagler.
     p.   cm.
1. Cleveland (Ohio)—Social life and customs—Anecdotes.
2. Feagler, Dick, 1938– —Anecdotes.  I. Title.
F499.C65F43  1996
977.1'32043'092—dc20                          96-35634


ISBN 1-886228-09-4 *hc*
ISBN 1-886228-10-8 *sc*
Printed in the United States of America
10  9  8  7  6  5  4  3  2

*First edition*

This book is gratefully dedicated to its readers,
and especially to those who've read these columns once before.

# Contents

# Editors' Preface

We knew Dick Feagler long before we met him. As natives of Cleveland, we got to know him the same way most of you did—by reading his enormously popular column in the *Cleveland Press*.

Even back then, he already was the city's star columnist. And why not? He had wit. He had insight. He had style. And he captured the essence of the city and put it into words like no one else.

He still does.

Twenty-five years later, the evening newspaper where we first discovered Dick Feagler is only a footnote in the 200-year history of Cleveland. Feagler, though, remains an institution.

Younger people may first have gotten to know him through his second life as a television commentator, anchorman, and chief interrogator. Or through one of his many newspaper venues after the *Press*—the *Beacon Journal* in Akron, the *Chronicle-Telegram* in Elyria, the *Journal* (now the *Morning Journal*) in Lorain, the *News-Herald* in Willoughby, or, of course, the *Plain Dealer*, where he now occupies the coveted upper-left-hand corner of Page 2—the spot reserved for the star.

Wherever they have appeared, his columns consistently have set a standard of excellence. Not just for his hometown, but for that elite group of writers in metropolitan areas throughout the country who lay claim to the envied title of "columnist."

Most of them can't touch Feagler. That is why, over a period of time, we became so deeply puzzled by a simple question: Why hasn't anyone published a collection of Dick Feagler's columns?

By the time we started asking the question, Dick had become a great friend and colleague. So we asked the question of the man himself. Though he seldom is lost for words, and equally seldom lost for explanations of why things are the way they are, his answer amounted to something like: "Dunno."

Which is another way of saying that he never quite got around to doing it. And it appeared he never would. So we decided to do it ourselves. You are holding the result.

It was and is our conviction that if Dick Feagler had written columns for his daily bread in, say, New York or Chicago or Los Angeles, by now several collections of his work would have been published in book form. It is high time, we think, that Cleveland showed off its star. He is, after all, an unsurpassed craftsman. He also happens to have provided Cleveland with a true, always entertaining, and often moving chronicle of its life in this last third of the 20th century.

He has done for Cleveland what other really gifted columnists have done for their cities—Runyon for New York, Royko for Chicago, Murray for Los Angeles. Now, finally, the man who arguably is the finest writer ever to string sentences into columns about Cleveland has his book. And we—all of us who enjoy his work and who are moved and inspired and entertained by it—do too.

We have our book because there were so many others who believed sincerely that it was a must-do project for Cleveland. Among them:

Nancy McArthur, who spent endless hours in the *Cleveland Press* archives at Cleveland State University, where she transposed early Feagler columns from microfilm to printed page. Tim Mueller and Dan Rose, partners who lead Vantage One, who provided early help and advice and who culled and converted columns from disks that Dick (miraculously) had saved. Miriam Carey, writer and editor, who similarly worked her electronic wizardry and gave essential guidance to the second- and third-worst technophobes in Cleveland (the first being Dick himself). Elizabeth Osborne who typed, Della Osborne who collated, Julie Haug who helped choose . . . . The list could go on. But this book already has been far too long in coming. Let's not delay it any further.

Just one final point: Any determination of "best" is by its nature subjective. These, then, are just a few of our favorites. In re-reading thousands of his columns as we made these choices, we were cheered by the thought that we could randomly pick any of them and still have what could honestly be called the best.

Dick Feagler is *always* at his best.

Enjoy reading him. We did. We do.

—Richard J. Osborne and Edward J. Walsh, *Editors*

# Introduction

I was a reporter for eight years and not a bad one. But then I went crooked. In the second half of the tumultuous '60s, I spent a lot of time standing, Forrest Gump-like, on the fringe of foreign war and domestic revolution. Many events and people irritated me and I committed the reporter's sin of mocking them in print.

In those days there was a bold line between commentary and reporting. Now that line has been kicked and scuffed and nearly erased like the line around a batter's box. But 25 years ago, reporters were expected to stick to "who, what, where, when and why." Newsmen weren't supposed to tack on a gratuitous "P.S. I think this stinks!"

But I started doing that. It seemed incurable. So, in a quandary about what to do with me, the *Cleveland Press* made me a newspaper columnist. The editors wisely decided to hedge their bet. They thought it risky to give me a prime piece of newspaper real estate to scribble on. So they awarded me a corner of Page 2—a page most readers skipped on their brisk journey from Page 1 to the interior of the newspaper.

Page 2 was not, however, unoccupied. Its primary tenant—a paying guest—was a huge May Company underwear ad which took up most of the page. The leftover space was assigned, on alternate days, to me and a columnist who signed himself E.Z. Strange.

E.Z. Strange never came into the office. No one I knew had ever seen him. It is possible that E.Z. Strange was a woman. It is probable that E.Z. Strange's name was a made-up name. But there was no uncertainty about E.Z. Strange's journalistic mandate. His/her job was to write columns about CB radio.

The CB radio fad had just taken the country by storm. Grandmothers were rushing to appliance stores, lugging home walkie-talkies, and conducting blissful conversational dalliances with the drivers of 18-wheelers:

"Breaker, breaker, this is Red Hot Granny."

"Hi, Granny. I read you five-by-five. My handle is Popeye."

"That's a big ten-four, Popeye."

It was E.Z. Strange's assignment to answer mail from CB-addicts and to give them tips on what equipment to buy to intensify their addiction. There were certain commercial overtones in this that were beneficial to the paper. E.Z. Strange was thought to be hot stuff. Of the three tenants on Page 2, the editors considered the underwear ad the most valuable and E.Z. Strange the most compelling. Then there was me. It was my task merely to fill the space on days when E.Z. Strange was absent.

"Write about anything you want," the editors told me.

This is not as easy as it sounds, though if you've never tried it you probably won't believe that. I quickly grew to envy E.Z. Strange. Soon I directed this envy, polluted with a sullen resentment, toward the other columnists on the newspaper. After all, if the movie critic was stuck for a column, he could always go and see a movie. The sports columnist could go to a prize fight. E.Z. Strange could rip open a crayoned envelope sent in by one of his good buddies. All these scribblers seemed to be working with safety nets. Whereas I, who could write about anything, kept waking up in the morning to peer, horror-stricken, into a gaping awareness that I had nothing to write about.

It was obvious to me that my career as a columnist could not last. I gave myself weeks at most. But deep inside me flickered a tiny flame of fierce determination. I resolved to outlast E.Z. Strange. I vowed, as a point of pride, to keep my act going as long as he/she did. I regarded the invisible Ms./Mr. Strange as my tangible opponent in a grim turf battle waged for possession of a corner of a slum page of the newspaper.

When the dust settled, E.Z. Strange, the fad, would be gone whence he/she had come. I, alone, would occupy the exalted rank of second most important thing on the page next to the underwear ad. Then I could quit with honor.

And that, dear reader, is why you are holding this book. I forced myself to write columns whether I had anything to write about or not.

And once I began I didn't stop. Somewhere along the line, E.Z. Strange faded into the ether and so, I am sorry to say, did the *Cleveland Press*. Many fads and fancies came and went. Even May Company disappeared. But, seeing no other options, I just kept on scribbling. I still wake up most mornings horror-stricken with the awareness that I have nothing to write about. And then I write it anyway. That's what we columnists do. Armed with one firm opinion a month, we grind out three columns a week. It ain't easy but it's certainly strange. I try not to think about it.

Well, after 25 years of this, two dear friends of mine, Rich Osborne and Ed Walsh, decided some of the columns should be collected in a book. I thought this an idea of dubious merit.

Columns are written a day at a time and should be read a day at a time.

Cramming a book full of them down a reader's throat seemed likely to invite some sort of bulimic reaction.

But Osborne and Walsh volunteered to do the horrible work of retrieving and assembling a selection of columns from two and a half decades. It was the kind of offer a lazy man can't refuse.

Columns in this book have been written for various periodicals. My thanks to editors Dale Allen of the *Akron Beacon Journal*, John Cole of the *Morning Journal*, Jim Collins of the *Lake County News-Herald*, Arnold Miller, managing editor of the *Elyria Chronicle-Telegram*, Liz Ludlow of *Cleveland Magazine* and, of course, to David Hall of the *Plain Dealer*, my current newspaper home.

When I signed on with the *PD*, there was some discussion about where my column would run.

"How about Page Two?" I suggested, slyly. I didn't tell them why. But the truth is I've grown comfortable on my old battleground, typing away, keeping a wary eye out for the return of E.Z. Strange or the arrival of senility.

And I guess that's the way it will continue. For as long as it does.

# FEAGLER'S
# CLEVELAND

# MAN ABOUT TOWN

## Where'd we go?

The day Cleveland came back, I was sitting in my bathrobe sucking on some coffee and trying to wake up. Then the telephone rang.

"We are calling from National Public Radio's 'Morning Edition' program," a nice young man from the East said. "We wonder if you will let us interview you. Cleveland has come back, you know."

"I know," I told him. "I read it in USA Today. They had a front-page story saying we were back, so we must be back."

The young man assured me that we were. "The only trouble is, I'm not sure I'm the right person to interview about it," I said. "I don't feel as if I've ever been away. I've been here all the time."

The young man considered this. But he announced it didn't worry him.

He didn't say this in so many words, but the impression I got was that he figured I had been away without realizing it. Cleveland had been away and, since I lived in Cleveland, I had been taken away with it. I had been like a passenger on a cruise ship who doesn't realize the ship has left port until it is way out at sea.

But even if this were true, I still wasn't crazy about being interviewed. I still had bad memories of the last time.

Back in 1980, they held the presidential debates in Cleveland. All the civic cheerleaders thought this was wonderful. They figured it was a sign that Cleveland had come back. Pretty soon they had me thinking so too.

Tom Brokaw came to town and wanted to interview me on the "Today" show. About how it felt to be back.

Full of confidence, I agreed. Soon after the interview started, Brokaw asked me about the weather in Cleveland. He had heard, he said, that it was pretty lousy between Christmas and Easter.

Flushed with pleasure at being back, I sprang to Cleveland's defense.

"That isn't our fault, Tom," I said. "You see, it isn't our weather. It comes here from someplace in the west. It stays around awhile and then it moves east. WE really aren't responsible for it at all."

I thought that was a pretty good answer and meteorologically sound, too. So you can imagine my dismay when, right after the show, all the civic cheerleaders gave me hell.

"What kind of a dumb thing was that to say?" they screamed at me. "Why didn't you talk about our orchestra and our art museum? How are we ever going to come back if people hear stupid things like that?"

"I thought we WERE back," I said.

"Not yet," they said. "We're coming back but we're not back. And what you just said set our comeback back. Shame on you."

I never got over that. So when the guy from Public Radio called, I was pretty nervous. Suppose we weren't really back yet? Suppose I again said something that blew us back out to sea right in the sight of land?

I knew I had to be pretty careful this time. So when the interviewer asked me how it felt to be back, I said this:

I said that back in grade school there was always one kid that everybody made fun of. Maybe they started making fun of him because of the way he walked or talked. But pretty soon they were making fun of him just because it made the rest of them feel like big men. Cleveland was like that kid, I said. And the rest of the country was like the other kids.

But then, I said, if there's justice and a God in heaven, that kid gets straight A's and a scholarship to Harvard. And he becomes a brain surgeon and makes 500 grand a year. And when he comes back to the class reunion, he's the only one with hair and he's got a blonde on his arm who looks like a model. And that's the way Cleveland feels today, I said.

That seemed to go over pretty well. At least nobody bawled me out for saying it.

But since we're friends, I'll tell you how I really feel.

I think Cleveland is like a pair of pleated pants. If you'd worn pleated pants three years ago, everybody would have laughed at you. But this year, pleated pants are the latest thing and so is Cleveland. It's all a matter of fad and fashion.

The thing for us Clevelanders to do with our new national respect is to enjoy it and wear it with pride.

And make damn sure we keep the fly zipped.

*— May 14, 1986*

## You have to murder a park

Mrs. Bernadette Walsh called the other day to complain that her neighborhood playground was dirty, dangerous and had been abandoned by the city.

"It's full of broken glass," she said. "The weeds along the fences haven't been cut.

"The trash barrels are overflowing. The trash didn't get collected last time because the barrels were padlocked to concrete posts and nobody had a key.

"It isn't safe to let a young kid play there. A little girl fell on the glass the other day and cut her arm from the wrist to the elbow. Our street club is going out to clean it up, but we can't keep doing that. We think the city ought to do more about the recreation facilities out here."

"What's the name of your street club?" I asked her.

"The Euclid Beach Civic Association," she said.

"You mean you live near old Euclid Beach Park?"

"We live on old Euclid Beach Park," she said. "On what was an old parking lot for it anyway. I live on Humphrey Ct."

Well, I got into a car and drove out to see her. We walked over to Grovewood Playground which is the playground that services her street.

It was littered with broken glass just as she said it was. Trash was lying where it had blown in the corners. It wasn't a very pretty place to play.

It has finally turned out just the way a lot of people said it would. The kids who live right on old Euclid Beach haven't got a decent place to play.

You could laugh about that if it didn't hurt so bad.

If you had a copy of the City Charter, you could pitch it from the playground and it would fall on the old Euclid Beach grounds.

I walked over there, past a sign that said NO TRESPASSING tacked on a tree.

It was a graveyard of broken-down trucks and twisted metal. Weeds grew over the old park paths and there were no landmarks to show you where the rides had been.

If you walked toward the Lake, you eventually came out on the bluff overlooking what had been the beach. The old pier stands there yet, but the end is broken off and stanchions poke out of the water like bones. The empty boulevard light sockets stare straight up like the eyes of a corpse. The old fountain is dry and discolored. It will collapse one of these days and nobody will be around to hear the sound.

Old women in wheelchairs are pushed along the edge of the park, on an outing from the high-rise old-age apartment near by. If they glance down at the beach they can see a litter of bricks and junk lining the shore. They do not look surprised at this. They are old enough to know how things all spoil in the end.

All this was once a part of everybody's childhood. It was everybody's birthday park and it would have been a park yet.

But politics got in the way. Politics and pettiness and racial fear and all the things we haven't unlearned yet. All the spoilers.

We get a lot of calls every summer about playgrounds. But Mrs. Walsh's call was a little different than most.

That call was in the works the day we decided to let the old park die. It is really quite a significant thing when a park dies, I think. Because you have to go out and kill it. That's Murder One, a capital offense.

It's a crime worth thinking about the day a lady calls to say the kids of Euclid Beach haven't got a decent playground.

— *June 28, 1974*

## Bad jokes

I got a letter from an angry nun. Instantly, I sat up straight at my desk, folded my hands, said "Good morning, Sister," and read it.

Sister M. Colette Link of Painesville wasn't sore at me though. It was another little boy who writes a column that she was angry at. A fellow named John Kelso who writes for the Austin, Texas *American-Statesman*.

Kelso had written a column knocking Cleveland. Someone had sent his column to the sister and she sent it on to me. "Isn't it worth a rebuttal?" Sister wanted to know.

Kelso's column was full of your normal Cleveland rubbish. It talked about how filthy the river is, about how dirty the air is and about how nothing ever happens in Cleveland. (Which left me burning with curiosity to know what happens in Austin. Fortunately, I extinguished myself.)

Every other week somebody sends me a column like Kelso's column. It seems that everywhere in the world somebody reads a column knocking Cleveland, they send it to some person in Cleveland—either someone they know or someone they pick out of the phone book. Then that person sends it to me. And then I throw it away.

I throw it away because as strong as my loyalty is to Cleveland, I have a stronger loyalty to my brother columnists everywhere.

When I see a column like Kelso's, I am sad because I know I'm looking at a column written by a man who doesn't know what else to write. Especially if the columnist works for a hyphenated newspaper. People who work for hyphenated newspapers tend to worry about job security.

For years now, the Kelsos and Rich Littles of the land have found relief for inadequacies by picking on Cleveland, the same way some little boys in Sister Colette's classes pick on other little boys who wear thick glasses. It all evens out in the end and the little boys with thick glasses grow up and drive Mercedes

with blondes in them. Cleveland is coming back, and next year
Kelso will have to pick on somebody else on one of his bad days.
I suggest he pick on Columbus.
That's what I do.

*— October 18, 1981*

## Plum crazy

Recently the *Miami Herald* printed an editorial calling for everybody to think of how to help improve the image of Florida.

This came as a surprise to people up North, whose image of Florida is pretty good, especially in December, January, February and March. But the *Herald* seems to feel that the image of Florida has suffered refugee problems.

Perhaps the most surprising thing the *Herald* said was that Florida should copy Cleveland, a city which had managed to turn its image around.

That was the first concrete word from out of town that the image of Cleveland has improved. Naturally, I wanted to know how that had happened, so I telephoned my best Cleveland source.

"Is this Mrs. Figment who lives in the old neighborhood behind Republic Steel where the fallout from the steel mills turns the laundry orange on the clothes line?" I said.

"No," said Mrs. Figment. "That is an outdated image of me."

"Aha," I said, "you have upgraded your image, then?"

"I've upgraded my laundry," said Mrs. Figment. "My son, Herbert, bought me an electric clothes dryer."

"Wait a minute," I said. "Let me write that down."

"You must really be hard up for news, Mr. Feagler," said Mrs. Figment. "But then again, you always were."

"Let me explain what I'm doing," I said. "The *Miami Herald* says that Cleveland has made a comeback. I'm trying to figure out all the things Clevelanders have done to improve the image of the city. Your new clothes dryer may be one of those things."

"I doubt it," said Mrs. Figment. "I don't really like it that much. Clothes come out of it all stuck together like they were magnetized."

"That's too bad," I said.

"Well, just don't let the *Miami Herald* find out," said Mrs. Figment.

"Maybe what I ought to do is just ask you to list things that are responsible for Cleveland's comeback," I said. "For example, do you think Cleveland's comeback has been a result of the slogan 'Cleveland's a Plum?'"

"Do I have to answer right away or can I think about it?" asked Mrs. Figment.

"Take your time," I said.

"All right," said Mrs. Figment. "I have an opinion."

"What?"

"No," Mrs. Figment said. "If oranges aren't helping Florida, plums aren't helping Cleveland. Prunes are a little helpful, I'll admit. Especially when you get to be my age. A little prune juice in the diet helps. A little Feen-A-Mint is also good if you can find it. But on days when you need a comeback, prunes are nice. Plums, on the other hand, do nothing for you."

"Mrs. Figment," I said, "I don't think you are taking Cleveland's comeback seriously."

"You have a point," said Mrs. Figment.

"But why not?"

"Because things on my street are pretty much the same now as they were five years ago. Or for that matter 25 years ago. The church needed a new roof. We built one. We got a new young minister and a lot of women weren't sure about him but then, when Elsie Rumbach's husband died, he went over the day after the funeral and said a prayer with her . . ."

"Mrs. Figment, wait a minute, I . . ."

"A lot of people got aluminum siding," Mrs. Figment said. "The market at the corner closed and they put up a Lawson's store. They finally fixed the sidewalk where the Randalls' elm tree roots came through. Emma Redlin broke her hip and now she uses a walker. The new *Press* boy doesn't deliver on time and I'm afraid I'll have to call his mother. There's a vacant house at the corner and we're worried about rats. The old *Press* boy is working for IBM and I think he's being moved to someplace in New York. And Charlie Bates, poor man, fell asleep in his chair and burned himself with a cigarette so Lizzie started hiding the bottles."

"Mrs. Figment," I said, "what has any of this got to do with Cleveland's comeback?"

"Why, Mr. Feagler," said Mrs. Figment, "don't ask me. I'm not the one who's been away. Ask the editorial writers. Now goodbye, because I hear my dryer buzzing."

And she hung up before I could wish her Happy Comeback.

*— December 11, 1981*

# A *farewell to Halle's*

"The removal of Halle's from the downtown scene presents not a problem but a significant opportunity for Playhouse Square and indeed for all of downtown Cleveland."
— John F. Lewis, member, Playhouse Square Foundation

Mrs. Samuel Halle liked flowers. She was especially partial to geraniums and on those afternoons when she entered the dark-varnished elegance of the store that was named for her husband—moving with a regalness softened by courtesy among men and women who worked there—the newest employees of what was always considered the Halle's "family" could identify her because of the salmon-pink flower pinned to her lapel.

She would ascend, in those years, the twisting series of escalators to the roof where Halle's maintained a solarium and a greenhouse. Members of the Halle family were encouraged, on their breaks, to bask in the sunshine of this solarium but they knew, and were amused by the knowledge, that it had not been built for them but had been created as an incubator for the gestation and early nurturing of Mrs. Halle's prize blossoms.

On the way out of the store, Mrs. Halle might stop at the Geranium Room, a restaurant which in Halle's was called a "tea room." If she had a suggestion to offer about store policy, it was offered constructively and gently. "At Halle's," a long-time employee recalls, "you never had the feeling you were being watched. You often had the feeling you were being taught."

"We see the closing as a positive thing for the area."
— Wesley Williams, president, Playhouse Square Business Council

Samuel Halle might enjoy his wife's flowers, but his passion was aviation. He became a licensed pilot at a time when to do so was considered oddly daring. When the Cleveland Air Races truly were a fascinating national event—before they had been replaced by the traveling circus of an air show that now lands here annually—Samuel Halle sponsored a trophy for the best woman aviator; thus pouring two kinds of progressive thought into one silver cup.

"Now that the fate of Halle's is reality rather than rumor, we can all move forward to create an exciting place to live, work and play in Playhouse Square."
— John F. Lewis

For all its elegance, Halle's did not shun what advantages it saw in modern technology or what opportunities it saw in its location in the city's theatrical district. A cordial relationship was maintained with Max Mink, impresario of the Palace Theater, so that a constant traffic of theatrical personalities was steered into Halle's for autograph parties and, perhaps, tea.

Halle's did not overdo this sort of thing, blending its flashier exploits with more refined and high-minded public projects. It ran an art contest for Cleveland school children and hung their paintings on its walls—the store always looked a bit like a gallery anyway. In the earlier days of television, Halle's sponsored a show featuring its own trademarked Christmas elf. Mr. Jing-a-Ling appeared with a co-host, an attractive lady dressed in a gown from Halle's formal shop.

After the first telecast, mothers telephoned to complain that the gown, while unquestionably fashionable, disclosed an upsetting amount of cleavage when Mr. Jing-a-Ling's consort bent to speak to child guests. Halle's provided her with a fur from its fur salon. As Samuel Halle often preached, the customer was always right.

Only once did Halle's theatrical pursuits create an incident that might have been considered un-Halle-like, which is to say regrettably intrusive. A television performer named Pinky Lee, who enjoyed a large and dedicated national following, began announcing on his program that he would soon appear at Halle's. An appalling number of children and their parents began telephoning the store to ask when they might come down-town to see Lee.

Halle's decided it might be better if it moved him across the street to the Statler Hotel. But this plan was inadequate to the problem. On the day of Lee's appearance, such a traffic jam froze the thoroughfares around Playhouse Square that Lee had to climb atop an immobilized Greyhound bus and show himself to his adoring public.

"It's not all gloom and doom."
— Bob Zion

From the top of his Greyhound bus, Pinky Lee, looking west on Euclid, might have seen B.R. Baker, the fine men's shop. He might have seen Cowell & Hubbard's imposing jewelry store and its competition, the Webb C. Ball Co. Bonwit Teller might have caught his eye as well as Sterling, Lindner Davis. He would have seen a Stouffer's Restaurant and Bonds Clothes. A number of quality shoe stores and a hat store.

Pinky Lee was a man of almost maniacal good cheer and ludicrous optimism. Had someone told him that all these fine stores would close and that finally Halle's itself would be purchased by a discount store from Columbus, Ohio, which would, having captured it, rape and abandon it, it is possible that even he would have been saddened by the news.

Anybody who isn't has less common sense than . . . than a geranium, let us say.

— *January 29, 1982*

## The rubber stamp

By now you know that Cleveland is going to build a 48-foot-high statue of a rubber stamp on Public Square in front of the Sohio building.

The big question on Clevelanders' minds is, is this good or bad?

Naturally, everybody is afraid to say what he really thinks because nobody wants to be accused of being an artistic dummy. Even the art critics are pussy-footing around the issue.

"It is impossible to predict what a five-story (rubber stamp) will look like once it's up," wrote one critic, cautiously.

I disagree.

Suppose six months ago I had come to you and said: "Hey, whaddaya suppose it would look like if we built a five-story-high statue of a rubber stamp next to the front door of the Sohio building?"

Do you suppose you would have said: "Gee, I can't imagine how that would look. Maybe nobody would even notice it."

Of course not. You probably would have said it would look pretty strange. And of course, it will. It will look predictably screwy and everybody knows that. But that isn't the question.

The question is, will it be art?

If it ain't art, we don't want it. But if it is art, we do want it. So how do you tell?

On the one hand, it seems like it might be art because the people who are going to build it are named Claes Oldenberg and his wife, Coosje Van Bruggen.

I know enough about sculpture to know that people with names like Claes and Coosje get paid for scattering things around the landscape that would get a guy named Willie Smith arrested for littering.

Claes and Coosje left a huge statue of a clothespin in downtown Philadelphia and nobody prosecuted. They left a 48-foot high statue of a flashlight in Las Vegas and it's still there. If Claes or Coosje threw away an old refrigerator, somebody would probably thank them, build a fence around it and put it on a post card. If it ain't art, how come nobody stops them?

On the other hand, people who know their art know enough to be a little wary of an artist who builds a statue of a rubber stamp. Great artists do not usually do this.

Take the great artist Isamu Noguchi for example. A couple of years ago, he was hired to put up a statue of something in front of the Justice Center. So he went to his studio and welded some pipe together and made a giant paper clip.

I and some of my fellow art-lovers went over to have a look at it. We knew it was a paper clip right off. But we couldn't get the snobs in town to agree with us.

"Noguchi calls it *Portal*," they said. "It is his vision of a door opening and closing. The shape of the aperture changes as you view the work from various angles."

What made Noguchi's paper clip art was that he didn't admit it was a paper clip. So naturally a lot of Clevelanders are uneasy about building a big rubber stamp and then admitting that it's a big rubber stamp.

Everybody is afraid that after it's up and paid for, some visitor will come to town and get off the airport rapid and say, "What's that big rubber stamp doing over there?" And nobody will know what to tell him.

That kind of thing probably happens all the time in Philadelphia and Las Vegas. But in those cities, you can yank a visitor off to see the Liberty Bell or a six-foot-high topless woman. In Cleveland, the best you can do is hustle him down the street to take a look at Noguchi's paper clip.

One way or another, Clevelanders will have to decide whether the big rubber stamp is art or it ain't. One way would be to try to find out what kind of stamp it is by looking at the bottom of it in a mirror.

If it says eeH-eeT, we're probably in trouble.

—*August 14, 1985*

# Lessons from Rockford

The New Cleveland Campaign is cranking out another series of ads designed to make people elsewhere feel good about Cleveland.

I hate these things. They embarrass me. I stay indoors and hide until they blow over.

A couple of years ago, this group or another like it came out with a big ad blitz around the slogan "New York May Be The Big Apple, but Cleveland's The Plum."

The idea was to have everybody elsewhere in the country thinking that. And soon everybody was. A friend of mine in Rockford, Ill. was the first person from elsewhere to call me.

"I awoke this morning with the nagging thought in my head that New York May Be The Big Apple But Cleveland's The Apricot," he said. "I don't know where the idea came from but I can't get rid of it. You live in Cleveland so I thought I'd call you to see if you know anything about it."

"Yes indeed I do," I said. "An ad agency in Cleveland decided to put that idea in everybody's mind. Only it's not supposed to be an apricot. It's supposed to be a plum."

"No, no," he said. "I distinctly feel 'apricot.'"

"Look," I said, "I don't want to be argumentative about it but we sent 'plum.' If you received 'apricot' you'd better check your receiver."

"But what does it mean?" said the Rockford man.

"Well," I said, "I guess it means that Cleveland isn't New York but in its own way it's very nice."

"We here in Rockford feel much the same way about Rockford," he said. "Oh, that's not to say we don't have our problems. Some blight in the downtown area. That sort of thing. But a very nice river called the Rock River flows through here. Some folks refer to Rockford as the Paris of Midwestern Illinois. Had you ever heard that?"

"No," I said. "I'm afraid I hadn't."

"Oh well," he said. "It's been nice talking to you about Cleveland. Now I know you're busy so if you'll just tell me how to get this apricot thing out of my mind, I'll let you go."

"Well," I said. "I'm not sure it's supposed to leave your mind. I think it's supposed to stay there."

"Stay here!" said the man from Rockford. "But it's driving me crazy. It keeps pounding in my head—'Cleveland's an apricot. Cleveland's an apricot.' It's worse than the theme from 'Rocky.'"

"Plum," I said.

"This is a terrible thing for a city to do to somebody," he said. "You ought to be ashamed of yourselves." And he hung up the phone. But he called back three minutes later.

"It wore off," he said. "I'm sorry I snapped at you. I'm not thinking of Cleveland at all anymore."

That's the trouble with these imaginative ad campaigns. They are all dazzle and no depth. I'm not sure my friend in Rockford thinks of us at all anymore and even when he did he never got the fruit right.

But from time to time, I find myself wondering why some people call Rockford the Paris of Midwestern Illinois. Someday, I may go there to find out. I think it was the soft sell that got me.

— *September 27, 1987*

# Don't rock the polka

While the yuppies are sitting around waiting for Cleveland to build its Rock and Roll Hall of Fame, the ethnics are promising a Slovenian Polka Hall of Fame by Thanksgiving.

And they'll deliver too. That's the wonderful thing about ethnics. They don't do a lot of bragging and they don't make a lot of noise. But when an ethnic says he's going to do something, he does it. That is the spirit that founded Parma.

If you ask me (and, strangely, nobody ever does) it makes a lot more sense for Cleveland to have a Polka Hall of Fame than a Rock and Roll Hall of Fame—Moondog or no Moondog.

Cleveland is a very ethnic town. All the politicians know that. When a politician wants to run for office in Cleveland, he's a dead duck unless he announces his candidacy at a Polish Woman's Hall. Around election time, a Polish Woman's Hall is so full of politicians, a Polish woman couldn't get standing room with a shoe horn.

Naturally, because of the big ethnic heritage in Cleveland, there's a big polka heritage. On Sunday, in the old days, AM radio was wall-to-wall polkas. Every ethnic group got a piece of air time. All day long, all you heard were polkas and speech in strange tongues. The only English words spoken on the radio on Sunday were the words "Factory Furniture on Broadway." Factory Furniture was to polka programs what Texaco was to the Metropolitan Opera or Longine was to the Symphonette.

In those days, most teen-age boys took accordion lessons. Nobody played the guitar. The only contact we had with a guitar was watching Gene Autry serenade his horse at the Saturday afternoon movie. A guitar was not a city instrument. The accordion was the big thing.

I have to admit I wasn't crazy about polkas in those days. In fact, they embarrassed me a little. Whenever we had a big family occasion—wedding or wedding anniversary—polkas would be on the program. I didn't mind the music so much. What I couldn't stand were the "yoo-hoo-hoos." People who are really enjoying polkas are supposed to give out with a "yoo-hoo-hoo." It bothered me to see people I was related to yelling "yoo-hoo-hoo." I thought it was socially gauche.

Ha! I didn't know what was coming. I didn't know that 10 years later, in the era of rock 'n' roll, people would be smashing instruments on stage and biting heads off birds and smoking dope and screaming songs whose lyrics sounded like the stuff written above the urinals in the men's room

Rock 'n' roll gave me a new appreciation for polkas. Polkas were simple and clean and their lyrics had a real message. Who can ever forget the immortal lines of the "Too Fat Polka"?

"Oh, I don't want her, you can have her, she's too fat for me. She's too fat for me. She's too fat for me. I don't want her you can have her, she's too fat for me. She's too fat . . . She's too fat . . . She's too fat for me!"

That's Hall of Fame material if I ever heard it. Some of you won't agree but let's hear a big Yoo-Hoo-Hoo from You Who Do.

*— June 19, 1988*

## Suspending artistic license

Near the front door of the People's Art Show at Cleveland State University is a bottle of urine. It is not on its way to some diabetes lab. It is one of the "works."

Urine, of course, is quite fashionable in art circles these days. Ever since the notorious artwork displaying a crucifix in a jar of urine, urine has replaced those pictures you used to see showing a bowl with a couple of pears in it.

But the urine was not the main attraction at the People's Art Show. The main attraction was an artist's rendering of a missing 17-year-old Cleveland-area teenager named Angel Ormston.

Ms. Ormston has been missing for some months now. Her family is sick with grief. The horrible suspicion is that she is dead. Posters displaying her graduation picture have been printed in the papers and displayed on television.

A Cleveland State art student named Steven Bostwick got hold of one of Ms. Ormston's fliers, copied her face and painted her body below it, nude from the waist up.

This is the same Steven Bostwick who, two years ago, hung a picture in the People's Art Show depicting another teenager, Diah Harris, in sexually explicit poses. Ms. Harris had been savagely murdered by her boyfriend. Her family, already tortured by her murder, found this piece of "artwork" agony. They asked that it be removed.

Cleveland State took the same position then that it did this time. That it would be a violation of Bostwick's artistic freedom to take the picture down. Bostwick, after reveling in the publicity, removed the Harris picture. Tuesday, he did the same thing with the Ormston nude, removing it from the exhibit.

But the hell with Bostwick. This column isn't about him and I'm sorry I had to put his name in it to set the scene for you. This column is about Cleveland State University—an institution my tax money involuntarily funds.

"This is one of those situations where you ask the general

public, 'What is art?'" a CSU spokesman was quoted as saying. He added that the university instructs artists they must bear the responsibility for work they bring to the show.

Uh-uh! It's a nice cop-out but life ain't like that. CSU hung the travesty, CSU is responsible for it. It's their nail, their wall, their problem.

It is obvious to anybody sane that what Cleveland State ought to do is lock the door and pull down the shades every time it sees Bostwick headed its way with an oblong package. But they aren't that smart. They are apparently idiots.

The country is full of idiots prattling about the First Amendment and censorship. None of which has anything to do with this slimy little matter.

If Bostwick, inspired by his ghoulish muse, wants to paint such pictures, he has a right to do so. Nobody can break into his house and burn them and whack him in the backside with a slat, delicious as that notion may be.

But he doesn't have a "right" to get them displayed in a gallery. And he doesn't bear the responsibility for what happens when he does. That right is granted and that responsibility is borne by CSU. I know that without checking the law. And they must know the law at CSU. There's a rumor they even teach it.

If CSU wanted that picture there, they are sicker than Bostwick. What's the question again? What is art?

It ain't Bostwick's picture. That ain't art. CSU is flunking art. And if it didn't want to flunk humanity, too, it would have taken the picture down. And, while it's at it, empty out the chamber pot. They know enough to do that in a backwoods brothel.

— *November 20, 1992*

## Rude awakening

Lakewood is a wonderful town. I grew up in Cleveland and stayed here and I've lived East, West and South. But my last 14 years in Lakewood have been the best.

You can feel the lake in Lakewood. The houses along its rocky cliffs are old and elegant. Lakewood Park is a painting by Norman Rockwell. Teams of little girls play marvelously inept softball on the park's diamonds. On Sunday nights, there are band concerts, and on the Fourth of July, the fireworks rival Cleveland's.

The downtown is pleasant and viable. The population is ethnically diverse. The schools are old but well-maintained, with mottos carved above their doors which praise the virtues of education and remind the reader that our children will determine our future.

There are mansions and rows of high-rise apartments and inexpensive walk-ups. There are streets of Victorian houses and tree-shaded blocks of nice, frame starter homes for young families. Young women jog alone and fearlessly along Lake Ave. well after dark. Public Square is a convenient 10 minutes away.

So it has been possible to live in Lakewood and dream the American dream—a dream made slightly fitful by headlines from other places. Yesterday morning, though, the citizens of Lakewood arose to confront the American nightmare on Page 1–B of this newspaper where a headline read:

"Teens took life, dollar, police say."

"Man stabbed to death on street in Lakewood."

The plot of the nightmare was this: A group of five teenagers, four of them from Lakewood, picked a 38-year-old man as their prey and allegedly stabbed him to death with a buck knife in a residential neighborhood.

Vincent Drost tried to cross the street when he saw the youths approaching but it didn't do him any good. According to police,

the youths who were arrested said they were out to "do" somebody. Police reported that they showed no remorse.

There it was. All of it. Dumped like toxic waste amid the
shade trees of Dreamland. Zombie youth, innocent victim, random selection, death.

The ripples of civic trauma began immediately. First, people
began calling the Lakewood police seeking some word of reas-
surance.

"They are saying things like, 'I usually like to take a little walk
down Lakeland and over to Detroit. Is that safe? Should I be
doing that?'" said Police Capt. Alan Clark, who investigated the
fatal knifing.

Clark is a Lakewood resident and a 30-year veteran of the
police force. What he sees happening to Lakewood, he doesn't
like. If you ask him what the problem is, the answer he gives you
is the same answer you've already heard. You've heard it from
cops in Cleveland and East Cleveland and Cleveland Heights.
You've heard it on your TV from cops in Los Angeles and
Miami—from sea to shining sea.

"The parents don't supervise them," Clark said. "They've got
too much money without working for it. They don't have a sense
of right and wrong. They just don't care."

One of the juveniles arrested told police he likes fights. He
pulled up his shirt sleeve and displayed old knife scars on his
arm.

"What do you want to be when you grow up?" a cop asked
him. "Besides a killer, I mean."

"A rapper," the kid said promptly. Then he complained that
he was tired and wanted to go to bed.

"They had just killed a man," a policeman said. "And they
were complaining that we wouldn't let them get a good night's
sleep."

If you ask around Lakewood, you will hear a lot of complaints
about too much rental property and too much Section 8 gov-
ernment-subsidized housing. You will hear fear and frustration
and racial distrust and ethnic distrust and distrust of the poor.

Beneath the town's idyllic landscape is that other American landscape. That ugly landscape ulcerated by anger and tired of political rhetoric empty of solutions.

But you have to ask. Because what happens in a place like Lakewood when the American nightmare arrives is not speeches. Oh, there are speeches all right. Speeches about putting more cops on the street. And speeches about how the death of Vincent Drost was just one of those isolated incidents that should not be blown out of proportion.

But beneath the surface where the real action is, little, telling changes take place. Fewer young women jog down Lake Ave. after dark. Mothers worry a little more about their kids in Lakewood Park. The "starter family" begins scanning the real estate section, looking at the prices of the houses in those new treeless developments an hour's commute from town.

Lakewood is the best place I've ever lived, which is why I almost didn't write this column. The Chamber of Commerce won't send me a fruit basket for it. I will not be serenaded by the Lakewood Rotary Club.

But I've been around long enough to know a turning point when I see one. In the Belle Barber Shop on Detroit Ave., a troubled customer told the barber he had always thought of Lakewood as a town that had it all.

"We do now," the barber said.

— *July 12, 1995*

# Two anniversaries

Two anniversaries in this column and a dash of humility. . . .

Tonight is opening night at Gund Arena, but you will not see me among the celebrants. I had my big arena opening night 20 years ago this month when Nick Mileti took the wrapping paper off that Big House on the Prairie, the Coliseum.

I was there and it was a lot like being in the cast of one of those epic disaster movies that Hollywood was turning out at the time. The Poseidon Adventure comes instantly to mind. Remember Shelley Winters, in her party dress, trying to scramble her way through the inverted labyrinth of an overturned ship? Well, the plot of the Coliseum opening was similar except Frank Sinatra was in it.

You should know, my children, that I am speaking of a time when taxpayers were not generous about giving their tax money to create sporting establishments. When Nick Mileti asked for some help to build his basketball arena, politicians thumbed their noses at him. But that was a mistake. In the ensuing nose-thumbing contest, Mileti turned out to be a thumber of Olympic caliber.

He led his basketball team into the wilderness and built himself a great concrete arena that loomed startlingly out of the meadows like the ruins of an ancient civilization that had been spiffed up by Bob Vila.

Opening night was invitation-only. Black tie. Frank Sinatra, backed by Woody Herman's band. All the people in Cleveland—most of them rich—who always go to such things went. And I went too, on an expense account that included a $35 rental for the tux I did not own. In those days I did not have the dazzling social calendar I have since acquired.

The moors of Richfield were off the beaten track for most of the swells who were used to having their pictures taken standing around with glasses in their hands at places like Severance Hall or the Art Museum. Traffic backed up and cars inched along.

Several overheated and were abandoned by their owners. It was obvious to all of us in the traffic jam that we were in danger of missing the start of the concert.

Somewhere, up over the highway embankment, was the Coliseum. We could feel Sinatra's spirit urging us on—telling us that if we could make it there, we could make it anywhere. So we abandoned our cars at the side of the road and climbed. Women with $1,000 dresses shoved the skirts between their knees and hitched them up and scrambled with their escorts up the slippery bank of dirt.

I scrambled too—feeling, in my rented tuxedo, like a waiter escaping from the Catskills. We got to the top of the slope and set off across the open field for the Coliseum. But when we got there the doors, most of them, were locked from the inside. We banged our fists against them, yelling blood-curdling war cries. We were on the point of finding a battering ram and breaking in when little ushers dressed in pixie suits came out to get us.

From then on, it was all OK. But we knew that there had been an ill omen in the evening's adventure. That this expanse of tundra was no place for an arena to be. Especially an arena for basketball.

Much of luck is timing, and Nick's dream was untimely. He came on the scene when our town was in a state of self-destructive depression. He couldn't get his message through. He was a man preaching fitness to a city in a coma. Or maybe I'm just biased because we both went to John Adams High School, which made us fellow Rebels.

\* \* \*

The Coliseum opening is nearing its anniversary. But I advertised two anniversaries and some humility.

One night, I was sitting next to Nick on a bar stool in the old Pewter Mug, which for a while was the chief drinking fountain for movers and shakers. And for the press that always circles them at their watering holes.

"Let me tell you something," Mileti said to me. "Do you want to know what's the matter with you news guys? All of you? You don't DO anything. People like me, we DO things. But what do people like you do? You hang around. You ask questions. You write whatever you want to write. You don't DO anything."

In 30 years in the news business, a lot of people have accused me of a lot of things. Like Mileti, I thumb my nose. The older I get, the less I care what people think of me. That is an unexpected and refreshing bonus of age I didn't know about when I was younger.

But what DO we do in this business? Especially columnists? Murray Kempton once said of editorial writers that they are the people who "ride down from the mountains after the battle to shoot the wounded." The same could surely be said of columnists. We peddle opinions no one has asked to hear beneath pictures of ourselves no one has asked to see.

A year ago today, this column first appeared in this newspaper. I want to thank the paper for the space and support. I want to humbly thank you for being so friendly.

I want to tell you that never in my life, on television or at any other paper, have I received the volume of kind sentiments and good will you have given me over the past year. Nor, I might add, have so many people, writing here and there, for reasons of philosophy or pathology, railed so hysterically against this column. It has been a wonderful year.

But what have I DONE? Have I made some of you feel that you're not alone? That you're not crazy? That somebody else feels like you do? I hope so. Because that's what you have done for me. And, Nick, wherever you are, that ain't chopped liver.

— *October 17, 1994*

# THE PASSING PARADE

## *The leader passes on*

When you watch the St. Patrick's Day parade go by tomorrow, look for the sign that isn't there.

It was a crazy sign—the sign that isn't there anymore. "OFFICIAL PARADE," it said. Doesn't make much sense when you think about it.

Yet for nearly 15 years, a big tall guy carried that sign right at the head of the parade. He was little more than a kid when he started carrying it. And he carried it in every St. Patrick's Day parade until he died.

I suppose most people thought he was Irish—that big guy with the meaningless sign. He was, after all, smartly turned out in a green silk top hat, a cutaway coat and green trousers. He looked as if he had just stepped off the auld sod.

But he wasn't Irish. He was a German Jew with a name that goes with that ancestry. You'll pardon me if I don't tell you his name. You'll see in a minute why.

It was back in 1958 when the big guy first carried the sign. In that year, Tom McManamon became chairman of the annual parade. And one day the phone rang in McManamon's office and there was a woman on the line.

"I have a boy," she said. "He's in his twenties. It's probably going to be hard for you to understand this, but he loves parades—anything about parades. I was wondering if it would be all right, if I got a costume for him, if he could march in the St. Patrick's Day parade this year."

"Well, I don't know," McManamon said. "We already have our roster of who is going to appear and . . ."

"You see, Sir," the woman said, "my boy is mentally retarded."

So that's how it began. The woman brought her son down to 13th and Chester. There was a great hustle and bustle of activity as marshals lined up floats and issued marching orders. Into the middle of this frenzy walked the big kid in his top hat.

Nobody was really sure what to do with him so somebody printed the sign. "OFFICIAL PARADE." And the kid, proudly holding his sign, was placed right up in front of the leading color guard.

And every year after that, he led the St. Patrick's Day parade.

Through the years, the parade people found out a little about the big guy. He worked as a messenger for a firm that specialized in hiring the handicapped.

After several years, his mother died. Then the big guy would get very nervous as parade time approached. He would keep calling the parade headquarters office, checking to make sure somebody would come and pick him up so he wouldn't have to miss his big day.

And they always would. Old news photos of the parade show the kid marching at its head looking like a big Irish leprechaun. But no newsman ever asked who he was and the parade people never gave away his secret.

He marched in his last parade a couple of years ago. Death takes people with his malady while they are still young.

This year, Tom McManamon will be the Grand Marshal of the parade. When you watch the parade go by, you'll see him there.

While you are watching, think about the sign that isn't there. A sign that meant nothing to most people.

And everything to one young man.

*— March 16, 1977*

# *The last picture*

Basil, the sidewalk preacher and itinerant portrait painter, is painting his last picture.

Painfully he daubs the colors on in a filthy and roach-infested house on E. 24th St.

A year ago the doctors told Basil he had three months to live unless they operated on him. He told them:

"I, Basil Kalashnikoff, will not let your knives touch my body. I belong to the Lord. It is His duty—His duty, I say—to heal me. I am His problem."

If you come downtown at all, you've probably seen Basil. He used to stand in front of May's store, clutching a Bible in one hand, the other hand raised on high, shouting to pedestrians to reckon with the Lord Jesus.

A couple of years ago, when the hippies held be-ins at the Art Museum lagoon, Basil became their self-appointed chaplain. He shrieked at them, telling them they were doomed. They loved him.

When he wasn't preaching, he would dash around town with his portraits—huge frames wrapped in brown paper. He would bring them into newspaper offices and show them to reporters short on lore about the arts of the Lord.

Neighbors near his house at 1415 E. 24th St. became alarmed about him. Rats and mice scurried from his windows. He was too weak to come outside. When he saved any strength it was for painting.

Mrs. Cangemi, who lives next door, was worried. She called the police who broke his door down and found him asleep on his bed on the second floor.

Basil's sensibilities were offended. He knew his neighbors were acting in his behalf. But he resented being invaded. So that night, he crept down the stairs, chose one of his brushes and some blue paint and painted on his front door:

"BASIL IS OK."

I went out to see him the other day. When he was still able to walk around town he haunted me for weeks, wanting me to tell his story. I listened to him and smiled when he left.

"You see," he said to me yesterday, "I knew in time you would come. I know you are a very busy man. I too am busy.

"You didn't know I had my own art school downtown for 25 years. The Kalashnikoff Art School! Established 1939!

"I, Kalashnikoff, was married to my art! So was Michelangelo! Art and God have had me in their clutches. Now let me show you something."

He walked slowly through the front door and over to an easel.

He drew back some dirty shirts hanging over it. Roaches scuttled in all directions. There was a half-finished portrait of Dr. Lewis Raymond, pastor of the Old Stone Church.

"There, you see? This I must finish. Dr. Raymond. A wonderful man. I knew him well. We both preached on Public Square, you know. He was my competition."

He let the shirts drop.

"They said to me if they didn't operate, I would die. You know what I told them? I said, great! That is what I want! For 55 years of my 73 years, I have been working to achieve Heaven and my salvation.

"Then I walked out on them. And here you see me. Still alive. Isn't it so?"

I asked him if there was something I could do for him.

"For me? No. No thank you. I need nothing."

But surely there must be something.

He thought hard. Then he smiled.

"Yes," he said. "You can perhaps go to the famous George's Restaurant and maybe bring me some very thin soup and a bowl of mashed potatoes with no gravy."

Where?

"George's Restaurant," he said. "Surely you have heard of it. It's on St. Clair. Its soup is the finest with the possible exception of the Forum Cafeteria, which has the best food in town."

I told him I would take care of it.

"Thank you, Mr. Feagler," he said. "It was very nice of you to visit me. But now, we are both busy."

And he shut his front door so that the last words from him were those he had painted on the door panel.

\* \* \*

Shortly after this interview, Basil Kalashnikoff was taken by his neighbors to Metropolitan General Hospital. He had fainted while at work in his home. The hospital reports his condition satisfactory.

*— September 4, 1973*

## Ariane packs her memories

What kind of a man will follow Sam in Ariane Sheppard's love life?

Your guess is as good as hers really. But she pondered the question in her Bay Village home yesterday as she prepared for the auction Saturday that will mark the beginning of the end of her ties to Cleveland and the Sheppard case.

There was a big ad in the paper last weekend advertising the auction. It said that Ariane was selling off Sam's medical jackets, suits, medical equipment, cocktail glasses, Nipon tureen and many other things including HUGE SELECTION OF TOP QUALITY PERFECT CONDITION WOMEN'S DRESSES AND NEGLIGEES FROM WORLD'S FAMOUS DESIGNERS.

For the benefit of any extra-terrestrial beings who didn't know who Ariane is, the ad was signed "Mrs. Ariane (Dr. Sam) Sheppard—owner."

The end of this month, Ariane will sail to an apartment in Antibes, leaving negligees and nostalgia behind her.

"I have been so very busy sorting through things you wouldn't believe it," she said. "There are a lot of Marilyn's things I am taking with me. Such as a lock of her hair, love letters she wrote Sam, yearbooks and dance programs. The boy (Sam's son, Chip) might want some of them.

"And then I got a call from Dr. Monroe. He operates the Bay Village Historical Museum and he wanted to know if I would donate some things of historical interest. So I don't know yet what I will give him. It has been a busy time."

It has, it has. The phone rings constantly and the mailbox is full of letters. People call Ariane to speak German to her, to ask her for dates, to ask for her hand in marriage. Inmates of prisons write to her expressing the wistful wish that she will come and pluck them from behind jail bars as she once did Sam Sheppard. For this there is no hope though.

"That was, of course, a one-time thing," she says.

Ariane admits that one of the reasons she is going to France is that she finds herself missing normal social contacts these days.

"I have dated men," she said, "but not too many. And most of them know who I am, of course. From time to time, out of town, I have dated men who didn't know who I was and the subject of the Sheppard case never came up.

"But I have always felt guilty about that. I dated a man once for two weeks in California. He didn't know who I was. I felt guilty for not telling him. So the last time I saw him, I gave him a copy of a speech I use for women's clubs—so he could read it after I was gone."

Ariane says she has no idea if she will marry again. But if she does, she says, the man would have to be intellectual, well-educated, gentle, non-violent, possessed of a quiet humor and not loud at parties.

A book about her life with Sam is still very much in Ariane's thoughts. She hasn't found an author yet though.

"I had a Harvard student who expressed interest," she said. "But his father, a judge, told him to go to law school instead. And a German author was interested but I haven't heard from him in some months.

"I want to find an author whom I can tell my heart to. I don't want a small man who lives in a suburb with a suburb mentality and thinks I am some kind of nut. I couldn't tell my inmost feelings to that kind of man."

One of Ariane's most inmost feelings is that Sam didn't kill his wife. She says they talked about that from time to time—he always brought it up—and he assured her he hadn't.

Her years with Sam, she says, were no bed of roses, complicated by his addiction to drugs and alcohol. She felt that prison had ruined Sam and that she couldn't help him.

As she looks back on her relationship with Sam, Ariane has a ready answer for what she got out of it all—for what moments of happiness she and Sam shared together.

"Nothing," she says, "None."

Just an ad in the paper saying, "Ariane (Dr. Sam) Sheppard."

— *April 3, 1974*

## The fall guy

Last year in this space, I wrote: "There will always be people who will remember that the battleship Iowa blew up because Cleveland sailor Clayton Hartwig had been jilted by his homosexual lover. And that he planted a bomb in the gun turret he served and blew himself away along with his shipmates.

But this was all a made-up story. A story concocted of 'psychological profiles' and guesses and malice. Made up by little, faceless people in the Navy Department who wanted the blame for the explosion to fall on somebody other than the Navy."

A year has passed since that column ran. Now the Navy has admitted that the Iowa explosion could have been an accident.

But the lines I wrote last year are as true today. The Navy did all it could to pin the disaster on Clayton Hartwig. And it did such an effective job of smearing him that it owes him a very loud apology.

Kathy Kubicina, Hartwig's sister, has worked tirelessly to clear her brother's name since the1989 explosion that killed 47 sailors.

Using the Freedom of Information Act, Ms. Kubicina managed to pry loose from the government documents pertaining to the Navy's investigation of her brother.

One such document she sent to me at Channel 3 News. Because it involves Channel 3 News in a bizarre and outrageous way.

The document, from the U.S. Naval Intelligence Service, contains an anonymous informant's description of an interview that Channel 3 happened to conduct with Clayton Hartwig a few years before the Iowa explosion.

Channel 3's Leon Bibb was covering a Memorial Day service aboard the U.S.S. Cod in Cleveland when he spotted Hartwig, in uniform, in the crowd. Bibb interviewed Hartwig briefly.

Atfer Hartwig died in the Iowa blast, Channel 3 rebroadcast the interview, which was less than a minute long.

The interview is described in Hartwig's intelligence file with the following phrases: "Hartwig acted in the interview as if he had an unnatural admiration for war heroes. The informant first noticed that Hartwig's hairstyle looked effeminate. This led him to notice his general mannerisms, which also seemed effeminate."

That's the way Hartwig's manner and conduct is described in an official Naval Intelligence document.

The description is such a lie and such a distortion that it's unbelievable to imagine it can be anything but a deliberate smear.

In the interview, Hartwig wears his sailor cap. The cap hides his hair. His sideburns are a little long. He looks about as effeminate as the driver of an 18-wheeler.

He speaks in a soft voice and says he decided to go to the Memorial Day ceremony to show his respect for servicemen, many of them his age, who gave their lives in Vietnam, Korea and World War II. If the Navy thinks those sentiments are "unnatural," the Navy ought to go work for another country.

This document may have played an insignificant part in the Navy's case against Hartwig. But it shows so much distortion and bias that it's obvious somebody was going to great lengths to make Hartwig the fall guy.

After the Navy apologizes, it ought to find out who that somebody was.

— *August 10, 1991*

## A *soldier's smile*

A photograph of Billy Garcher has been on my wall for 28 years. I confess that vanity made me frame it and hang it there. I am no photographer, and I shot the picture with a cheap, early Instamatic camera. By luck, it came out well. Good enough, I have always privately thought, for the cover of a magazine. The old *Life* magazine is the one I have in mind.

What I like best about the picture of Billy Garcher is his smile. There isn't much good to say about the rest of him. His clothes are as dirty as a coal miner's. He badly needs a shave, maybe two shaves. Where his beard stubble stops, grime takes over. If you washed his face with a wash rag, you'd want to throw the rag away.

But the smile illuminates the middle of the picture and the smile is genuine. It is not the kind of smile dutifully produced when a photographer says, "Say cheese!" It is the kind of spontaneous smile a young man smiles when there is a good joke and it is on somebody else. It is as natural as a sunrise.

Twenty-eight years ago, I met Billy Garcher and talked to him for 10 minutes. Then I never spoke to him or heard from him again. I didn't know whether he was alive or dead. Until last week. Last week I got a letter from him.

I want to tell you how startling the arrival of that letter was, but I don't think I can manage it. First, of course, it jerked me back without warning through 28 years of time. Second, it was written by a man who had no idea his picture hung on my wall. So that, when I read the letter, the effect was that the picture, frozen and silent for so long, suddenly cleared its throat and began to speak. It said:

"Dear Mr. Feagler. It was a December day in 1967 when I bumped into you at a helo pad in Dong Ha, S. Vietnam . . ."

(Yes it was, Billy. You had just been dumped off with a load of wounded coming down from Con Thien.)

"You brought joy to my face because you were from Cleveland, Ohio, and I had relatives there and you agreed to let them know I was OK . . ."

(And there was joy on my face, too, Billy, because I was trying to hitch a ride up to Con Thien but it was fogged in and nobody was flying. I put on a big act of being disappointed but I was happy as hell because mortar rounds were falling like sleet up there and it was a day when I wasn't feeling particularly lucky.)

"You did better. You put my picture and that of my friend, Dave Bailey, on the front page of the *Cleveland Press* on Dec. 20, 1967. I have the newspaper article embossed on a plaque in my game room and I'm very proud that I served my country in an unpopular conflict. My friends tell me it was not a war. How very foolish and naive they are . . ."

(And how very young we were, Billy. How very young we were.)

"I never thanked you for my little claim to fame and publicity. Thank you. It's taken 28 years to write this letter but I still get tears in my eyes thinking of all the good friends I lost over there."

(You're welcome, Billy. You're welcome to the lucky photo with the cheap camera on a day when I was feeling chicken and glad not to go up to the place where you had come from. You're more than welcome, Billy, so don't mention it.)

"I'm also writing for your help in trying to locate the other gentleman in the article, Dave Bailey. The 3rd Marine Division is having its annual reunion in mid-July and I would like to meet Dave Bailey at this reunion. Of course, he might not be interested, but I pray he is. We still have some unanswered feelings in our closet. God bless you and thanks again. Bill Garcher. P.S., Semper Fi!"

He lives in Pennsylvania. He left a telephone number. I knew if I called, a spell would break and time would vandalize us and make us almost old men. But I had a question I wanted to ask Billy Garcher.

A young woman answered. I thought maybe it was his wife but it turned out to be his daughter.

"Do you want Bill Garcher Jr. or Senior?" she asked.

"I don't know," I said. "The one who was in Vietnam."

"That's Senior, then," she said. And there he was on the line. He said he's 53 now. His wife is Sandy. They got to know each other through letters she wrote him in Vietnam. They had four children. He sells pharmaceuticals now. He's been to the Wall. He has friends there.

He'd like to find Dave Bailey. He has six possible phone numbers in Florida but he's afraid to call. Bailey lost an eye in a bayonet attack. It's hard to know how people feel about things. He has one friend who feels bad because when his position was overrun, this friend played dead in the bottom of a foxhole and he lived, and now he's guilty about it. We talked of such matters. And then, half-ashamed of myself, I asked him my sneaky little journalistic question.

"What do you think about what McNamara said?" I asked him.

Because former Defense Secretary Robert McNamara said this week that he knew the war was wrong and unwinnable. Knew it the day Billy Garcher and I met. Knew it the day Dave Bailey lost his eye. Knew it the night the guilty young man played dead in the terror of the foxhole.

It was a dumb, journalistic question but I asked it anyway. And Billy Garcher gave it the answer it deserved.

"No comment," he said.

I hope McNamara knows that is an answer. I hope they all know it. It is an answer made of the ice of contempt and the thunder of rage. And I will add to it and deliver the message Billy Garcher asked me to deliver in the mud of that landing strip years and youth ago.

He's OK. Billy Garcher is OK. They couldn't wipe the smile off his face. Damn them all to hell, he's OK. And P.S., *Semper Fi*.

*— April 14, 1995*

## Miss Herbert

The word was spread by telephone. Some of the calls were long-distance. Many of the callers phoned people they hadn't seen for years. Some callers apologized because they were telephoning people they scarcely knew at all.

"Hello, I'm so-and-so," these latter callers would say. "You probably don't remember me. But I thought you would want to know that Elizabeth Herbert is dead. She died last weekend."

Across the city and the state and the country, people who got such calls paused for a moment to absorb the news. In that moment, a face took shape, quickly, in the photo bath of memory. A handsome, no-nonsense kind of face. A face that managed the trick of combining fierceness and gentleness. Silver hair. Eyes that could flash or twinkle. What color eyes? Blue, certainly. Or brown?

The years blur the picture, but not the style. The style was aristocratic but not aloof. The style invited you to speak up but warned you not to talk nonsense. The style demanded your best as a fair exchange for what she was giving. The word for this used to be class. But the word is almost quaint now, and she wouldn't have liked it much anyway. Too imprecise. Too dangerously close to slang.

With the memory of the face came snippets of sound.

A harsh bell ringing. Feet shuffling. A locker door clanging open to release the vapors of somebody's lunch. Salami.

"Who do you have for English this year?"

"Herbert."

"Oh, brother. She don't let up . . ."

Ah, but she did let up. If you had to go see her for something after class, if she sent for you to visit her in the little office no bigger than a broom closet in a nook at the end of the hall. In there, she was a general at ease after the battle.

If she sent for you, that meant she had hope for you. She

wanted to know your plans. She insisted you have some. You supplied the plans and she, if necessary, steered them.

"Where are you going to college, Richard? You have been lucky enough to receive a small scholarship, I know."

(Of course she knew. She had helped me get it.)

"I have a scholarship to Kent and a smaller one to Ohio University, Miss Herbert."

"My advice would be to go to Ohio University if you can manage it. They have an excellent journalism school there. But my advice would be not to major in journalism. I don't quite understand how that could take four years."

"Uh, OK."

"Good. Let me know if I can be of any help."

That old showman, memory, brings all of this back through 40 years—the face, the conversation, the empty, polished, after-class hallway, even the dust motes discovered in the air by the slanting rays of the afternoon sun. It's all here in an instant because of the special effects of the mind and the circuitry of the heart. Only seconds have passed and, on the phone, the woman you don't know just got through telling you that Miss Herbert died last weekend. And now it's supposed to be your turn to say something.

"Thank you for telling me," I said.

The kid intelligence network at John Adams High tried to do a job on Miss Herbert, but came up woefully short. She was not married, lived in an apartment somewhere over near Shaker Square. She was . . . get this! . . . the sister of a man who had been governor of Ohio. And . . . you won't believe this! . . . she's got a little Ford and she drives it like a bat out of hell.

That last part was hard to believe. Its wild abandon didn't fit with the classroom where Shakespeare had been entrusted to Miss Herbert and it was her sacred duty to grimly inoculate us. We were unlikely candidates, with our greased-back hair and rolled-up cuffs and poodle skirts and giggles at all the fancy passages, which Miss Herbert beat out in iambic pentameter with a ruler.

She knew she must try to convince us of one essential truth in a world that turns away and sneers. That taste can be improved. That the struggle to improve it is as important as the struggle for food or air. That lives are lost through spiritual malnourishment.

So she bundled us in a bus and took us downtown to watch Olivier do *Hamlet*. She hoped, perhaps, that his sex appeal would jump-start the girls in poodle skirts, which would, in turn, arouse interest in the boys. After this cultural safari, we returned to the classroom. "Good night, sweet prince . . . ," she declaimed, beating time with the ruler, ". . . and-Flights-of-Angels-Sing-Thee-To-Thy-Rest."

And there, my memory spool runs out.

There was a memorial service today. The agate obit in the paper reveals that Miss Herbert came in with the century and lived to be 94 and died in a retirement home. She was president of the Greater Cleveland English Teachers Association. She was an active Ohio University alumna (aha!).

After I left Adams, she went to Nigeria to teach them the secret of taste. So there will certainly be some calls made to Nigeria from people who will say, "You don't know me, but . . ."

The obit says she had lots of relatives. But no children. No children, is what it says. Oh, my.

All over town this week, her aging children stood for a moment with telephones to their ears. Then they went quietly and thoughtfully back to their dinner tables. "My old English teacher died," they told their questioning wives or husbands.

But they were thinking about flights of angels. Flights of angels.

— *March 24, 1995*

## Symbol of glory

Frank D. Centanni's symbol of eternal glory turned up in a junked auto a couple of weeks ago.

Leonard Heil found it. Leonard Heil works in the Harvard Yards where city vehicles are serviced. One of his jobs is to dispose of cars that can't be saved.

A car came in a couple of weeks ago and Leonard Heil looked at it and he knew it would have to be destroyed. It was a total wreck. But he frisked its body before he sentenced it to death.

In the trunk, wrapped in an old jacket, Heil found a bronze plaque. On it were the words:

TO THE MEMORY OF FRANK D. CENTANNI, FIRST GRADE FIREMAN OF ENGINE 28 WITH THE RANK OF CAPTAIN, HEADQUARTERS COMPANY, 34TH INF. KILLED IN ACTION LEADING HIS TROOPS AT THE FOOT OF MALINTA HILL, CORREGIDOR, FEB. 17, 1945.

Leonard Heil stared at the plaque.

What was it doing here? Who was Frank D. Centanni? Where had the plaque hung? Who would want it now?

He carried it out of the junkyard into his office. He called me. "It shouldn't be here," he said. "Find out if anybody wants it."

I called the fire chief's office.

No, said a man there, I don't remember a Frank Centanni. Yes, we had an Engine 28 but it doesn't exist anymore. Got reorganized out.

Maybe the *Press* library would have a trace of Frank Centanni. The *Press* has a very good library.

Buried in drawers of white envelopes are the minor deeds of the long-dead. Traffic accidents, court suits, neighborhood squabbles, heroic acts, births, deaths — all these lie in suspended animation ready to live again for anybody curious enough to press a button.

But there is no white envelope for the ghost of Frank Centanni, killed at the foot of Malinta Hill.

I called Leonard Heil back.

"So far, no good," I said.

"Well," he said, "You know, there's a chance he's not even from Cleveland. It doesn't say Cleveland anywhere on this plaque."

"God," I said.

The old city directories are lined on a shelf on a wall of the library. Turn their pages slowly because they crumble. The pages are yellow and the print is blurry. Ads for dead businesses border the pages. They don't call the library the "morgue" for nothing.

In 1942, Frank D. Centanni, firefighter, lived at 3578 W. 49th St.

"Okay, Frank," I thought. "There's a war on and it has just started. And it's going to last a long time. Here it is, 1942, and you're a fireman. I'll bet you haven't even heard of Malinta Hill yet. But there's no sign here you are married. Things are waiting to happen to you, Frank. Let's see what happens next year."

Probably to save paper the 1943 and 1944 city directories were combined in one book. And something had happened to Frank in a year all right. He was closer to Corregidor.

CENTANNI, FRANK D., 3578 W. 49th St. U.S.A.

And under that, a new listing:

CENTANNI, GUSTAVE, 3578 W. 49th St. U.S.A.

A whisper in time.

Gustave Centanni now lives at 7335 Beresford Ave. His son answered the phone.

"That's my Uncle Frank," he said. "But I better give you my dad's number at work. I don't know much about him. He died way before I was born, you see. I'm 24."

So I called Gustave Centanni at work. I told him about Leonard Heil and the Harvard Yards. About the car that had been demolished and the jacket in the trunk. And about Frank D. Centanni's symbol of eternal glory.

"What do you know," he said. "Sure, I'd like to have that."

"Tell me about Frank," I said. I sounded eager and it must have seemed strange to him.

"Well," he said. "Well, hang on a minute. You know, you're asking me to go back 30 years.

"I was in the Navy, you know. And he was in the Army. He was a fireman, all right. He went to West Tech so maybe the plaque is from West Tech. Or some fire station.

"I don't know anymore if he enlisted or was drafted. I know he was in the Pacific. I think he got the Bronze Star. Seems to me that's right. The Bronze Star.

"He's buried over there on some island. They sent a picture of his grave to my sister. Somewhere in the Philippines. Some island there."

He paused.

"You know," he said, "That's about all I can think to tell you. I'll tell you this. He was a helluva nice guy."

I hung up. I was disappointed. It wasn't Gustave Centanni's fault. It wasn't anybody's fault. It was silly of me, in fact. Frank Centanni was dead 31 years.

I called Gustave back.

"I forgot to ask you how old he was when he died," I said.

Gustave didn't answer. He was thinking.

"He was killed Feb. 17, 1945," I said.

"Well," he said. "Then he's 28."

— *January 5, 1976*

# A *tree of love*

It was a pretty good party. A 12-piece band was playing all the good, old tunes. The entree was strip steak. The cast of *All Night Strut* showed up and did a few numbers. The bar leaked top-shelf stuff all night long. Everybody's wife looked sexy.

The lady on my right was a lady I like to talk to. Her maiden name was Mary Kenney and she was raised with the rest of the Irish over in the neighborhood of St. Pat's parish on the West Side. She looked pretty elegant but we all felt pretty elegant and reasonably pleased with ourselves the way you ought to be at a Christmas party.

"Got your tree up yet, Mary?" I asked her.

"Yes," she said, "Norman put it up Friday. We paid 14 dollars for the privilege of going to somebody's farm and cutting one down."

"They aren't cheap," I said. "Mine cost me nine bucks and I thought that was high. For 14 bucks you must have a helluva tree."

"It's nice," she said. "But it's not the best tree I ever had. The best tree I ever had cost exactly 25 cents."

"That must have been back a while."

"It was," she said.

It was back when the old tunes weren't old and even on Clinton Ave. you could hear the big bands. If you had a radio. With a radio, you could fill your house with the sounds of parties at the Cafe Rouge in New York City and songs about stardust and moonlight cocktails. It was interesting to learn that, at the Cafe Rouge, there wasn't any Depression going on apparently. Strange.

Because there was a Depression going on on Clinton Ave., that was for sure. There were five kids in the shingle house with the iron fence. Mary Kenney was the second youngest kid but she was not too young to know about the Depression and what it did.

What it did was, it threatened love.

Oh, there was plenty of love in the house. But things were always happening to threaten it. Ralph Kenney was laid off from a good job at Republic Steel. He took a job as a water boy for a WPA project and was lucky to get it. He hurt his back. He was tired nights.

There were family meetings. Ralph Kenney presiding. A lot of the times the family meetings were about how-to-stretch-the-money. Such meetings put a drain on the best of spirits. Such meetings meant that the Depression was getting in the house. It had gotten past the iron fence and was right there in the house, hurting people.

What you did when you were hurt was, you tried your hardest not to show it.

One night Ralph Kenney came home and hung his hat on the clothes tree in the hall and called a family meeting and said, in a businesslike way:

"Now the way it is, this Christmas either everybody can have one present apiece, or we can have a Christmas tree. One or the other, but not both. How do we vote?"

How did you vote?

There had always been a Christmas tree. Dripping with tinsel and ornaments and, way on top, the old cardboard angel from the attic who came out once a year to reign over the Kenney household. How could there be Christmas without a Christmas tree—without the angel?

But how could there be Christmas without presents? Without hoping and praying for the thing you wanted most and ripping the paper off your very own packaged dream on Christmas morning?

How could you vote on such a proposition? How could you possibly . . . ?

Unless you had to.

The kids voted. The vote was 5-0 in favor of one present apiece. And it was done.

So the days passed. And you could see the Christmas trees

beginning to appear in the houses on Clinton Ave. Not just in the houses where the St. Pat people lived either. In some of the houses that the newcomers had bought—the people who were not even Irish. The people who had bought the McCluskys' house and who came from somewhere down south. Even they had a tree.

If you wanted to, you could pretend that there was magic and that the magic would produce a tree in the Kenney house. But you could only pretend that for a very little while. Because you knew better.

Mary Kenney's brother had a quarter.

And on Christmas Eve, he took his coaster wagon and pulled it over to the West Side Market.

All the stalls were shutting down but there was a place that sold Christmas trees. And on the ground at this place there were broken branches and pine needles—the crumbs of somebody else's Christmas.

Mary Kenney's brother gave the tree man his quarter. Then he picked up the bits and pieces of branches. They smelled of pine and they were green. He loaded them in his wagon and pulled them home. He had the idea that, if he couldn't have a Christmas tree, at least he could have a something like a Christmas tree.

But he knew that it wasn't a very good idea. In fact, it was a very bad idea. Because the pitiful pile of branches only made things worse somehow. It mocked the idea of a Christmas tree. It was as if the Depression was saying, "Try as you may, I win."

So the Kenney children went to bed. And then it was Christmas morning.

Mary Kenney went into the living room to claim her "one present apiece."

And there she saw a small pile of packages beneath a Christmas tree. A Christmas tree!

But like no Christmas tree she had ever seen before. Its trunk was perfectly round like a pole. Three legs grew out of the bottom of the trunk to hold the tree upright. Fastened to this round trunk were the bits of branches that her brother had brought home. Between the branches were brass hooks—this tree grew brass hooks.

It was the clothes tree from the hallway.

And on top was the cardboard angel from the attic—the finishing touch placed there by Ralph Kenney in the hours when his children slept.

"And that," Mary told me, "was the best tree I ever had. And it only cost 25 cents."

What do you say to that?

"Mary," I said, "may I have this dance?"

— *December 22, 1976*

## Welcome back, Kotter

Janet Brasty is a social studies teacher. She teaches at Glenville High and has her master's degree and Monday she began her first full week back on the job since a student beat her bloody in a stairwell.

There wasn't an awful lot of blood. Mainly it was the rabbit punches to the jaw and the side of the head that injured Janet Brasty. A friend of hers—a teacher in the chemistry department—drove her to St. Alexis Hospital.

"Do you want to make out a police report on this?" somebody in the emergency room asked her.

"I think I do," Janet Brasty said. And so she filled out the forms. Then she went to see her own private doctor and then she went home for a while.

There was a lot to think about at home. Janet Brasty had wanted to be a school teacher for almost as long as she could remember. Certainly since the first grade in St. Wenceslas School in Maple Heights. Back in the first grade, whenever the sister had to leave the room for any reason, Janet would take over—playing teacher. She sensed it was a job that brought with it a dignity and quiet pride.

She never changed that opinion. She got her bachelor's degree from Ursuline College and her master's in social sciences from John Carroll. She taught social studies at South High for 10 years and was transferred to Glenville two years ago.

There were a lot of good kids at Glenville and good kids— kids eager and wanting to learn—are as necessary to Janet Brasty's existence as the air she breathes. There were good kids.

There was also hall duty.

Janet Brasty and a platoon of her fellow teachers fan out for hall duty every third period with the precision of a well-trained infantry rifle squad. The idea is to make certain that students are not loitering in the hallways when they should be in class. Or smoking dope in the bathrooms. Each teacher has an area and the areas overlap.

"It's like a game in a way," Janet Brasty says. "We really chase kids around until we tire them out."

About a month ago, Janet spotted a student walking aimlessly.

"If you're just waiting for the bell to ring," she said, "you better wait downstairs."

He pushed her, then began clubbing her with the side of his hand. He knocked her glasses off and cut her forehead. Janet began to fall and as she fell she tried to protect her head because it seemed to her the young man was trying to hit her in the temple.

She fell behind a trash can and used it for cover as best she could. What saved her, she thinks, is that somewhere in the hallway a door slammed. The student heard the noise and ran. Janet made her way down to the school dispensary and her friend drove her to the hospital. She stayed away from school for 22 days and when she returned, she found those days had been deducted from her sick pay.

Monday, at the beginning of her first full day back, Janet conducted homeroom in the art room. Then she went to her class in Comparative Political Systems. Then it was time for hall duty.

"I went to a neurologist," she said as she patrolled her section of hallway. "He said I should beware of the assault leaving some permanent psychological damage. I asked him if he meant that I might hide under the desk when the kids came in the room and he said something like that."

She shook her head ruefully.

"I never wanted to be a policeman," she said. "You try and try to build up a rapport with your students in the classroom. Then you go out and play warden in the halls. And you lose what you've built up."

Down the hall, a student fumbled at a locker. Janet began to walk toward him.

And at that moment, another student sprang from somewhere and grabbed the first young man. He slammed him into the locker once, twice, three times until the hall was filled with clanging.

The teachers in Janet Brasty's little platoon converged on the fighters. Classroom doors opened and more teachers ran out. They tried to pull the boys apart and finally did.

Janet Brasty walked back to me. She held her grade book in her right hand and held her left hand stiffly in front of her.

"Would you mind holding this?" she asked. "I have to wash my sleeve."

And she left me standing in the middle of the hall as she went to wash blood—somebody else's this time—from her arm.

"Welcome back, Kotter," I said.

And she turned and grinned. I think you'd have to say it was an admirable grin.

— *April 6, 1977*

# A *single rose*

I came back from lunch and a single red rose was nestled in the clutter of papers on top of my desk.

It was a perfect rose, long-stemmed and the color of blood. The appearance of this rose had aroused a certain curiosity in my neighbors. I am not known as one who gets roses.

"A little old lady in a black straw bonnet left it," Cele Hughes said. "She said it was to say thank you."

I knew then that this was not a rose to be happy about. It was a rose I did not want—payment for a favor that merited no payment.

It must have cost her at least a dollar. More money than she would care to spend casually. For she is a lady who knows exactly how much money she has in her purse at all times. She budgets carefully.

She came in one afternoon a couple of weeks ago. She was dressed in black but, if her clothes were in mourning, her eyes sparkled in celebration of life. She barged up to me, grabbed my hand, pumped it and told me she was glad to see me as if we were effecting some kind of reunion.

"I have a problem and I know you can help me," she said.

I live above a store over off St. Clair," she said. "Here is a list I have made. You can see what I pay for rent and what I pay for food. I go to Mass every morning and it costs me this little bit because I take the bus in rush hour.

"Now, here is my Social Security check. You can see that my expenses come to a little more than I get from Social Security."

When people say this you are studiously polite.

"I'm sorry about that, Ma'am," I said politely. "But there is nothing I can do about it. Maybe if you go over . . ."

"There is something you can do," she said. "I wouldn't have walked all the way over here if I didn't know there was something you could do."

"What do you have in mind?"

"Every month they take about eight dollars out of my check for Medicare," she said. "If I had that eight dollars I would have just what I need. I want them to stop taking it out."

"Now wait a minute," I said.

"I went over to see them and they promised to stop deducting it," she said. "But still it comes out. I don't think they understand me. So I want you to call and tell them I mean it."

"But what will happen if you get sick?"

"God will take care of me," she said.

"Well, how can we count on that?"

"I have counted on it for more than 70 years."

"I don't know if I want to make a call like that."

"That is probably because you don't have to live on my check," she said. And she laughed, gaily like a girl.

And I called. I got a man with a tired voice. The tired voice told me that, yes, he remembered the lady. Yes, she was within her rights in wishing to stop her Medicare payments. He would check the records, the tired voice said, and make sure her next check did not contain the deduction.

"You did it," the lady said when I hung up.

"Yeah."

"I will light a candle for the Infant Jesus for you."

She went away. I don't know if she lit the candle. But a few weeks later she left the rose. The rose made me uneasy when I saw it.

But then I got a glass of water and propped the rose in it on the desk top.

When someone leaves you a rose, you should care for it, after all. It is a responsibility of roses.

—*July 8, 1977*

## *Out of job, out of life*

I probably wouldn't have written this story except for an item I saw in the paper the other day.

The item carried the headline, "Funds for Perk are sought."

The story began:

"Long-time friends of Mayor Perk are being asked to contribute $250 each to a trust fund to help the mayor after he leaves office Nov. 14."

And farther down, the story said:

"'The mayor just can't retire,' Bennett said. 'He doesn't have any accumulated wealth or any great assets. His house is paid off. That's about it.'"

When I saw that story, I thought about a phone conversation I'd had earlier in the week.

The woman who called gave me her name. Then she proceeded uncertainly.

"I don't know what I want from you," she said. "Somebody suggested I call you. It's about my husband.

"Another company bought the company he works for and they gave him notice that he's through at the end of the month. He's only 55."

"What does he do?" I asked.

"He's an art director," she said. "He's an art director for a wallpaper company."

I might have been amused at that. It has a ring to it that sounds like one of those routines they used to do on the "It Pays to be Ignorant" radio show. "I used to woik in that town," the comedian would say. "I was an art director for a wallpaper company until I got too wrapped up in my woik."

But I wasn't amused. There had been pride in the woman's voice when she had said the words "art director." Pride and a sort of desperation.

"It's killing him," she said.

"What is?"

"He can't find a job."

"Oh."

"I don't know how many interviews he's had," she said. "I think he's had more than a dozen now. Maybe 20.

"At first it wasn't so bad. He would leave in the morning with his portfolio. I helped him put it together. He didn't have any trouble getting interviews. And he came home happy because a lot of the people he talked to seemed impressed with him and his work. I mean, he's had a lot of experience.

"But then nobody would call him. And when he called back they would say they were sorry but they'd hired somebody else. And the somebody else was always a younger man."

"Oh."

"I try to keep his spirits up. I'm a fighter by nature, you see. But he acts funny. He just sits now. He comes home and sits in front of the television set and sometimes he cries.

"We have a mortgage on this house and we have payments on the car and who would have thought this could happen? When you get to be 55, you don't want too much. But you want to be able to count on things being set, you know?"

She hesitated.

"He tells me maybe it would be better if he did something and I got the insurance," she said.

She said this with awe in her voice. The kind of awe people use when they speak of the greatest of tragedies—scarcely believing them but knowing they are true.

And I didn't want to hear it. My phone rings. I pick it up and here is a lady trying to draw me into her desperation. I can resist this to a point but the point passes when she says "he tells me maybe it would be better if he did something and I got the insurance." She has told me a terrible secret and once you know someone's terrible secret you are bound to that person whether you like it or not.

"Is there a priest he can talk to or a minister?"

"I don't know," she says.

"It isn't his fault this happened to him. Somebody should make him see that."

My own words ring hollow. What this lady wants is a job for her husband. She wants him to be art director at somebody else's wallpaper company. She wants him to make the car payments and the mortgage payment and grumble about the interest. She wants some order in life again. After 55 years, she thinks he's earned that. She wants her husband's dignity back.

"I don't think he'd want his name in the paper," she says.

And there is my escape clause.

"Well," I say, "if I wrote a story I'd probably have to use his name."

"I just don't know how he'd feel about that," she said.

"Well," I say, quickly. "I'm sure everything will be all right. He'll weather it . . ."

And, in a scramble of words, I hang up.

I wouldn't have written about the call if I hadn't seen the story about how city employees have been urged to donate $15 or $250 to a special dinner for Ralph Perk.

The wallpaper artist deserves equal time. You wouldn't call his story news. But then news is often just a pale shadow of the larger story which is life.

— *October 26, 1977*

# It's expensive to be a hero

Heroism has its price.

Alfred Antenucci knows what it has cost him so far to be a hero. But he doesn't want to talk about it. He doesn't want the figure printed. He's afraid he will seem ungrateful.

Being a hero has cost Alfred Antenucci several thousand dollars. It has cost him enough to buy a new car—a moderately priced one.

A little can be revealed. Fifty-three organizations have presented Alfred Antenucci with plaques proclaiming their eternal gratitude for him. Each plaque was presented at a dinner; each dinner sold tickets and, almost every time, Antenucci insisted on paying his way in.

"That's a little over a thousand right there," he said. "They offered me free tickets, of course, but what are you gonna do? These organizations need to raise funds. You have your political fund-raisers and your service organizations and all that. So, naturally, I felt I should pay."

At each of these affairs, Antenucci had heard judges, presidents, businessmen, chairmen, mayors and politicians talk about his heroism and recall the day he helped save the president of the United States from assassination. Then Antenucci is called upon to say a few words.

"It's not that big a thing," he always says.

His wife gets sore at this. She thinks such a response lacks a certain finesse. It would be better, she thinks, if he crafted a more lyrical comment. He worries she's right.

But what can he say:

"I saw the gun and I heard two shots. Then I started pounding on the kid. I kept pounding him right into the ground. They pulled me off the pile. The Secret Service kept me there talking to me for two hours. Then they let me go and I went back to the hotel and I passed out.

"I woke up in the hospital and there are two Secret Service men in my room. Nobody else gets in. I heard Chris Wallace yelling from the corridor he wants to talk to me. But nobody gets to talk to me. I started getting scared."

"Why?"

"I don't know. It was like they thought I knew something. But I didn't know anything. What did I know? The whole thing only took seconds. But they didn't let anybody talk to me for 10 days. My wife they'd let in the room, but they didn't let her talk about the shooting. Everybody was trying to call me on the phone, but nobody got through. Only Bob Hughes got through. How he got through, I don't know.

"When they took me out of the hospital, they drove me in a limousine down a driveway lined with cops. I kept feeling scared. 'What did I do?' I asked myself. Then I took a plane to Cleveland and on the plane I met this reporter and cameraman from Channel 8. They said they rode down so's they could be sure to interview me on the way back. Then, at the airport, there were hundreds of people."

Alfred Antenucci found himself officially labeled a hero. People then had to figure out what honors befitting his status should be supplied.

A street in Garfield Heights was renamed Antenucci Blvd.

The sweater and hat he wore the day he pounded on the gunman were requisitioned and encased, behind glass, in the Senior Citizens Hall of Fame in Columbus.

The governor appointed Antenucci to the Unemployment Service Commission.

People started to point to Antenucci in restaurants. Letters came to him asking for autographs—some from Italy and Mexico.

In the men's room in Hopkins Airport, a stranger approached. "I want to shake your hand," he said. Then he remembered his manners. "As soon as I wash my hands, of course," he said.

The president sent word he would like to meet Antenucci.

"I stayed awake all night trying to figure out what I would say to him," Antenucci says. He was ushered into the president's room. "Relax, Al," the president said. "What I did wasn't that big a thing," said Antenucci, modestly.

Then after a while, it got quiet. For a couple of months it stayed quiet. Then, a week or so ago, Antenucci's phone rang and it was a newspaper reporter. The phone rang the bell signalling the start of Round Two.

"He wanted to do a story about how it was a year since the assassination attempt," Antenucci said. "I didn't want to talk to him because I knew it would start up again. But he said, 'Just a few words.'"

And, of course, it did start up again. By now, Antenucci had seen enough reporters to be wise in the ways of the press—much the way a man who sees enough children playing hopscotch becomes wise in the ways of hopscotch.

All day yesterday, reporters and television crews washed in to Antenucci's office like waves wash against a bank of sand; taking a little bit of him away when they left.

"It was no big thing," Antenucci told them. And, in fact, many of them agreed with him. But the truth was that whether it was a big thing or not did not matter. It was the "year-since" stories that mattered, the presentation of plaques that mattered, the ability to somehow use a little piece of Antenucci that mattered.

"Once, I wondered, did I do right? Or did I do wrong? Or should I have minded my own business," Antenucci says. But he has stopped asking. He doesn't want to sound ungrateful. Heroes must be grateful. You wouldn't think so, but that's the way it is.

— *March 31, 1982*

## Christmas Angels

Christmas week began with the story of the funeral of Angel Ormston, a young woman from Mentor, missing since last summer, whose body was found in a ditch by a couple of raccoon hunters.

TV reporters, newspaper headline writers and the people who write photo captions made great use of her name, Angel. "Fallen Angel" and "An Angel Laid To Rest," the newsprint poets wrote. That kind of thing.

Angel was stabbed to death. Police have some duct tape and clothes line that was used to bind her. But no leads yet. And a cold trail. Another headline said that. "Trail to Angel's Murderer Cold," it said.

Then, late in the week, another angel entered the news. This was a newborn baby girl, its cord still attached, abandoned by her mother to die. And she almost did die. This second angel was found in a pile of leaves by a woman who heard it crying, uncovered it, and promptly named her Christmas Angel. And Angel, unofficially, has become the little girl's name.

It was a week crowded with angels. The news shows were full of accounts of the two angels just mentioned. And, in deference to Christmas, the disk jockeys suspended their normal play list of songs about sex and revolution and substituted Christmas carols instead.

So, between bulletins about the murdered Angel and the abandoned Angel, we heard songs about "Angels From the Realms of Glory." And "Angels We Have Heard on High." And "Hark, the Herald Angels Sing."

The herald angels in the latter carol were sent to earth to bring good news. "Fear not!" was their message. They brought with them a promise that peace and good will would triumph over evil and death.

But the two Angels that dominated the newscasts—innocent though they were themselves—were the heralds of an entirely different kind of story. The story of a society filled with random, slashing violence and murderous, criminal neglect.

And the holy week was a week in which we found ourselves caught between heaven and hell. Listening to both sides of the old story. Our hopes and fears met here as another one of the ancient carols says.

In a week dedicated to universal love, it was harsh to remember but impossible to forget that, while some angels sing, other angels die here.

*— December 25, 1992*

## Do not disturb

On a small island called Johnson's Island, linked by a short causeway to the Marblehead peninsula near Sandusky, there is a tiny Confederate cemetery.

People who don't know about it are surprised to find Confederate soldiers buried here in Ohio. A plaque tells them that Johnson's Island was a Civil War prison camp for Confederate officers. They were treated well until news filtered north of the atrocities at the Andersonville prison camp in Georgia. Then, conditions on Johnson's Island were allowed to deteriorate. Many of the soldiers died, and some were left here beneath weathering stones.

There is a local tale that the cemetery is haunted. And, of course it is. The dead haunt us regularly. My Aunt Dorothy, a humorous but opinionated woman with a peppery tongue, appears often—usually when I've done something I know she would think was stupid.

"You know what Dorothy would say," I ruefully tell people who knew her. And they gleefully agree that, yes, they know what she would say. In fact, we can hear her saying it and see her saying it, even though she has been dead for 10 years. For when we get older, many of the people we know best are the dead, and they visit us often without invitation, and their visits are never unwelcome.

In a haunted cemetery of the military dead, there is a special stillness. Gaze down on a gravestone on Johnson's Island or in the green and white vastness of Arlington, and you are overcome with a deep imperative of quiet, as if you were in the room with a sleeping child. Pvt. Smith, the stone tells you, lived 18 years before he died in 1918 or 1943 or 1966. In some mysterious way, the stone, no matter how old, is as fresh as yesterday.

The barriers and distances of time dissolve. Here is a soldier born before you were born, and yet you are old and he is young. You know things he never got to know. And vice versa. What happened to him might have happened to you if you had been born in an unlucky year. There have been a lot of unlucky years for 18-year-olds to have been born in. There was 1900, for instance. Or 1925. Or 1948.

That was a banner year for Cleveland, 1948. After a rollicking summer of baseball at the Stadium, the Indians beat Boston in a one-game playoff and then beat the other Boston in the Series. Truman beat Dewey too, but had a harder time of it. Automobiles, back again after the war, bedecked themselves in growing excesses of chrome. Suburbs were explored and tamed. Schools were excellent. The Russians hadn't figured out the Bomb yet. Vietnam was Indo-China and few knew that, and fewer cared.

Into this happy world came Pvt. Smith, who would grow up and get all his shots (except the longed-for polio shot—and finally even that). He was born of a doting mother, raised by Dr. Spock. He knew about propeller beanies and Hopalong Cassidy pistols and hula-hoops. He ran through lawn sprinklers and watched Howdy Doody and worried about his pimples and bought a girl a corsage and delayed college and joined the Army and used up all his luck and went to Vietnam and . . .

Here he is. Under a marker. In a place that makes you want to be very quiet. As if there were a "Do Not Disturb" sign hanging on each stone in this corridor of stones.

This column is because of Robert McNamara's book. I wasn't going to buy the book and then I did. I didn't think there would be anything new in it and there wasn't. I marked passages with toilet paper, getting ready to write about the book. But I never did. Others wrote columns about it and I figured, let them.

I watched him, though. I watched him compulsively appear on every television show that would have him. I watched him talk about the Vietnam War and analyze it with his dispassionate engineer's mind as if it were a malfunction on the great assembly line of wars and he was reviewing the problem to try to get the bugs out. I saw him in studios and I saw him on campuses. I saw him everywhere but in a cemetery. I heard him say everything but "I'm sorry."

And then he began to disappear from the talk shows and the

news columns. Soon the book will disappear from the best-seller list. And finally, it will be just a half-forgotten, strangely wooden mea culpa and it will join all the other mea culpas that have ascended toward heaven since the dawn of time. Toward the ear of a God who has heard it all before.

But McNamara disturbed. He disturbed people who have been badly hurt already. And today my heart, and I hope yours, is with the families he disturbed. They are in quiet cemeteries all over America. They are looking down at young men they know. Young men who will haunt them all their days.

What can we wish but that good memories come back often to overcome part of the pain. And that their sons and husbands and fathers visit, unburdened by politics or the rightness or wrongness of a cause they did not shape, anymore than the young men on Johnson's Island shaped the cause that sent them to war.

Let them come back warmly and happily and just as they were. The way my Aunt Dorothy drops in now and then with a blessing from a place that cannot be so very far away.

— *May 25, 1995*

# PUBLIC SERVANTS

## *Rockefeller's cool*

On Vine Ave. and 29th St. in Lorain—a section of pavement called "Puerto Rican Blvd."—Angel Lozano, 18, stood last night in judgment of one of the richest men in the nation.

Angel was born in Puerto Rico and works in a Lorain steel mill and he stood in a crowd last night and eyed Nelson Rockefeller critically and listened to him speak Spanish and said:

"I was for Bobby Kennedy. This guy sounds like he is trying to be Bobby Kennedy. But he sounds cool, man. His accent isn't bad. Maybe I'm for him now."

Had Nelson Rockefeller heard that remark last night he would presumably have been happy. Because he spent the day in Cleveland yesterday trying to be cool—trying to capture the common man.

His road to the presidency is paved with such intentions and Rockefeller traveled the road yesterday—allowing the crowd to pull and pummel him like a good guy; eating roast beef in a Cleveland steakhouse while a group of Negro ministers amened him; pumping the hand of almost every Republican in Lorain County—seeing and being seen.

He started as soon as his plane landed at Burke Downtown Airport yesterday—plunging into the heart of the crowd with all pretense of security gone.

"This is the way he has been operating," said a newsman who has been traveling with Rocky and his friends. "He has 21 bodyguards following him constantly but when he hits a crowd he leaves them all behind. It scares all of us."

Rockefeller scorned the use of limousines. He arrived at the Lancer Restaurant, 7707 Carnegie Ave., in a Greyhound bus.

In a hot room bulging with people, he sat in front of a mural of pine trees, his head modestly bent and nodding while clergymen said nice things about him.

And then he delivered his sermon—the same message he had given the crowd on Public Square while a band of Negro hecklers waved flags at him and beat tom-toms and chanted "Umgawa, soul, power."

"The time for the old politics is past," he said. "I bring you the new politics."

Then Rocky bused to Elyria.

His wife, Happy, arrived and didn't look it. She stood next to her husband as he presented an endless parade of Republicans to her in a receiving line, pumping their hands, whispering their names and passing them on. She rewarded each with a slight smile.

Then they got back on the bus, riding in the front seat, waving at the crowds and a presidential campaign was borne to Angel Lozano as he stood on Puerto Rican Blvd. and listened to Rocky speak Spanish.

Rocky pushed back to the bus through the crowd of Puerto Ricans and a photographer shoved Angel up to him and their groping hands met in a handshake.

Then the bus pulled away and turned a corner. And Angel and the little crowd of voters drifted to their homes a little bewildered that this man, who seemed to have everything, had come to ask them for help.

— *June 20, 1968*

# Two years later

*Déja vu.*

It is quite possible that Andrew Dono, executive assistant to Mayor Stokes, has never used that term in his life. This is not a criticism of Andrew Dono's articulation. It is merely that the term is French and there is no significant French vote in Cleveland.

And yet the other night as Andrew Dono stood in the lower room of Settler's Tavern on Buckeye Rd., he must have had a feeling of deja vu, a feeling that he had been here before with cigar smoke and gypsy music swirling around him, doing his best for his boss. A feeling that he was reliving the past.

Which up to a point he was. Andrew Dono had been in this room two years ago and when he looked around the other night, everything was just the same — almost.

There was Councilman Jack Russell, who owns the 16th Ward and all the fullness thereof, whispering in the Mayor's ear. There was Zoltan Gombos, publisher of nationality newspapers. There was Jonas Shondor and his magic violin playing gay tunes. There was William Murar, president of the Cleveland Hungarian Democratic League waiting to announce that his group had endorsed the Mayor for reelection.

There were the steaming bowls of csiga soup and the plates of veal porkolt. There were all the leaders of the Hungarian community. It was all the same cast of characters, same menu. Just as it had been in 1967 when Andrew Dono hosted the party in support of Ralph Locher for mayor.

But soft! There were some differences. The little buttons on everybody's lapel had been red and white last time and now they were orange. And last time the party had been all white and this year somebody had let some Negroes in. Yes, somebody had let some Negroes in and (will wonders never cease) one of them was the Mayor of Cleveland. Andrew Dono's boss. Two years ago you wouldn't have believed it. But a lot has changed in two years.

Two years ago Carl Stokes was running for his life. Now he's drifting along toward the primary date, listening to the music of violins in gypsy restaurants, listening to the singing of Joel Grey at the Music Hall. Paying no attention whatsoever to Robert Kelly who is running against him.

The other night Robert Kelly was making a speech about Carl Stokes. He was saying that Carl Stokes' only aim was self-aggrandizement; that his aides keep being sent to jail; that he is a frightened man; that he is responsible for the city's high homicide rate . . .

And while Kelly was saying all this, Stokes was going to the theater.

He was sitting up there in the front seat of his big Lincoln with Tony Midolo at the wheel and he was on his way to catch the second act of "George M" and George M. Cohan was the only Irishman he was interested in that night.

"What about Kelly?" a newsman asked.

Stokes turned around in the seat, propping one expertly tailored, properly rolled sleeve on the seat back and said:

"I don't recognize Kelly."

That's all. That took care of the whole primary election. That is what is known as confidence. So the reporter, having been so greatly informed with such an economy of words, tried again:

"What about Perk?"

"Perk," the mayor said, "I worry about."

But that's another election. Carl Stokes was going to the theater this night and after the theater he was going to a party given by George Steinbrenner up in the Top of the Town.

He had come from the Liberty Tower on the East Side where he had given a little talk in behalf of the NDP program, not once mentioning that he was running for re-election. He had fought his way gaily out through the crowd of people who wanted a touch of him.

And now Midolo was driving toward the theater.

Things have changed a lot in two years all right. There was a night two years ago when Carl Stokes, driving his own car toward a house party in the Mt. Pleasant area, looking tired from his day said:

"The only issue in this campaign is whether enough white people will vote for a Negro, even if they believe the Negro is the best qualified man."

He looked at the reporter's face searchingly as if the reporter, being white, could answer that question. Which he couldn't.

The party had snubbed him. The party was printing newsletters saying that white voters must turn out Oct. 3 for Ralph S. Locher to save Cleveland. There was an organization and the organization was party-controlled and Locher-controlled. Carl B. Stokes was locked out.

That was two years ago and a lot had changed.

So the other night Mayor Stokes swept into Music Hall and was ushered to his fourth row seat and enjoyed the show hugely—especially a portion of it when two pretty black chorus girls trotted out on stage.

"Look at that," the mayor said. "Old George M. Cohan would roll over in his grave if he could see those girls in one of his shows."

And then he went on to the Steinbrenner party and then he went home to bed.

The following night, Andrew Dono and Jack Russell stood in the lower room at Settler's Tavern waiting for their mayor to arrive. Russell called a reporter over and said to Dono, "Andy, fill him in on how things are."

Andrew Dono is paid to know how things are in the nationality areas of Cleveland. Ralph Locher paid him to know how things were. Carl Stokes pays him to know how things are. Andrew Dono is the keeper of the nationality flags in City Hall. He can lay his hands on an imperial Polish eagle in 10 minutes. He is the author of a City Hall document titled: "Personnel of Ethnic Background in Responsible Positions Administration of Carl B. Stokes."

Andrew Dono can tell you there are six Bohemians in responsible positions at City Hall and four Hungarians, with Andrew Dono at the head of the latter category.

So Andrew Dono told how things are:

"I got the Hungarians, the Croatians, the Slovaks," Dono said. "I even got the Czechs, even though Perk is a Czech. Of course the Hungarians don't like him because he's a Czech. Things are real fine."

"How many votes did Stokes lose this area by last time?" the reporter asked.

"About 600," Andrew Dono said. Then he frowned because last time he had been working for Ralph Locher and those 600 votes had been some of his doing and now things had changed.

So Carl Stokes made his entrance—star of the party he couldn't have gotten into to wait tables two years ago.

He ate his csiga soup. He ate his veal porkolt. And then he got up and said:

"Folks, you know since I just live over on the other street, I'm interested in dropping by here just to see if you keep your property up." (No laughter.)

"This has been a pretty active year at the Hall. But it's a lot quieter than it was when the Big Boss here (nodding at Russell) was in the saddle.

"I think I'm just going to let Jack Russell tell you if he thinks these past two years have been productive ones. Jack, why don't you tell the folks."

So Russell slowly got to his feet—two years ago he endorsed no one in the primary—and he started speaking softly.

"We can't hear you, Jack," shouted a woman in the back of the room.

"Then buy a hearing aid," Russell said and he went on talking softly about how the Stokes administration had resurfaced streets in the area and replaced sidewalks.

And Stokes stood there, hands at his sides, beaming up at the television lights and wearing a smile of rapture.

"Jack," Stokes said. "That was beautiful. And now I'm going to sit down here and relax and when I get good and relaxed I'm gonna go around the corner and go home."

And that's what he did.

*— September 19, 1969*

## Perk brushes up

"A lot of the secret of politics is style."
— Carl Stokes on his last working day as mayor.

About 4 1/2 hours after he was sworn in as mayor, Ralph Perk was in a blue, nondescript car, heading toward the Allen Theater on Playhouse Square to daub the marquee with paint.

A ladder had been set up against the marquee. Glidden Co. had supplied two gallons of white paint. Somebody from the Playhouse Square Assn. was on hand with a couple of painter's hats — one with red lettering and one with black — to crown the new mayor if he wanted to play a frisky role for the television cameras.

And the cameras were there. All the stations and both newspapers were represented. Putting a daub of paint on the marquee would be Ralph Perk's first ceremonial act as mayor. And the media was there to record his style.

The television executives who launched the cameramen were in possession of a very great truth. They knew that, in this day of video-photogenics, the way Ralph Perk painted that marquee would be very important to their viewers.

Because, for the boob tube media, and perhaps for all of us, politics has become a question of theatrics. It is not what a candidate says that counts anymore as much as it is how he plays — how he enters the living room; the composite of a million dots of electrons.

It has been this way since 1960. Since John Kennedy bested Richard Nixon in a series of television debates. Bested him, not so much because of what he said but how he said it. And because of lighting and makeup and the closeness of a shave.

Style has become the stuff winners are made of. And that's why Ralph Perk fooled all the media in the election he just won.

To the members of the media (myself included) Perk just didn't seem to play well enough to be a winner.

Carl Stokes appeared to be the model of a winner. Carl Stokes, the master elocutionist, smooth, sexy, the man who, when once a reporter kidded him about his $200 suits, said:

"I wouldn't own a $200 suit. I bought one once and it didn't wear well and I'm sorry I bought it."

For the media, Carl Stokes became the model of what a winner should be. Ralph Perk wasn't even in the running.

But Ralph Perk won. And if style is the secret of politics, Ralph Perk won because of his style—the style of the little guy.

He isn't a good speaker. Neither are most of us.

He doesn't wear $200 suits. Who in the 14th Ward does?

He is maybe some kind of square. But these days, the so-called squares feel persecuted and have huddled for self-preservation; feeling sore because nobody appreciates their values anymore.

It was the Ralph Perk style that won this election. And his style was one that appealed to all the little guys out there who felt that they had been snubbed for the past four years.

And the little guys turned out yesterday to celebrate in City Hall. The Anton Blaze Post 2079, Veterans of Foreign Wars; the Polish Legion of American Veterans, Pulaski Post No. 30; Mrs. Frances Tesny, president of the Association of Polish Women of America; the Singing Angels (who sang "This Is My Country," and "The Lord's Prayer") and gaily dressed girls in embroidered skirts dispatched by the American Nationalities Movement representing 26 nationality groups.

These were representatives of the people who put Ralph Perk in office, and the media (myself again included) can like it or lump it.

Still trying to decide which, the media gathered in front of the Allen Theater today to watch Ralph Perk show his style.

Bert LeGrand, once a newsman and now a public relations man, held the ladder for Perk—suffering under the responsibility of being just one heartbeat away from being lynched.

Ralph Perk pulled up in front of the theater in his nondescript blue car and hurried out. He wore a blue suit, blue topcoat, white shirt, blue figured tie.

A man stepped out of the crowd and whispered something in Perk's ear.

"My wish for you," Perk told him, "is may you have good health and happiness."

Then he walked back to the ladder, spurned both the red and the black painters' hats, scurried up and slapped some paint on the marquee.

And got some on his coat sleeve and dropped some on two people standing below him.

The kind of thing that could happen to anybody.

*— November 9, 1971*

## Ralph Perk's boat

The other day, Mayor Perk proposed that the city buy a couple of ocean liners and tie them at the foot of E. Ninth St. to help the hotel situation here.

A lot of people thought this was ridiculous, but I didn't.

It is always easy to criticize any new idea. But if everybody just sat back and criticized, nothing would ever get done.

Look at Wade Shurtleff of the Port Authority, for example. He criticized the mayor's plan just because the Welland Canal locks are only 80 feet wide and the mayor wants to sail a boat through them that is 84 feet wide.

It is that kind of narrow-minded carping that prevents this city from getting ahead. Here the mayor has a plan to get about 96% of his boat through, and Shurtleff is knocking him because he may have some difficulty with the other 4%.

And some people criticized the mayor because the water is only 18 feet deep where he wants to park his boat and the boat needs 28 feet of parking depth.

But nobody bothered to point out that almost 66% of the mayor's boat will fit, leaving a mere 34% that won't fit.

I have no patience with people who resort to this kind of irresponsible criticism. It is easy to find fault with any idea. But consider the implications of the mayor's idea if it works.

If the mayor is successful in bringing a boat in here for use as a hotel, the way will be paved for bringing other boats here for use as other things.

The mayor could, for example, bring an aircraft carrier in and tie it up at Ninth St. That would go a long way toward solving all the furor that was raised about a jetport in the lake.

Now there will be those who will object to this aircraft carrier plan. I can hear them now. "How will he get it through the locks?" they will say. "How will he find enough room to park it?"

The same way he got the hotel boat through, that's how.

Lots of people will fly to Cleveland just because they have

never landed on an aircraft carrier before. And they will stay in the hotel boat just because they have never played shuffleboard before on a cold January day with the wind blowing 60 mph in a blinding snowstorm.

But all of this is just the beginning. Enough of frills and gimmicks for the tourists. Think of what the mayor's boat-buying program could do for the citizens of Cleveland.

The mayor could buy a battleship.

Now there will be some who will say, "What good is a battleship?" Ah, these are the people who have not given careful thought to the project.

Can you imagine the effect a battleship would have on the city's crime rate? A battleship anchored at the foot of E. Ninth St. between the aircraft carrier and the ocean liner would make any crook stop and think twice, I'll tell you.

Furthermore, there are plenty of battleships around that can be had for a song, 16-inch guns and all. They are in mothballs now, but a thorough airing in the brisk lake breezes will drive away the smell of camphor. In time of riots, entire city blocks could be pacified with merely a round or two.

I'm sure if you consider all this carefully, you will see, as I have seen, how far-thinking the mayor was in his plan to buy some ocean liners. I became so excited about the idea that I called Prudential Grace Lines in New York to find out how fast the mayor could get his hands on two boats he wants to buy from them.

I was transferred to the office of the president, a Mr. Skouras. He was out so I asked his secretary what she could tell me about the mayor's plan.

"The mayor of what wants to do what?" she asked. "Boy, that's a new one on me. But then again, I don't know everything that goes on around here. I am constantly being surprised."

She oughta live here.

— *September 7, 1972*

## Rating a crisis

I had to find out how Clevelanders were reacting to the crisis at City Hall. But the only Clevelander I know who works here was off sick.

So I telephoned Mrs. Figment who lives in the old neighborhood behind Republic Steel where the fallout from the steel mills turns the laundry orange on the clothes lines.

"Mrs. Figment," I said. "I have a question for you. Keep in mind you are speaking for the record."

"Don't worry, Mr. Big Pants," she said. "You never call me unless you want something. You could once in a while simply call just to ask how I am."

"How are you?" I said.

"Don't ask," she said. "What with all that is going on in this city."

"What troubles you most about the situation?"

"What troubles me most? Why they got rid of Dennis. They should have their heads examined. I'm not saying Dennis was perfect but who knows how great he might have been if they hadn't gotten rid of him. I'm sick over it."

"But Mrs. Figment, they haven't gotten rid of him yet. They may not get rid of him at all," I said.

"Yes they did," she said. "He went to Boston. I read it in your newspaper."

"Wait a minute," I said. "Are you talking about Dennis Kucinich the mayor?"

"I'm talking," she said, "about Dennis Eckersley the no-hit pitcher. What is this? Another one of your silly politics calls?"

"Mrs. Figment," I said, "please. There's a crisis going on in city government. My question to you is, would you recall the mayor?"

"Which one?" she said. "I recall most of them. I recall more mayors than you ever heard of. But that's because I'm older than you are so I'm not blaming you for that."

"Mrs. Figment," I said, "you aren't being seri . . . "

"What I recall about most of them is," she said, "that they all had some kind of crisis going on. Why don't you ask me how I rate this crisis compared to some past crisises."

"All right."

"All right, what? You make such a big point of this being on the record."

"All right, how do you rate this crisis compared to some past crisises—crises?"

"This may be the best. I give this four stars."

"What is there about this crisis that makes it maybe the best?"

"My son-in-law, Melvin," said Mrs. Figment.

"I don't understand," I said.

"My son-in-law Melvin gave me a color television for my birthday, when you might have called to say how are you but I won't mention that. This is the first crisis I've seen on color TV so for me this one is the best."

"Mrs. Figment, I'm trying to . . . "

"I recall when there were only newspapers," Mrs. Figment said. "In those days you could take or leave a crisis. With radio, crisises got bigger and better. Television helped them a lot. But color television is absolutely best for crisises. Tell me, what color eyes has Hongisto got?"

"What has that got to do with . . . ?"

"I'm still on warranty," Mrs. Figment said. "Does the mayor really look pale or is something the matter with my chroma-color?"

"Mrs. Figment will you . . . ?"

"Then of course," said Mrs. Figment, "there is more news on than there used to be. Channel Three where you are has a whole hour. And the rest of them have shows at noon and in the afternoon. That helps the crisis along. Then they all have those little messages that crawl and beep across the bottom of the screen. That really helps a crisis. So I'd say, no question about it, this is the best crisis I've seen."

"I will quote you on that, Mrs. Figment."

"I'll be interested to see how it comes out this time," she said.

"Now, Mrs. Figment," I said. "I only have one more question. Please try to answer this plainly. If this is the biggest crisis you've ever seen, do you think we ought to get rid of the mayor? Should the mayor be removed from office?"

"Why?" said Mrs. Figment. "Did he do something wrong?"

— *April 3, 1978*

# Tale of two speeches

It was quiet in Dennis Kucinich's living room last night—so quiet you could hear the crickets chirping outside on Milan Ave. It was nice sitting there listening to the crickets. It was nicer than listening to the returns.

Listening to the returns was, in fact, against the rules. The big combination television-phonograph in the living room was off and it stayed off. The election numbers—beamed through the ether from the television studios and the news radio stations— arrived at the Kucinich house and bounced off the mayoral roof.

It was, truth be told, a little spooky. For weeks, for months the churning, crazy politics of the entire city had been racing toward this night. The night of Showdown Sunday,

Now the polls were closed. The voters had spoken but the sound wasn't carrying here. Upstairs, the mayor was sitting in his bedroom—the only room in the house with air conditioning. He was working on his victory speech and his concession speech. He had a manila folder for each one. Down in the living room, Sandy Kucinich sat in a rocking chair. Carol Juniewicz, wife of the mayor's press secretary, was keeping her company.

Earlier, the house had been full of McCarthys—Sandy's mother and father, sister and brother and nephews. Four-year-old nephew David had left a huge, stuffed pink panther propped against the stair rail. The panther gave me a blank stare. Upstairs, the floor creaked. The mayor was pacing over his speeches. Outside the crickets of Milan Ave. sounded sad.

Sandy Kucinich turned on her player piano—a birthday gift from the mayor. The piano began to beat out a tune. "It's a Small World After All." It was. It was too small for my tastes.

"Dennis never listens to the television returns on election night," Sandy said. "He waits until somebody calls him."

The mayor galloped down the stairs.

"I don't hear anything," he said. "What do you think if I put in the speech a line from A *Tale of Two Cities?* Somebody sends a message and the message reads 'Recalled to Live.' If I win, I've been recalled to life."

He liked it. He went back upstairs. Sandy put a new roll on the piano. "Waiting for the Robert E. Lee."

I couldn't wait though. So I went out into the soft warm night with a portable radio. I turned it on low so as not to distract the mayor with news of his election.

Half the precincts were in and he had a 3,000-vote lead. Then, the crickets and I listened to his lead drop like a stone.

"We don't know where the mayor is at this moment," a girl on the radio was saying. "Those gathered here at his victory party expect him soon." Inside, a telephone rang.

The mayor came out with his manila folders. "Time to go over," he said. In the car, the driver had the radio on. The lead was almost gone. The mayor grabbed his mobile phone and made a call. "Get somebody guarding those ballots," he said.

The radio carried the sound of a victory party. The people at the Bond Court Hotel were celebrating. They thought they had plenty to celebrate. Their man had beaten the newspapers, the television stations, the big unions. Happy noises came out of the radio and then we were at the hotel and the sound was real and right there.

But the truth of the night lay somewhere between the shouting and the silence. There would be a recount. An election had been won by a whisper but Dennis Kucinich could not say he had been recalled to life. He could only say he seemed to have survived.

— *August 14, 1978*

# So long, Dennis

You know how it is. If there's a guy you've worked with and you hear he's leaving, you make it a point to stop and say so long to him, just in case you miss him on his last day.

So long, Dennis.

I hear you are leaving. All the polls say so. I don't usually hold much with polls but this time I think they are right.

You ought to see the looks on the faces of the out-of-town reporters. They started straggling in late this week the way they've straggled in for two years while you've been fighting to keep your job.

(Two years. My God. It seems longer than that to me. Doesn't it to you?)

Yeah, the reporters came in this week and by now they know where the good restaurants are. And they put the arm on the local newsmen and take them out on expense account lunches. They open their notebooks and put them next to their salad plates. They uncap their Bics and buy a Scotch. They tell the waitress they'll order in about 10 minutes. Then they are ready for work.

"Is he really gonna lose to this Voinovich?" they say.

"Yeah," you tell them.

"No kidding," they say. "Losing to an unknown."

(That's the way it is with out-of-town reporters. If they don't know a person, that person isn't known.)

And they know you, Dennis, and they know Carl Stokes and they know Ralph Nader and they can't figure out who is beating you.

I wonder what you think, reading the polls.

Do you really think somebody bought this election? Do you think the town sold you out? All your life, from the time you were a very little kid, you fought extra hard for whatever you got. You were small and life was tough and the lesson you learned early was that life was a struggle. They used to call what you have

Moxie. Somewhere you picked up the idea that life was grim and dirty like the Korean War. Rich kids don't grow up thinking that way. They expect everything will turn out all right. In your world it won't.

It won't Tuesday but how will you read that?

Will you yell foul? Will you claim you won on points? The out-of-town reporters think you did. You beat the recall. You saved the light plant. You took on the banks and the utilities. Total that up and it looks like you are ahead. The out-of-town reporters know what you did and they are puzzled.

But then, they don't have to live here. Anybody who lives here wants to live in a city. Nobody wants to live in a sociological laboratory. Nobody wants to live in Debate 101. This is not the set for the stone-throwing scene from "David and Goliath." This is a place to live.

You won your fights but you wore out the town. The town is out of breath. The town can't keep up with you. The town wants a rest. You don't offer that. You don't know how. You haven't got the vocabulary for it.

It's a big stew of a town and everybody needs everybody. The thin cats need the fat cats. The black cats need the white cats. And vice-versa. And et cetera. The Mayor has the tough job of keeping it all in balance.

You scorn balance. You've kept it all off balance. You rock it like a canoe in the rapids. You are like the guy who fights when he drinks. Enough of that and people edge away from you. Enough of that and they seat you near the door so they can get you out in a hurry.

When people live together they have to have harmony and cooperation. You never had much and you don't miss it. The town does though. That's what's happening to you.

People have been telling you that all along. You didn't trust them. Maybe you thought they were out to trick you. The people you listen to don't know harmony from Spike Jones. The people you listen to would blow a police whistle at a funeral mass. The people around you get on everybody's nerves.

You wore out your welcome in the end. The polls say the end

is coming Tuesday. But for you it's just a chapter. You had a lot of what you needed but you didn't have enough. You're young and you'll be back.

You won on points and you had the heart. You lacked the humility. To you, that was excess baggage. To you that was weakness. You never learned humility but you'll get a lesson in it Tuesday night.

When it comes, treat it like a gift. When you come back, bring it with you.

— *November 3, 1979*

## A *bitter city votes*

The town looks bad when the winter rains start to come. The days are gray and the nights turn glistening black. The city George Voinovich inherited last night was wet and cold. And bitter, very bitter.

Yesterday it voted bitter. It knew what it wanted to get rid of. It wanted to get rid of Dennis Kucinich and it turned out to do that job.

The town was a hit man yesterday. It terminated Dennis Kucinich with extreme prejudice, to use the campy hit-man term. The city knocked Dennis Kucinich down and that left George Voinovich standing alone. And so he became the mayor.

Minutes before Dennis Kucinich conceded the race, George Voinovich stood alone in the middle of the rug in the middle of the 10th-floor corridor of the Cleveland Plaza Hotel. In a suite behind him, his wife Janet sat with friends. "She's holding up pretty well," he said of his wife. "I took her to lunch at Settler's Tavern today. That's kind of an Election Day ritual with us. Lunch at Settler's. Then dinner at the Bridge Tavern. But we skipped that. That brought back too many memories. We had dinner at my mother's."

His little girl's death is still a fresh wound. He would begin his acceptance speech with a reference to it. He stood in the hall like a sentry, guarding his wife and her sorrow.

"What I need now is time," he said. "I have to have time to find the right people. I've got to keep the people around me from panicking. I have to find a finance man. I have to have a guy who has some credibility with the banks. A guy who can walk into the banks. That's the first job, and the tough job. Finding the people to straighten out the finances."

He looked grim. Downstairs in the ballroom, the crowd was building. It was a noisy crowd and the noise it made changed as the evening grew later and the crowd grew bigger. Early in the evening it had been happy noise—up-tempo noise. But as people came out of the night the noise changed to hubbub. Just noise. Racket.

Then the racket became a roar. There was a television set in the middle of the crowd and the set suddenly showed Dennis Kucinich standing in a hotel across town. You could not hear what he was saying but the word was passed that he was conceding the election. The crowd roared at that because the grinding and tragic and bitter campaign was over.

George Voinovich did not enter the ballroom through the crowd. He came in through a back door near the stage. He struggled to quiet his supporters but never was able to do it. He started his speech in the middle of that noise. His speech was short phrases hurled against the sound.

The crowd began to boo. That was the first sign that Dennis Kucinich had entered the hall. He had come to surrender and the Voinovich crowd wanted the surrender to be unconditional. It was not a night for sportsmanship. Gestures did not count. No frills last night, only harsh realities.

George Voinovich knows them. Dennis is gone and George is left—and it's still a sour town. What has ended is still more significant—more definable—than what he has begun.

Dennis used his two years to point out the villains. He showed the bitterness that is Cleveland today. He ended his term at a ballroom where there were metal detectors at the doors, presumably to sniff out weapons.

When Dennis left the Voinovich ballroom there were some policemen on the sidewalk in front of the Cleveland Plaza Hotel. The mayor's car had difficulty pulling out into traffic.

"Goodbye," the policemen yelled sarcastically. Then one of them left his friends and walked into the street.

"I'll get you out of here," he said. He put his fingers in his mouth and whistled. "I'll stop traffic for you," he said. He held up his arms and the oncoming traffic stopped.

"Now go, you — —-," he yelled at Dennis Kucinich.

And that was the way something ended yesterday. With a curse in the rain.

It wasn't pleasant. Things aren't here. From now on it's all

George Voinovich's fault. From now on, he's the target. He is a man worried about time. Yeah. And they call that winning.

— *November 7, 1979*

## Jim Rhodes goes fishing

Last week somebody sent Gov. Dick Celeste an envelope with a newspaper clipping in it. The clipping was yellowed and old, which didn't make me feel so hot because I wrote it.

Celeste handed it to me with a grin.

"Thanks," he said. "Here's another vote for me."

It was a story written in 1969 about a day in the life of then-Gov. Jim Rhodes. A day he went fishing.

Let me set the scene for you . . .

It is early morning somewhere on the Chagrin River. The only sounds are of birds twittering in the trees and the babbling of the flowing water . . .

Whoops! Wait a minute. That isn't the river babbling. That babbling is coming from a crowd of people who now appear from over the horizon. There are a couple of state troopers in the crowd and a gaggle of officials from the state wildlife commission. A few politicians are there, sticking close to a younger Jim Rhodes and a couple of newspaper reporters including a younger me.

We have gathered at the river to watch the governor catch a fish. The fish he is after is a fish he more or less invented. The coho salmon.

This is a year when Lake Erie is a stagnant pond. Its fish have died in it or left town. Rhodes is trying to show that all is not lost. He has stocked the river with coho salmon—a new kind of fish to most of us who are only used to salmon in cans. Now he has come to pull one of his fish out of the water and regard it and call it good.

So the governor and his troopers and the crowd of state officials and the political hangers-on all struggle into waders. They enter the water. And the governor begins to fish.

Nothing's biting.

The wildlife people begin to eye each other nervously.

Finally, one of them splashes out of the water and squishes, in his waders, upstream. Bored, I follow him.

Around the bend, a man crouches next to some kind of electrical device. The wildlife man marches up to him.

"The governor hasn't gotten a nibble," he says, sternly. "Did you shock the fish to stun them like you were supposed to?"

"Yeah," says the crouching electrician.

""Well, do it again," says the wildlife man.

Then he marches back to the fishing party and I follow him. Everybody gets out of the water. Around the bend the electric man zaps the river. And soon some groggy coho salmon come floating around the bend, resting on their sides.

Jim Rhodes hops back into the river. He hoists a fish by the gills and turns, grinning to the cameras. He addresses the reporters.

"Here boys," he says. "Have some feesh . . . "

I finished reading the story. I remembered it all. Attached to the clipping was a note from a voter. The voter said she was writing to tell Dick Celeste that she had come across the story in a drawer and, after reading it, was certainly not going to vote for Jim Rhodes.

I handed the clipping to Celeste.

"Why don't you ever do anything like that?" I said.

"Like what?" he said.

"Stun fish," I said. "It probably would never occur to you, that's your trouble!"

Celeste looked puzzled. And I guess I don't blame him.

But the truth is, I'm going to miss Jim Rhodes. I can see that some of you want to argue about that, but I'm not interested. I didn't say I'd vote for him.

But miss him . . . hell, yes.

— *November 2, 1986*

## Ask the consultant

When I saw that the Cleveland school system was facing a massive reorganizational crisis, I telephoned the famous out-of-town consultant Charlie (The Dip) Scarducci, sometimes known as Vacuum Cleaner Charlie, to see if he had any advice.

"It'll cost ya," Charlie said.

"Money is no object," I said.

"Yes it is, too," said Charlie. "It is a small, rectangular object with numbers on it and one week's worth of my consulting gives me enough objects to buy a nice CD."

"The only thing we in Cleveland care about is the future and well-being of our children," I said. "We are always willing to pay, even if we are broke."

"Well," said Charlie, "I can give you two kinds of advice. I can give you the normal consultant advice, which sounds pretty good but which doesn't mean anything. And then, for a higher fee, I can give you some revolutionary consultant advice which sounds so bold and daring you might be afraid to take it."

"Can I get a preview of some of the cheap advice?"

"Cheaper, not cheap," said Charlie.

"Can I get a preview of some of the cheaper advice?"

"OK," Charlie said. "Try this. 'The goal of the Cleveland school system should be to supply a support system tailored to address the divergent backgrounds and socio-economic levels of the educable population in such a manner as to facilitate its desirable assimilation by society as a whole while at the same time provide non-threatening motivational challenges which, when subtly administered, will direct and hopefully stimulate those exposed to them toward useful career choices and living modes.'"

"I like that one," I said. "How much is that one?"

"Wait a sec while I look at the meter," said Charlie. "OK. That advice comes to 50 grand."

"Can I get a sample of some of the high-priced advice?" I said.

"Sure," said Charlie. "Are you ready?"

"Ready."

"OK. Teach 'em to read, write and do math."

"My God!" I gasped.

"Kind of startling when you first hear it, ain't it?" said Charlie.

"It's far out," I said. "I can't grasp the enormity of it all at once. It's too bold and daring a concept."

"It's new," said Charlie. "It ain't on the market long. People are afraid of it."

"It's . . . it's . . . it's awesome," I said. "Who teaches them?"

"Teachers," said Charlie.

"Good Lord!" I said. "Who advises the teachers?"

"Principals," said Charlie.

"I can't believe what I'm hearing," I said. "Who advises the principals?"

"You got an overall school superintendent," said Charlie. "Then you got heads of departments like a reading head and a writing head and a math head. Then you got other people in charge of stuff like lunches and buses and music and art and those things."

"Astonishing," I said. "What does the school board do?"

"It gets elected," Charlie said.

"That's all?"

"Well, it raises hell from time to time so it can get elected," said Charlie. "But otherwise it keeps its hands off."

"Charlie," I said, "revolutionary as it sounds, there may be something to it. Of course I'll have to think about it. I'm still a little stunned by it. What does it cost?"

"A hunnerd million dollars," said Charlie.

"That seems a little high," I said.

"I got to price it high," said Charlie. "It's a one-shot transaction. The only thing wrong with it is there ain't no future in it."

"For the kids?" I said.

"For the consultants," said Charlie. "What kids? Am I a kid?"

— *June 5, 1981*

# Who's watching the children?

The people of Cleveland had better lock up their children. There are four candidates for school superintendent in town. It is not a sight for youthful eyes.

You've got to wonder about anybody who wants the job. The last school superintendent killed himself. There were, you may remember, two schools of thought about why.

Some people said the job drove him out of his mind. Other people said he was mentally disturbed all along but it didn't show.

I tend toward the latter opinion. In the chaos of the Cleveland schools, mental illness does not stand out. It blends in.

The miracle of modern communication being what it is, the word soon spread that Cleveland's school superintendent had shot himself and blamed the town. You might have thought such news would discourage applicants. But it didn't.

It would have in the old days. In the old days, a school superintendent was a little like the pope. He was considered infallible in matters of education. He was a paragon of dignity. He kept the accumulated knowledge of human civilization downtown in his office. He doled it out to the school children a spoonful at a time.

But then education fell into the hands of the hucksters and the hacks. Businessmen and politicians discovered the potential of ignorance and segregation. They began to peddle the quick fix. With proper marketing, virtue can be made to pay even better than vice.

We got busing and the New Math. Fancy reading programs were sold to the school systems for fancy figures. In the meantime, the children got dumber and truancy rose.

The old breed of educator, the one who believed that teaching was almost holy, was replaced by the new guy. The new guy comes on like a vacuum cleaner salesman. He holds press con-

ferences and stands with his nose quivering in the political
breezes like a Beagle scenting Alpo.

Cleveland has played host to a string of passing school super-
intendents, some of whom exploited the children in a manner
that makes the Pied Piper look as caring as Captain Kangaroo.

One guy left a trail of bar bills that would have awed Foster
Brooks. Another guy spent most of his time trying to peddle his
own reading program. The school board finally read the hand-
writing on the wall and he was replaced. With Fred Holliday.
Who killed himself.

Now the job is open again—a job that comes open more
often than the presidency of a banana republic. Four candidates
were in town this week talking about why they should get it.

We heard that one should get it because she's a woman. That
another should get it because he's a black. That another should
get it because he knows how to mix politics and education.

We didn't hear very much talk about children.

But then, some people don't like children.

*— August 21, 1985*

# The cost of caring

Well, the bribe didn't work.

I got into a lot of trouble last spring for calling it a bribe. Boy, was I lectured!

"It's not a bribe, it's an incentive," said a caring, sharing woman who, strangely, is a friend of mine. "There's a big difference between a bribe and an incentive."

"That's what the lobbyist said when he handed the senator the envelope," I said.

"Go ahead, be sarcastic. But it is not a bribe to pay Cleveland school children to go to summer school," said the caring, sharing woman. "If they don't pass the state proficiency test, a third of them will not graduate from high school. They need an incentive. A bribe is paying somebody to do something that maybe he shouldn't do. In this case we're merely paying the children to do something they should do."

"Then it's worse than a bribe," I said. "It's a corruption of their entire value system. You get a kid used to the idea that he gets money for doing what he ought to do, he'll want a paycheck for not robbing old ladies. Bribe a kid to go to summer school and he'll want a bribe to go to regular school. Why wouldn't he?"

"You are hopeless," said the caring, sharing woman. "Try looking at it this way. If these kids weren't going to summer school, they would be working this summer. Isn't it right to pay them at least as much as they'd make if they were working?"

"No," I said.

"No!" she said. "How can you say no to that?"

"Because in the old days kids went to summer school and worked too," I said. "Besides, suppose a kid says he can make $800 a week as a drug lookout. Are you going to try to match that salary in math class? Once you start talking about money, you're talking about money. The laws of capitalism take over. And there are a lot of capitalists out there on the street who are flunking biology."

"Well, I can see it's pointless to discuss this any further with you," said the caring, sharing woman.

So we didn't discuss it any further. Until yesterday. When a *PD* story said that not many Cleveland school kids had gone to summer school, incentive or no incentive. And that a third of them still hadn't passed the state test and were in danger of not getting a diploma.

I telephoned the caring, sharing woman to see what she'd have to say about that. One of the advantages you have if you ration your caring and sharing is the freedom to say I told you so.

But now the caring, sharing woman had changed her tack.

"The problem is with the test," she said. "I agree with the NAACP that the test unfairly discriminates against black students."

"Except the ones who passed it," I said.

"Well, we're not talking about the ones who passed it," she said.

"I know we're not," I said. "What I don't know is why we're not."

"What's your point?"

"The Cleveland school system is largely black," I said. "Two thirds of the seniors passed the test. I presume that means that many more black kids passed the test than failed it. It's also pretty safe to assume that some white kids failed it. Or don't you want to assume that?"

"Of course I want to assume that," said the caring, sharing woman, shocked at the question.

"So do I," I said. "So we're talking about a test that more black kids passed than failed. And that some white kids failed. I don't see how you can say such a test discriminates against black kids. But I'm certainly willing to say such a test discriminates against some white kids."

"Well, at least you used the word 'discrimination.' That's something," said the caring, sharing woman.

"Sure," I said. "In the first place, the test discriminates against dumb kids. All tests do."

At that, the caring, sharing woman let out a squawk like a smoke detector.

"Dumb!" she yelled. "What a stupid, bigoted, distorted, unfeeling thing to say."

"No more stupid, bigoted or distorted than saying that the state rigged a test too hard for black kids to pass even though most of them have passed it," I said. "And as far as feelings go, I was trying to spare yours."

"What do you mean?" she said.

"I mean that the real victims of the test are the victims of your caring," I said. "It was your so-called caring that allowed kids to think that bad English is as acceptable as good English. That rap records are as valid a learning source as books. It was your 'caring' that promoted a kid to the next grade even if he wasn't ready because you didn't want to damage his self-esteem. It was your 'caring' that encouraged standards in city schools you wouldn't for a minute allow out in Bay Village where you live."

"The kids in city schools are victims of historic discrimination," she snapped.

"Yes," I said. "And they will continue to be as long as you call for a double standard. Why do you think the kids are doing so poorly in math? Because math is one thing you can't fudge. Maybe you can slide through with bad grammar and borderline illiteracy. But it's simple arithmetic that you can't use a six-foot ladder to get to a 12-foot shelf. And if you water down this test, that's what you're doing. You're giving these kids short ladders and sending them out into a world of high shelves. If that isn't institutional racism, what the hell is?"

At which point the caring, sharing woman hung up on me.

Oh well. The effect of caring and sharing on society is overrated anyway. Arsenic would produce the same results.

*— January 14, 1994*

## Winning the west

Those of us who covered the mayoral campaign of Carl Stokes way back in 1967 knew we were witnessing history—the election of the first black mayor of a major American city.

But the Forbes-White mayoral campaign is historic too. This is the first time two black candidates have competed for the mayor's chair. And that fact is producing a phenomenon we've never seen here before.

In most Cleveland mayoral campaigns, two white candidates take the field. Soon they trot over to the East Side of town to woo black power brokers and try to form an emotional bond with voters in the black neighborhoods.

But this is the first time that two contending black contestants have crossed the river, east-to-west, to court white voters. And no wonder.

Cleveland's white West Side holds the key to this election. It's as simple as this:

If the white voters stay home, George Forbes wins the election.

If the white voters go to the polls, Mike White wins the election.

That may be distasteful, but it's reality. Cleveland mayoral elections are not to be confused with Brotherhood Week.

"If the election were held tomorrow, we'd lose 60–40," a top Forbes campaign advisor told me.

The Forbes people know there is no way their candidate can win the west. When they sent him across the river into Mike White's promised land, it was to deliver a simple message:

"I'm not as dirty as you think I am. Mike White isn't as clean as you think he is."

Forbes isn't trying to convert white voters. He knows he can't. He's trying to drain their batteries. He's hoping to create enough indifference to keep them home on election day—to make them say, "aw, the hell with it." In a democracy where less than half the people vote, that's not an impossible goal.

White, on the other hand, has been campaigning as the candidate with a dream. But, as election day nears, I predict he will talk less about his dream and more about the dream of his white constituency:

"For years you've dreamed of a way to get rid of George Forbes. At last your dreams have come true. I am the way." That, dressed up in fancy clothes, will be White's message.

In order for Forbes to put the voters to sleep, he has to throw dirt on White. In order for White to get the voters charged up, he has to throw dirt on Forbes. Given that set of imperatives, let me see a show of hands from those of you who think the rest of this campaign will be (a) clean, or (b) dirty.

Right.

I predicted on primary night that Mike White would be the next mayor of Cleveland. Nothing has happened since to change my mind.

The Forbes people sent an army of housing inspectors out to climb around on some rental properties White owns. Guess what? They found housing violations. If they came to your house they'd find some too. That was a yawner.

White has been willing to talk about this. Perhaps too willing. He confessed that, while married, he'd once had a months-long affair with a woman but could not remember her name. That, I found damaging. It's a sign of a man who's not keeping his mind on his work.

But these are razor nicks. It will take some deep and gushing wounds to weaken White's lead among white voters. And he hasn't really started on Forbes yet. That bell is about to sound.

And the prize ring is on the sunset side of the river, with a campaign strategy written 100 years ago by Horace Greeley. Go west, young man. And go armed.

— *October 18, 1989*

## A *more fitting tribute*

Politicians take tax money and build skyscrapers, which they name after each other. Millionaires carve their names on ballparks. Everybody itches for a little posterity.

Today, they named a piece of sidewalk after Louie Seltzer. The bit of pavement between the Galleria and the Ameritech Building will be called Seltzer Way.

A piece of sidewalk is a third-class ticket to immortality. It doesn't seem like much for a man who was once called "Mr. Cleveland." The real Mr. Cleveland—Moses—landed here, took a quick look around and left forever. Yet he rates a statue on Public Square. Seltzer was editor of the *Cleveland Press* for 38 years. He gets a shortcut. But you settle for what fame you can get in this, the age of Snoop Doggy Dogg.

A tunnel might have been a more appropriate namesake. Some people used to believe there was a tunnel between the *Press* and City Hall. Through this dank cavern, so legend went, Seltzer would summon the current mayor so he could issue instructions on how to steer the city.

But there was no tunnel, except in a metaphoric sense. Seltzer, it was true, had a good deal to say about who became mayor. Former Mayors Frank Lausche and Anthony Celebrezze Sr. owed much of their political fortunes to Seltzer's sponsorship. Dick Maher, the *Press* politics writer, once told me about an earnest conversation in which Seltzer wondered whether the city was "ready for an Italian mayor." Seltzer trusted himself to answer his own questions at such times, and Celebrezze got the paper's backing. Today, Celebrezze, a moving spirit behind "Seltzer Way," returned the favor. In city politics, concrete is often a medium of exchange.

Lausche, who also served as both governor and senator, was a free spirit Seltzer plucked from the Triple-A league of City Council. If the *Press* had something on its mind back then, it would often unload it over eight columns across the top of the front page in an editorial signed "L.B.S." Even an egomaniac politician was awed by such backing.

Lausche was a savvy campaigner in his own right. He liked to wear Homburg hats and was given to campaigning in saloons. Often, he would leave his hat behind on purpose.

"If you make a speech in a tavern," he once explained to me, "they're apt to forget about you as soon as you go out the door. But if you leave your hat there, the bartender will point at it a couple of times a day and say, 'See that hat? . . .' Lausche's spirited oratory sometimes took wing and broke the tether of his thought process. He once ended a speech to a group of mothers whose sons were in service by saying warmly, "I hope all you Blue Star mothers become Gold Star mothers." A frenzied aide explained to Lausche that he had just uttered the hope that his audience's sons would be killed in action. But Lausche trusted that they would know what he meant.

But I am wandering away from the subject of Seltzer. Not surprising when you consider that the path he took for 38 years wound all over the city and touched every part of it. In 1964, *Time* magazine named his newspaper one of the 10 best in the country. "No cause is too large or too small for the *Cleveland Press*," *Time* said. But if you worked for Seltzer, you knew that.

When I was hired, an old hand wryly explained to me that Seltzer's mission was to follow his readers from the cradle to the grave. We picked them up at birth with a "cradle roll" feature, saw them through puberty with a "Teen-Press" department, let them alone while they were working for a living and picked them up again in Marie Daerr's "golden-age" column. And when they died, we strove mightily to make poetry out of their obits.

Seltzer was a public titan, but in the little family circle of his newspaper, he was a benign and fun-loving uncle. His secretary kept a list of the names and ages of the children of the staff members and, at Christmas, there was a personal and tasteful gift from Louie to your kids. He threw firecrackers around the city room and the staff retaliated by dumping him in a wastebasket. Once, they locked him in a men's room stall and there existed, for a while, a famous photo of him escaping over its wall.

It's no wonder he thought of a newspaper office as a family home—he had been in one since he was 12, when he quit school. He regarded us all as beloved but somewhat unstable children, many of whom drank too much.

It was a pretty good drinking staff and, at a famous Christmas party that I did not attend, Seltzer experimented by leaving the bar open for only an hour. The staff coped by ordering scores of drinks during that hour and hiding them around the hotel ballroom, behind drapes and under tables. As the evening progressed, Louie watched, puzzled, as his troops got more and more oiled even though the well presumably had been capped. Their condition became undeniable when an editor did a belly slide across a banquet table.

Scripps-Howard owned the *Press* in name only. In 1960, when the chain decided to endorse Nixon, the paper published the corporate endorsement, then endorsed Kennedy across the page in an editorial signed "L.B.S." There was a lighthouse on the front page, but Seltzer's was the real flame.

But not an eternal flame. History has a short attention span. Most of the kids in the food court of the Galleria have never heard of Louie Seltzer. Today's household word is tomorrow's trivia question. Dorothy Fuldheim is now a meeting room in the Sheraton. Louie Seltzer is a piece of sidewalk. His paper is gone and he is gone and so is the Seltzer Way, no matter what the street sign says.

— *July 29, 1994*

# *The senator from Ohio*

There was a little going-out-of-business party for Howard Metzenbaum Monday night in a small room at Harlan Diamond's pleasure palace, Landerhaven.

The event was strictly nonpolitical. Old friends from way back when, some of them Republicans, gathered to wish the senator well as he retires from the Senate. The affair was engineered by Metzenbaum's longtime aide—a dynamic woman who bears the unusual and savory name of Candy Korn.

A dozen friends stood to say a few nice words about Metzenbaum and throw a few digs. Most were cronies from his old law firm. Some were partners from the small parking lot business Metzenbaum started years ago with his pal Ted Bonda.

"Our first parking lot had a name," one of these old friends said. "It was called E. 12th St." What he meant was that the first parking lot the company owned was too small to hold enough cars to generate a profit.

So if you pulled into the lot, an attendant greeted you and asked you casually how long you planned to park. If you said several hours, the attendant would wait until you were out of sight, then hustle your car out to the street and park it at a meter. That freed a parking space for the next guy. The imperative was to get the car back in the lot before the customer came for it. That parlor trick grew up to be APCOA.

Metzenbaum had several million dollars when he decided to run for the Senate. A story I contributed to Monday night's party was about a campaign trip we took way downstate past the "booosh line," which is the point, at about Mansfield, where Ohioans start saying "boooshes" for bushes and "feeesch" for fish. Ohio turns into a big and varied state when you campaign in it.

Nobody else was traveling with us and we visited a little town with a name something like Hobnob. At a meeting of about 14 lukewarm Hobnobians, Candidate Metzenbaum made a speech denouncing the evils of abortion. When we got back to the motel, I asked him about it.

"I thought you were kind of pro-choice," I said.

"Look," he said, "I'm a Jewish millionaire from Cleveland. That's enough bad news for Hobnob for one night."

Metzenbaum worked hard. But he always had. He paid his way through Ohio State peddling soap and razor blades and mums for football games. There was a persistent rumor, muttered by his opponents, that he also sold condoms for after the game. If there's any truth in that, it only shows you how yesterday's outrage is considered today's public service.

He was ambitious but he was lucky, too. Certainly lucky to have his wife, Shirley, and his four daughters. Also lucky in matters of the wallet.

"Different people have different knacks," he once told me. "I have a knack of making money." This remark left me pretty dissatisfied with my own knack, which was the ability to play bad piano by ear.

But back in 1974, Metzenbaum drew a bad hand. He had to run in the primary against John Glenn. I remember watching him stand on the street in Ashland with a campaign button the size of a dinner plate on his lapel. Grabbing at the hands of shoppers. Trying to get them familiar with the name "Metzenbaum."

They were, of course, already familiar with the name "John Glenn." Glenn was in Ashland, too. In the library, already in the history books. Metzenbaum had to wait two years to get there. Glenn beat him, but he came back to beat Bob Taft Jr. Maybe he was having a bad day, but Bob Taft Jr. was the dullest man I ever met in politics. They've called Metzenbaum a lot of things, but dull isn't one of them.

But now it's curtain time, and over in the Federal Building, Candy Korn is taking the pictures down from the walls and packing them away. The old political photos of handshakes and grins with this president and that one. Down they come, leaving bare patches on the wallpaper.

At the party the other night in Landerhaven, a young man

named Marc Weagraff from the Institute of Music sang "The Impossible Dream," which is a song they sing to you when it's time to cash in your chips, whether you've won or lost.

Metzenbaum grew up poor and Jewish and listening to the sculpted, hopeful phrases of FDR on the radio. He made himself rich but hung onto his boyhood politics. He was the last of the ferocious New Deal liberals, and the country is closing that book, and he's getting out at a good time. He hoped his son-in-law would replace him but, at this writing, that doesn't seem likely.

It took Howard two trips around the state to make it. In Ohio politics, there is no parking-lot shuffle that helps you make it in one.

My politics are not Metzenbaum's but I'll tell you this: You knew where he was. You knew what he was going to do. In an age of hacks who trade their convictions for poll results, he would have none of that. And that alone is damn refreshing.

So I would have played him some Sinatra. He did it his way. So long, Howard. Best wishes. And so long, era, too.

— *November 9, 1994*

# SHADES OF DIFFERENCE

## *Reminders of violence*

What kind of monument can you make to a riot?

The people in Hough have two monuments to the week of terror and death which began three years ago tonight.

One of them is the $1,015,000 Thurgood Marshall Recreation Center, conceived after the Hough Riot and not yet dedicated—a plaything for the living.

The other is a small plaque, dedicated today on the baseball diamond at the center. A committee of Hough citizens led by Louis Robinson proclaimed the patch of ground "Joyce Arnett Square" in honor of the first of four Negroes killed during the riot—a monument to the dead.

Which one is the real monument?

Take a ride on Hough Ave. today. It smolders and steams in the hot sun. The people are out on their porches and in the houses that have windows, the windows are open. Some houses don't have windows—that is Hough's air conditioning.

Watermelon and cold beer are selling well in the grocery stores where the pay phones all have crayon signs over them: "Please limit your call to five minutes"—grocery store telephones—Hough's communications system.

It is peaceful and quiet today under the hot sun where little boys are rolling hot auto tires (Hough's playthings) and the bigger boys are shooting baskets. Their baskets are the battered garbage cans planted along the curb (Hough's tree lawn).

Quiet and peaceful—nothing like it was the night Joyce Arnett saw it for the last time. There was shooting in the air that night and bright, hot searchlights, and police helicopters overhead.

The Joyce Arnett named on the plaque on the ball diamond was 26 years old. When they put her on the slab at the morgue she was noted as five feet nine inches tall and she weighed 139 pounds.

Those statistics were also on file at Central Police Station which Joyce Arnett had visited a couple of times—once after a man shot her during a quarrel. She survived her first gunshot wound but she wasn't going to survive her second one.

Joyce Arnett was a mother, and she had—musically—named her daughters Jynette and Lynette , which she thought went very well with Arnett. Jynette and Lynette were seven and Joyce's other daughter was Laura, who was five.

The night that she was killed, Joyce Arnett was trying to get home to her children because, whatever else she was, she was a concerned mother and people were shooting at police in her neighborhood and police were shooting back and her children were home alone.

She had left her home on E. 81st St. to go out and see what all the commotion was about. On the sidewalk she met her cousin, Leon McCord and his wife Barbara, and they all walked down Hough to E. 73rd St. There police were dodging and running around and a big policeman yelled to the McCords and Joyce Arnett to get the hell into an apartment building and out of the line of fire.

So they ran into an apartment building on the corner and up to the second floor. The shooting outside was loud, deadly popcorn now, and Joyce Arnett became nervous and began to cry because she was there and her children were home.

She ran to a window and outside was full of smoke. She filled her lungs with air and screamed out the last words she was ever going to say which were:

"My God, I want to go home to my kids."

The bullet struck her at the top of her head and exited through her temple. There was so much shooting going on that the McCords just thought that was another shot until they saw her fall. A couple of small pieces of lead were removed from her brain but it was impossible to tell whether police or snipers had killed her.

Jynette, Lynette and Laura were put in the care of their grandmother who spent that evening telling them:

"Your momma went off to heaven, off to heaven."

"Will she come back and see us sometimes?"

"She went off to heaven."

That is part of the story of Joyce Arnett which is also the story of Hough, in many ways.

And today they made a monument out of her memory and that is one of the two monuments to the riot.

The other is the splendid, streamlined Thurgood Marshall Recreation Center, a Taj Mahal of tennis shoes which looms at Hough and Crawford for the use of the children who roll auto tires and shoot baskets in garbage cans. Yesterday morning, however, those kids were playing their own games and the center was almost empty.

Well, not really, because Harland Jones was there and his anger filled the place. Harland Jones, goateed and fezzed, is Harllel Jones' brother. Harland is a licensed engineer and the city put him out at the recreation center to keep the place clean, which he does.

It was very clean and empty, and Harland Jones said:

"This place is nothing but a shell. They bring college students in here and tell them, 'Look what a fine building the city built for the poor kids.' Then those college kids go away feeling all good inside."

Then Harland Jones bounded up and began to walk rapidly around his well-waxed monument. As he did he talked, like a tour guide, in a steady spurt of angry words.

"This is our boys' toilets. They haven't worked right since the center opened. They been out of order for weeks. You can't flush them. I've called the city and complained but nothing is done.

"This is our game room. Don't see any games, do you? They're all broken or stolen. You got to have supervision for these kids but the city just put this thing here and no supervision. Sometimes kids bring marbles to the game room and play. Ha!

"This is the ping-pong and poolroom. We got one pool cue and six balls. We got three ping-pong tables and no paddles. When I try to get paddles, you know what I get?

"They sent me this beautiful electronic golf set. Wonderful thing. It's still in the box. If I set it up, it would take up half the gym floor. But I won't. Golf set, yeah! What do they think these kids know about golf?

"Most of them never played golf. What are they gonna do, join country clubs? Ping-pong paddles, that's what I need.

"Now this here is the shower room. They stole all the faucet handles so I bought new ones—harder to get off. Cost me $12.42. They stole those. I'm not going to buy any more.

"This is our flagpole. Notice something missing? Yeah, the flag. Supervisor say if he puts it up, who's goin' to take it down? Flag's all balled up behind the counter.

"This is our pay phone. Only phone we got. Somebody's drowned in the pool, I got to run up and down Hough Ave. lookin' for a dime to call the ambulance. Woman got raped out in front here two months ago. Nobody had a dime. We couldn't call anybody."

He stopped for air.

"I want you to put all this in the paper. The city put this thing out here and forgot about it. Did their job."

"Maybe if this gets in the paper, it'll wake up some people," said another center worker.

"Nope," said Harland Jones. "You can't wake the dead."

Three years ago tonight, the riot started. Today there are two monuments to it—the million-dollar monument and the monument to Joyce Arnett.

Two monuments and two questions:

What has changed?

Which is the real monument?

*— July 19, 1969*

# Ghosts of the past

A lot of the ghosts from my past are flitting around in Federal Court these days in the NAACP schools desegregation case.

I read the stories in the paper and I close my eyes and I can hear a lawn mower whirring. It is 23 years ago and my father is cutting the grass in front of our house on Invermere Ave. on the fringe of what is to become known as the Harvard-Lee area.

A car cruises slowly down the street. It stops and a man in a business suit gets out. He walks up to my father who reins in his lawn mower and eyes the stranger curiously.

"How much do you want for your house?" the businessman says.

"What makes you think it's for sale?" my father asks.

"What would you say to about $18,000?" the businessman asks, ignoring my father's question.

"It isn't for sale."

The businessman eyes him. His lip curls in a smile and his eyes show scorn.

"Come on, now," he says. And he laughs softly.

"Come," he says. "If it isn't for sale now, it's gonna be. You know that and I know it. You know the Negroes are moving into this neighborhood."

My father stares at the man. It is a startling statement. Because the businessman is quite black himself. And yet it is apparent that no kinship of soul got him out of that automobile. The color he is really interested in is the grey-green hue of money.

And a couple of weeks later, all the mailboxes on the street are leafleted with mimeographed pieces of paper that read:

HARVARD AND LEE BY '53.

NEGROES MAKE GOOD NEIGHBORS.

They ran finally, all those neighbors of my youth. First they tried signing petitions that swore they wouldn't sell their homes. But fear, economic and racial, eroded those blustering pledges.

One by one they left, shipping out, trying at first to sell only to white families. Then, a household at a time was sold to blacks.

The pressure stayed on from the real estate blockbusters, white and black, who were after the fast buck—the high turnover. Black families moved in—paying top dollar at first—seeking a stable neighborhood, a decent house, a better life. But there was no stability, there was only fear. There was only panic and the dream, that somehow this would be better, slipped away like sand through their fingers. If you weren't in it for the money, you lost.

The fear became like a great crawling beast and the people rode out on its back. The businessmen felt the fear and shuttered their shops. The people moved eastward—farther away from the city—and settled on streets in Warrensville Heights, clumps of them living in the same order they had lived in on old streets. Living in ranch-house developments built in a hurry to accommodate them.

And, of course, the schools changed.

From all-white they turned to tan and from tan to all-black. The high school first, then the junior high, then the elementary school.

When I was a kid I hated the thing that made the people run. If they only stayed, I thought then, we could have learned to have lived together and been better for the learning.

I didn't know then that fear drives all reason away before and didn't know that, in its midst, nobody triumphs.

The suit that is in Federal Court this week is there because of the fear that was in the neighborhoods 20 years ago.

This time perhaps we can control it. The time will have to come when we control it.

*— December 15, 1975*

## *Solomon's choice*

I wouldn't want to be Frank J. Battisti.

The sun comes up and the sun goes down and over in that green and gold federal courtroom decorated with Babylonian splendor, perched on his bench in front of a mural of the signing of the Magna Carta, Frank J. Battisti listens to testimony.

Looking up, he can see arrayed in front of him, men of good will and high standing in the community. Schools Supt. Paul Briggs is there and John Bustamonte. Charles Clarke of the distinguished law firm of Squire, Sanders & Dempsey is there. NAACP lawyers from Boston and New York are there. Gordon Foster, an expert in desegregation is there.

And past them—beyond the rail—an assortment from the community is there in the gallery. The black preacher who stands on the corner in front of Higbee's and yells: "Jesus knows what you are doing!," he's there. Some nuns and a priest are there. Lawyers who happen to be in the building stop off to listen. Because this is a big case.

One of these days, Frank J. Battisti is going to have to make a decision I wouldn't want to make.

He is going to have to say: "The Cleveland School Board deliberately caused the schools in this town to be segregated."

Or say that it didn't . . .

That's a problem I wouldn't want.

It sure was easier some years back. It sure was easier when we were talking about lunch counters in Atlanta or busses in Montgomery, Ala. or drinking fountains in Augusta, Ga. or rest rooms in Charlotte, N.C.

It spoke for itself, that sign. You didn't need to know its history to know all there was to know about it. To know that the person who had ordered it placed there denied the humanity of the person it was meant for.

But it isn't that easy to figure it all out, sitting there in that federal courtroom. This is no drinking fountain segregation we're talking about here.

What the NAACP is saying is that there is a sign on every school in town. Some of the signs say "Black" and some of them say "White" and a few of them say "For the time being, both."

Just like the drinking fountain days, says the NAACP, the black kids form a line in front of their sign and the white kids in front of theirs.

And the school board, says the NAACP, put the signs there. Never mind all this talk about school boundaries drawn for reasons of safety or whatever. What the schools people did, says the NAACP, was to segregate.

I listened for two days to the charges and it wasn't easy to understand them. As a matter of fact, it would be easy to brand them farfetched except . . .

Except there ARE black schools. There ARE white schools. The evidence is in the corridors. And separate but equal isn't equal. And something will probably have to be done about that. And that something may be busing.

And if it is, there are going to be white people opposed to it. And black people opposed to it. And plenty of both colors who don't understand it. Who don't understand the reasons for it. Who don't understand what the school board could have done to prevent it.

I don't for example. I can't read the minds of the people who drew the boundary lines years ago. People who aren't even on the witness stand in Federal court. I can't look into their hearts and guess their motives.

They were people who lived in their time and did what seemed to be the thing to do at that time. We fumble along, year after year, trying to find the solution that will allow human dignity and brotherhood. We change our minds and things that once seemed fair and natural change, too, somehow and go on trial.

I'm glad I don't have to make this ruling. Judge Battisti does. He has to read minds. He has to play Solomon. He's been listening in that Babylonian courtroom for a month and the trial drags and he gets weary. He slumps in that studied slump judges learn in judge school. He listens to the testimony of good-hearted men. And he has to decide whether to blame anybody for the results of years of human mistrust and fear.

I wouldn't want to be Frank Battisti.

*— January 21, 1976*

## Surprise ending: no surprise

See if you can guess the way this story comes out before you get through reading it.

It happened last Saturday shortly after noon. Mac McKelvey, 67, of South Euclid, had driven downtown to pick up his daughter who had a doctor's appointment at 30th and Euclid.

McKelvey's daughter came out of the doctor's office and joined her father in his auto. McKelvey turned the ignition key and his car wouldn't start. It wouldn't even try to start.

The town is pretty empty on Saturday morning. McKelvey is no mechanic. He sat there wondering what to do.

Then, from out of nowhere, two black men walked up to his auto.

One was about 35 and the other maybe 10 years younger. They had come up from different directions, but McKelvey had the feeling they knew each other and he wasn't sure why.

The older of the two asked McKelvey what his problem was. He didn't know. Maybe there's something wrong with your battery cable, the older fellow said. Just you wait here.

He left. The younger fellow stood idly by McKelvey's car. McKelvey's daughter had an appointment at the library so she boarded a bus and left her father alone with the stranger.

After about 15 minutes, the older man came back. He had a new part and he tried to install it in McKelvey's car. But the car still wouldn't start.

"Tell you what," said the older man. "There's a gas station at 30th and Chester. I'll get in my car and push your car over there." He nodded at the younger man. "You steer his car," he said.

So they went to the gas station. But there was no mechanic on duty. They pushed McKelvey's auto into an honor park lot near the station.

The older man eyed McKelvey. Pondering something.

"I think it's your starter," he said. "I know a place on the near

West Side I can get one cheap. How about if I drive you there?"
He glanced at the younger man and smiled. "He'll stay here and
watch your car," he said.

McKelvey was uncertain.

"Look," he said. "I've only got about seven dollars in my
pocket. I don't have my check book with me."

"Don't worry about it," said the older man.

So they drove to an auto parts store on the West Side.
McKelvey noted that the people there seemed to know his companion. The man bought a starter and signed for it.

They drove back to McKelvey's car. The older man produced
some newspapers and spread them on the dirty pavement under
the auto. He crawled beneath the car and installed the new
starter.

"Try it now," he suggested.

McKelvey turned the key and the car started.

"Say, that's really nice of you," McKelvey said. "If you follow
me home, I'll write you a check." He turned to the younger
man. "I'd drop you somewhere," he said, "but I guess you fellows
are together."

"Nope," said the older man. "We just met right here at your
car."

"You can drop me at 105th and Chester," said the younger
man. "I'll get a bus from there."

So McKelvey dropped the younger man off. He ren-
dezvoused with the older man at Belvoir and Princeton and the
man followed him home.

"What do I owe you?" McKelvey said.

"Just what's on the bill," said the older man.

But McKelvey insisted on giving him a little more. It was
when he went to write the check that he realized he didn't know
his helper's name. The older man said his name was Harry Staples. The younger man had been Michael Smart.

Harry Staples took his check and left. And Mac McKelvey
thought it was a wonderful story.

Until he began telling it.

He's told it maybe a dozen times now. When he gets to the

part about the two black men approaching his car, his listener usually rolls his eyes and says something like:

"Boy, I would have run away screaming for the cops."

When he gets to the part about leaving his car in the care of the younger man, his listener is apt to say:

"And when you got back, the car was gone, right?"

Everybody thinks he knows the way the story comes out. Everybody guesses wrong. I did, when McKelvey told it to me. Maybe you did too.

You think maybe we ought to let that bother us?

*— May 21, 1976*

## Bus ride to bigotry

I used to ride the No. 24 bus from the end of the Van Aken rapid to Solon. I had to stop doing that, though, because of the winters.

The bus and the rapid did not always make good connections and there were some winter nights when, going home later than usual, I would stand alone in an icy darkness wondering what frostbite of the nose felt like, hoping I had none in progress.

I remember best an especially bad night. Stores had closed early. Businesses had sent their employees home in mid-afternoon. My wait for the bus was an unusually anxious one. When it finally arrived, sighed and opened its door, I felt grateful to be welcomed aboard into the warmth.

I was the only passenger. But the bus was cozy. Its windows were steamed like windows in a winter kitchen with a turkey in the oven. There was a faint sound of music in the air and I saw that it was coming from a large, portable radio propped near the dashboard.

"If it bothers you, I'll turn it off," the driver said softly.

"Listen," I said. "Now that I'm finally out of the cold, nothing's gonna bother me."

The driver smiled. He was a man of about 60 with a kind face. His hair was white, streaked with pewter. He pointed toward his radio.

"A lot of nights it's the only company I've got," he said.

I sat down on the side seat across from him and looked at the radio. It was one of those big, multiband jobs, the kind that sell for around $100.

"It's a beauty," I said.

The driver smiled shyly and put the bus in gear. We moved off into the snowy night. Flakes of snow flew at the windshield like moths. The windshield wiper thumped a steady beat. The driver smiled over at me.

"I like company," he said. "I like somebody to talk to. But

these days people are too busy to talk, or too mad about something. So that's why I bought the radio."

"I can understand that," I said.

"You'd be surprised what you can hear on a radio like that," he said. "Sometimes, this time of night you can pick up stations way down in South America. They play interesting music down there. Have you ever heard it?"

"I don't know if I have or not," I said.

"Well it is different than anything you hear around here," he said. "Usually the talking is all in a foreign language. But did you know that some of those countries give the news in English for anybody who might be listening?"

"Yes," I said, "I had heard that."

"It's funny when you stop to think about it," he said. "People in some other country talking into the air not knowing who's listening. And me up here in this bus using them to keep me company."

"Yes, it is," I said.

"I like this run," he said. "I drive my route and then I go home. I work in my yard. I plant my tomatoes. That's the only thing that really bothers me in weather like this. Working out in the yard."

"Well," I said, "you seem like a man who doesn't get bothered easily."

"Yes," he said, "I think you could say that. There's really only one thing that gets on my nerves."

I smiled at him. "What's that," I said.

"Niggers," he said.

I looked at him, startled.

He was staring ahead at the whirl of snow, still smiling slightly.

"What?" I said.

"Niggers," he said. "I don't like them."

I said nothing.

"I used to have a run in the city," he said. "It was really bad there. They get on your bus, you don't know what they are gonna do. They look at you."

I said nothing.

"On a night like this or on a night when it was raining, if I was alone on the bus and saw one of them standing at the bus stop, you know what I'd do?"

I said nothing.

He glanced at me.

"Know what I'd do?" he said.

"What?" I said.

"I'd drive right on by and leave him there," he said, his voice rasping like a file on a piece of pipe.

"What do you think of that?" he asked me.

I said nothing.

"Huh?" he said.

"That's really something," I said.

He nodded and we drove on.

He was a very interesting conversationalist. I'll give him that. He started me thinking. I began by trying to figure him out. Was he an evil man with a touch of good in him, or a good man with a touch of evil in him? Sane with a touch of madness, or crazy with a coating of sanity?

I think of him every once in a while. When I think of this town, I think of him. The character of this town is a lot like his character. There are a lot of people like him, black and white. Hating, politely. Sharing their hate only with people they feel are kindred souls.

As he felt I was. Yes. As he felt I was. I, who said nothing.

When the bus reached my stop, I rose and he turned and said, "Next year, if I see you, I'll give you a basket of tomatoes."

But I drive to work now.

*— October 15, 1980*

# Missing the bus

Little Nickie Howard has a remarkable brain. But it isn't as remarkable as the school system thinks it is.

Nickie (short for Nichole) is 10 years old. The last time anybody checked, she had an IQ of 130. She is very smart, but doesn't have ESP. The school system thinks she has ESP.

Because of Nickie's brain—and because her mother is the kind of mother who pushes hard for her kids—Nickie was put into a major work program a couple of years ago.

At that time, her parents lived on St. Clair. Nickie was assigned to Gracemount Elementary School, which is pretty far from St. Clair. Every morning, Nickie's mother drove her to school.

Then busing started. Mrs. Howard was happy about that. For a simple and practical reason.

"I thought it would save me some gas," she says.

Nickie was reassigned to Fullerton Elementary School and the Howards moved to Gaylord over in the 93rd and Miles area. And Nickie began riding the bus to school.

The trouble is, the bus doesn't always come when it should. In fact, the bus often does not come when it should. In fact, the bus so often does not come when it should that Mrs. Howard and Nickie never know when to expect it. Or if.

Monday morning, for instance, Mrs. Howard saw Nickie off to the bus stop at what seemed to be the right time. A half hour later, Nickie came home. The bus hadn't come. So Mrs. Howard, who has become an old hand at this, called the bus garage.

"Yes, yes, yes," said a bus guy, "I know. We've had a problem this morning. The driver who was supposed to drive that bus didn't come in. We've had some trouble finding anybody to drive that bus. Tell her to go back and the bus will be there within 30 minutes."

So Mrs. Howard sent Nickie back to the bus stop. Thirty minutes later the phone rang. It was Nickie calling from the payphone on the corner to say there was still no bus.

Mrs. Howard called the bus people again.

"Well," said the bus man, "as I explained to you, we're trying to find somebody to drive that bus."

"But you said it would be here in a half hour," Mrs. Howard said. "What do you expect my daughter to do?"

It was then that the bus man showed just how remarkable he thought Nickie's brain was.

"Tell her to come home," he said. "Tell her to wait until she thinks the bus is coming and then go and catch it."

Mrs. Howard sort of went berserk then. She picked up the phone and began calling everybody she could think of. On the third or fourth call, she thought of me.

She had a lot to say. She wasn't against busing, she said. But busing had become such a big problem that it seemed to dominate all other aspects of Nickie's school work.

The purpose of going to school seemed to be to get there. The major work program has suffered, too. A lot was wrong.

Four times last year, Nickie had been marked absent when she wasn't absent. She had merely arrived at school after attendance had been taken. Mrs. Howard had got that straightened out. Then she called downtown to say she had a suggestion on how to reduce the absentee problem.

A woman on the other end of the phone had been polite until Mrs. Howard had mentioned the bus business. "This isn't a suggestion, it's a complaint," the woman had said icily.

It is my opinion that the school headquarters building on E. 6th would make a marvelous hotel. A small luxury hotel like the Sheraton-Carlton in Washington or the Hay-Adams.

At present, of course, it is not a hotel. It is an operations center full of consultants who draw charts, conduct studies, submit reports, hire lawyers, squabble and bicker, hold press conferences and burn money.

There is a master plan in that building and its success

depends, in the long run, on the ability of Nickie's remarkable brain and the remarkable brains of her classmates and their parents.

What is remarkable is that they still try. Nickie is in school today. This column is for her.

— *May 5, 1982*

## Facing racism

In Cleveland, as a general rule, white people don't want to live with black people. This is as true now as it was 30 years ago. It is as true in Cleveland as it was—and perhaps still is—in Selma, Alabama.

It is an ugly truth and you will hear it denied. It is denied by white people who don't want to admit it and it is denied by black people who don't want to make trouble. But such denials are like putting paint over rust. Sooner or later, the rust will show through.

Sooner or later, in the neighborhoods of Cleveland, the racism shows through—blood seeping through a bandage. Just the way it did during the Miracle of West 88th Street last week.

The miracle was that nobody died. Six shotgun blasts were fired. Eight people were hit. Nobody was seriously injured. The police came—late. Then the ambulances. Then the media. Jimmy Breslin, who was passing through town, visited West 88th Street seeking material for a sermon. The street became a flea market for bargain commentaries. West 88th Street led the 11 o'clock news. Except it wasn't news. It was the same old story.

Well, almost. There were a couple of new angles this time. The black family didn't just move to the all-white street. Marlene Armstrong and her children were placed there by the Metropolitan Housing Authority.

This was part of a program to move low-income people out of housing projects and into homes scattered throughout the city's neighborhoods. This is the kind of program that looks very good on paper. Humanitarian. Sensitive.

The people in charge of brotherhood and integration like to have luncheons at downtown hotels and award each other plaques in honor of how humanitarian and sensitive everything is getting to be. But the truth is closer to the first paragraph of this column and you don't see that on plaques.

On West 88th Street, the first thing that happened was that

workmen came out to fix up Marlene Armstrong's house-to-be. They put it in better shape than many of the houses on the street.

Astonishingly, the white people on West 88th Street did not react positively to this action. They did not rejoice that in America, tax money is spent to fix up a poor woman's house. Had they been invited to a couple of those downtown luncheons, they might have been happy about it. But they weren't invited and they weren't happy. Especially the ones with leaky roofs.

Then Marlene Armstrong moved in and the usual atrocities started. Some people shouted "nigger" at her and somebody spray-painted bad words on the side of her house after dark. Very soon, Marlene Armstrong decided she wanted to move out. But she says the housing authority wouldn't move her.

Well, they moved her now all right. They moved her after a young man who was visiting her—a black man who (truth being stranger than fiction) lives in Parma—fired four or six shots from his shotgun at a crowd of taunting white people. He's up on charges and Marlene Armstrong is back in an all-black neighborhood. All's well that ends well, as Hitler might have said.

The guy in charge of the housing program was asked if maybe it would have helped if West 88th Street had been prepared somehow for the arrival of a black woman.

"The Emancipation Proclamation should have prepared them," he said, using logic which, if followed, implies that Martin Luther King was just fooling around for his own amusement. Then the housing guy blamed the cops and the city blamed the housing guy and everybody kind of kicked it around, waiting for it to get lost which it will until the next time.

But the truth is still under there—rust seeping through—an infection beneath the bandage. The truth is in the first paragraph and unless we let the air get at it, it won't heal. The truth is that West 88th Street is the longest street in the country. More people live there than are willing to say so. And if you follow the street to the end, that commotion you see, that's South Africa.

— *June 18, 1986*

# A *snob is a snob*

I grew up in Cleveland one block away from Shaker Heights. Everybody on my street knew the people in Shaker Heights were snobs.

Not that they acted snooty, really. But back in those days, Shaker Heights was the richest community in the United States. So naturally, we all resented them. Shaker Heights boys wore white tennis shoes. Now everybody does, but back then a Cleveland kid wouldn't have been caught dead wearing anything but black tennis shoes that laced up over the ankles.

If a Cleveland kid had paraded around in low, white tennis shoes, the other kids would have yelled at him. "What are ya', some kinda nurse?" they would have inquired.

In summer, Shaker Heights girls wore boxy-looking Bermuda shorts with long socks pulled up to their knees. No Cleveland girl would have worn such things. When a Cleveland girl wore a pair of shorts, she didn't do it to show off the shorts. She did it to show off the stuffing. Shaker Heights girls were not motivated to show off the stuffing. This confirmed our belief that they all had arranged marriages over there.

Well, time passed and some things changed. My old Cleveland neighborhood is all black now and a lot of black people live in Shaker Heights too. Now there is a big flap brewing about some traffic barricades that the people in Shaker have built to keep people from Cleveland from cruising through their neighborhoods.

The people on both sides of these barricades are black, most of them. But guess what the people on the Cleveland side—led by George Forbes—are calling the people on the Shaker side? If you are not familiar with Cleveland you will never guess. If you are familiar with Cleveland, you have guessed already.

Racists! The black people in Cleveland are calling the black people in Shaker racists.

Now I realize I'm white and dumb, but what's the matter with

the word "snob"? It seems like a perfectly good word to me.
When WASPs lived in Shaker, they were called snobs. When
the Jewish population grew large, the Jews were called snobs
also. Now that blacks have moved into Shaker it seems to me
they ought to have an equal right to be snobs too. To deny them
that right seems clearly un-American.

But in Cleveland, we just love that word racism. We use it like
a kind of verbal A-1 Sauce. I have a friend who is so crazy about
A-1 Sauce he pours it on all kinds of things where it doesn't
belong like scrambled eggs and cottage cheese. Sometimes,
when I watch him eat, I suspect he owns stock in the company.
And sometimes, when I watch our civic leaders flavor everything
with racism, I figure they own stock in the company too.

Now, the trouble is, there is plenty of real racism around waiting to be found. It is in the neighborhoods. It is on the police
force. It is in the work place. It is even in some of the churches.
With all the places there are to look for it, why look among a
bunch of Shaker Heights residents who are just trying to be
snobs?

Don't get me wrong. I'm against the Shaker barricades. I told
you where I grew up. But I think the problem in Shaker Heights
is an ego problem, not a racism problem. And sending George
Forbes out to fix somebody's ego problem is like sending Joan
Rivers over to shush a Trappist monastery.

The cure compounds the problem.

— *June 24, 1987*

## Inside the closet

When I was in high school the words were fairy and fruit. Occasionally you'd hear the word queer—sometimes homo. Never gay. Gay meant carefree.

If you carried your books across your chest like a girl, you were certain to be called a fairy. If you wore green on Thursday you could be called a fairy for reasons never clarified. If you wore white tennis shoes, somebody would call you a fruit. For that was pre-Nike and male gym shoes were black.

For all the talk of fairies, fruits and queers, none of us really thought we knew anybody who was homosexual. But we did know people who were the victims of what, in those days, would have had to be called fairy-bashing.

The two I remember best were a boy named Edward Pond and his friend Benny Roberts. I have changed both their names for reasons that will be obvious.

Edward Pond was a quiet, delicate boy who was a terrific artist. Benny Roberts was a plump, outgoing boy with a nice sense of humor. He was an artist, too, but not as good as Edward Pond.

They had a nickname for Benny Roberts in that school. The nickname was "Bubbles." It is true that Benny Roberts jiggled a little when he walked. It is true that he carried his books the wrong way, like a girl. And, looking back on it now, I think it is probably true that Benny Roberts was homosexual. And that Edward Pond was, too.

At the time it never occurred to me to think so. It was a pretty rough school, as schools went then, and Benny Roberts and Edward Pond were members of a small group of kids who were well-behaved and studied hard and got good grades and, because of all that, were constantly being harassed by the school thugs. We all got a little of it. But nobody got more than Benny Roberts.

They would come up behind him in the hall and rip his

books from the cradle of his arms and throw them on the floor and kick them away. And then, at the sight of a teacher hurrying through the crowded hallway, they would scatter.

We felt sorry for Benny because he was our friend. We also secretly felt a little of the shameful "better you than me" feeling that you get in a world full of bullies. Benny would always laugh it off with us. But he would turn, for comfort, to Edward Pond.

This little story is almost over. We graduated from high school and went out into the world and did OK, most of us. Many of us became engineers, because that was a hot thing to be then. I went off to pursue a career as some kind of a writer. Edward Pond got a full scholarship to a prestigious art school in the East.

Benny Roberts went home one night and hanged himself in his bedroom closet.

All of that was more than 30 years ago. And I, who like to think I am such a smart fellow, never really understood it until very recently. Which shows you, I guess, how much we really have to learn about each other.

My guess is that Edward Pond had his art to see him through. The last I heard of him he was very successful. But all Benny Roberts had was Edward Pond, who went away. We thought he had us for support, but he didn't. He hanged himself in the closet and it took 25 years for me, his friend, to understand what that meant.

I have a lot of concerns about the gay rights agenda. I think it's a can of worms. And I saw a lot of people on the Mall last weekend who, frankly, I don't think I'd want running a Boy Scout troop. But . . .

I wish I'd seen Benny Roberts there. Walking any way he wanted to walk. Still alive and still my friend. Unmolested, untortured. Gay.

*— April 29, 1993*

# Kiss the rules goodbye

My pal George is the head of security for a downtown office building. From time to time, he escorts young women who work there to their cars after work.

During the holiday season, a couple of these young women gave George a little kiss. These smooches did not bother George at all. In fact, he rather enjoyed them.

But as he thought about them, he realized they had put him in a kind of philosophical quandary. Which he shared at lunch with a couple of us the other day.

"Now, it was the most innocent kind of thing," George said. "They knew me slightly. I knew them slightly. When I got them to their cars, they just kind of gave my arm a little squeeze and reached up and gave me a little kiss and said, 'Have a real nice Christmas.'

"So?" we said.

"So," said George, "I got to wondering what would have happened if I had done that to one of them. I walk her to her car. I stop. I give her arm a little squeeze. I kiss her and I say, 'Have a nice Christmas, Sally' or whatever her name is. Is that sexual harassment?'

"Yes," we all said. We were men but we were struggling toward enlightenment and salvation.

"But them kissing me was not sexual harassment?" George asked.

"No," we all said, very pleased with our progress toward awareness.

"Why?" said George. "What's the difference?"

This question slowed down the rhythm of the conversation. In fact, it came to a dead stop. Finally, a man named Bruce spoke up. We gave Bruce our full attention because he is a corporate executive who has been to several company-run sensitivity sessions.

"You, George, as a security man, carry with you a certain aura of power and authority. Had you presumed to kiss the woman, she might have felt helpless and victimized by your power and trapped within the aura of your authority. So, in any interaction between the two of you, she becomes the victim. Unless, of course, she initiates the kiss, as happened in your case."

Bruce sat back and we gave him a round of applause and ordered another cup of coffee all around.

"Suppose I had just kissed her back?" George said.

"You mean kissed her on the back?" one of us asked.

"No," said George. "I mean suppose after she kissed me, I then took her in my arms and kissed her back and said, 'You have a Merry Christmas, too.'"

We all looked at Bruce.

"That wasn't covered in the sensitivity session," he said.

"At that point," said a man named Sam, "I think she's traveling at her own risk. If she kissed you first, you have a right to assume she's asking for it."

We all booed lustily. One of us called the maitre d' and Sam was ejected from the restaurant. After several minutes, order was restored and we returned to the topic.

"Surely, George, you know the difference between a little Christmas kiss on the cheek and 'taking her into your arms' as you put it,' one of us said. "If you take her into your arms, you have escalated and intensified the encounter. You have taken advantage of a little kiss which is harmless."

"Harmless unless I do it," said George.

"Yes," we all said.

"Because of my aura of authority," George said.

"Yes," we all said.

"What if she was a vice president of the company and had a bigger aura of authority than I have and had the power to fire me and kissed me on the cheek? Would she be harassing me?"

"Who wants dessert?" somebody said.

"I might try some of the apple pie," somebody else said.

"Well?" said George.

"She might be," one of us said. "It would depend on how you felt about it."

"Listen," said George. "I was a cop for 20 years. Rules are rules. Rules don't depend on how people feel about them. I'm looking for some kind of rule here. A rule that would apply to everybody. Besides, I wouldn't know how I felt about it until she did it. And then the damage, if any, would be done."

Bill spoke up. He lives in Cleveland Heights and therefore is regarded as a great authority on matters like these.

"I have two things to say," he said. "In the first place, we are trivializing a very important issue. Sexual harassment is a big problem in America. The workplace is full of stalkers, gropers and fondlers. The kind of little incident you describe isn't even on the scope. Second, if you want a rule, treat co-workers like family. She gave you a sisterly little kiss and you know it. So treat her like a sister. Your little story is making a mockery out of the larger issue."

Bill glared at George. We all glared at George.

Silence happened for a while.

"So I get to kiss them like a brother," George said.

"No, man!" said Bill. "Your aura! Your aura!"

"If this is so trivial," said George, "why are you getting so excited?"

"Because," said Bill, "to use the line the women use, you just don't get it."

"But I'm trying to get it," said George. "That's why I brought it up. Ten years ago, I wouldn't have thought anything about it. I'm trying to grow. Besides, how many of you really get it? Lemme see a show of hands."

We all raised our hands.

"Liars," said George.

The pie came then and we ate it with relief. It's like the old song says, a kiss is still a kiss, a pie is just a pie. The fundamental things apply as time goes by.

One of those fundamental things being we ain't never gonna fully get it. But don't quote me.

— *February 11, 1994*

## Gender rules

One summer I belonged to a club called the All-Bad Club. Girls were not invited to join. If such a bizarre idea even crossed our minds, it crossed quickly, like a cat crossing a freeway, and vanished.

We did not often think of girls, though some of them lived on our block. A few of us had them for sisters. Occasionally, one or two girls would emerge from a house and stand silently watching us as we played baseball in the street. They did not ask to play and, if they had, we would have been struck dumb with amazement. We assumed we bored them as much as they bored us. The sexes on our street were kept in balance through a doctrine of mutually assured indifference.

A girl lived across the street from me and, on rare occasions, I would be sent across to play with her. She was a year older than I and therefore much bigger. It was through infrequent and uncomfortable encounters with her that I gained my insight into girls' strange play habits.

As soon as we were alone together, she began pacing about like a Hollywood film director, barking out stage directions and dictating episodes of a rather drab little saga in which we would be the principal players.

"You are the daddy coming home from work," she would say. "When you come home, you must kiss your wife and your little baby." She would indicate a doll, propped up in a chair. "Now we must all sit down and have dinner," she would say, distributing little tin dishes in front of us. It was terrible theater with no discernable story line. Any agent would have urged me to turn down the part, since I only had about two more lines than the doll and had to squirm out of the way of the kiss to boot.

Sometimes, she would be a teacher and I would be the pupil. This was a slightly better role, since I was awarded more to say. But after a couple of episodes, I noticed an irritating and, to me, outrageous pattern to this fantasy.

"What is the capital of Ohio?" she might ask, standing at a little blackboard and pointing at me with a ruler.

"Columbus," I would respond, promptly.

"You are wrong," she would say. "You have not done your homework. Now you must go and stand in the cloakroom." And she would point her ruler at a clothes closet.

"It is too Columbus," I would say, hotly. I knew she knew this. But the fact that I was right was not going to be allowed to interfere with her agenda. In fact, she made my protests seem like quibbling. I was to run across this maddening phenomenon plenty in later years. But it, plus her insistence that she always be the teacher, drove me happily back to the more rational company of the All-Bad Club.

We sawed on our fingertips with knives and bled into each other, thus becoming blood brothers. Then we all started making crossbows from a set of plans in *Sports Afield*. We never finished these. Our major project was to dig a clubhouse underground in the vacant lot on the corner. We tunneled four feet into the earth and propped up the dirt ceiling with flimsy boards. We brought in candle stubs and stuck them in cracks in the clay. We made a spy-hole and put a periscope in it and through the periscope, we saw a couple of girls standing quietly watching us.

And the next thing we knew, our horrified mothers were invading us with picks and hoes. They routed us out of the hole and knocked its roof in. The All-Bad Club was disbanded forever. The last time I looked, a run-down Hot Sauce Williams stood on its site at Invermere and Lee. The girls, we knew, had ratted on us. But we bore them no malice. Girls did things like that.

Almost 50 years of enlightenment have passed between the summer of the All-Bad Club and the summer of the Citadel. I've been illuminated with feminist manifestos and women's liberation and activism in behalf of equality and rights. I've been taught to assume that inside that girl playing teacher was a SWAT team member crying to get out. And that neither of us knew it.

So I can say I'm for equal rights and mean it. But do I have to say that I think the sexes are the same? Or is it enough to say that women ought to have a fair shot at doing anything they want. And they certainly . . . Certainly! . . . ought to be allowed to enroll in a school supported by taxes they pay.

I don't know exactly where women are going, but what I do know is: neither do they. They are still working on their scripts, and I'm still trying to adjust to the changes. In the years since the All-Bad Club, sometimes I've been the daddy and sometimes I've been the pupil. And sometimes, to my consternation, I've been assigned the role of oppressor.

Wherever we're going, we're going together. But do I always understand the rules of their game? What do you want me to do, lie to you?

— *August 25, 1995*

# *Bodhi benediction*

Good morning and Happy Bodhi Day. I was hoping for snow. I always like to see a little dusting of snow on Bodhi Day. But you know how it is in our town. We get all our snow in January—too late for the holiday season.

So what are you planning to do to celebrate? Anything special?

Me neither. Bodhi Day kind of snuck up on me this year. Mainly because I never heard of it until yesterday.

But yesterday, somebody sent me a copy of the *Lewis News*, the house organ of the NASA Lewis Research Center out by the airport. The newsletter contained the following item, which somebody had outlined in black and highlighted in yellow:

"VALUING DIVERSITY: Wed., Dec. 8 is Bodhi Day (Buddhist celebration of the Enlightenment of founder Shakyamuni Buddha, ca. 596 B.C.) Please consider scheduling meetings outside this date."

With the newsletter was the following anonymous note:

"Dear Mr. Feagler. If one wonders why it takes so long to get things accomplished in government, the necessity for recognizing such events as Bodhi Day and abstaining from meetings on these days may offer some explanation. Just think how many other special days could be recognized if someone really put an effort into it. Discretion being the better part of valor, I leave this note unsigned."

Valuing diversity, I called Lewis Research Center and spoke to a helpful and friendly woman named Doreen Zudell, the newsletter editor, to get the scoop on Bodhi Day and any other enlightenment she could give me. Which was plenty.

Ms. Zudell pointed out that the work force is becoming more and more diverse. She reminded me that, after the turn of the century, the overwhelming number of Americans will be diverse and non-diverse people will be in a minority.

For that reason, the folks at Lewis had decided to pay more

respect to the diversity of the Lewis family. So they had begun to have classes in diversity. At one such class, for example, a Native American had come in to do a Native American dance for the enlightenment of the non-diverse who were lucky if they could foxtrot.

And then, since there had been some complaints from the diverse that short-shrift was being given to their holidays, Lewis had obtained a calendar of meaningful diverse occasions. One such was Bodhi Day. Hence the item.

Out of respect for the beliefs of the diverse, it was decided to suggest that meetings not be scheduled on these special days which number, said Ms. Zudell, about 12. Twelve and counting, as they say in the space program.

I was so riveted by this information that I forgot to ask Ms. Zudell whether the ban on meetings cut across diversity lines. Whether, for example, it was all right for a couple of Presbyterians to have a meeting on Bodhi Day. Or whether this would be considered counter-diversity.

Nor did I ask whether the attention to diversity had taken time away from other things. Could the problems with the Hubble Space Telescope stem from the fact that, instead of checking its prescription for bifocals, the workers who built it were off somewhere watching a rain dance?

Instead, I just felt gloomy and out of touch, as I so often do these days. Because I had always assumed I knew a lot about diversity. And now I realize I know nothing at all.

I grew up near 154th and Kinsman, which, back in the '40s and '50s, was as diverse a neighborhood as you could find. It was racially and ethnically mixed and was full of spumoni joints, great delicatessens and Yiddish movie houses all lumped together on one street.

Radio and early television were full of comedy shows that poked fun at diversity. Nobody escaped stereotyping for a gag. There was "Life With Luigi," "Amos 'n' Andy" (white actors on radio replaced by black actors on television), "The Goldbergs," and "Allen's Alley," which kidded almost every ethnic strain.

My own heritage was German. Germans were usually portrayed either as cold-blooded murderers ("Ve haf vays uf making you talk") or roly-poly featherbrains, like Sgt. Shultz on "Hogan's Heroes."

We knew when to razz each other and when to take each other seriously. And what we were serious about wasn't the lack of respect for diversity. It was the lack of respect for inclusion.

The idea back then was the "melting pot" idea. All Americans, no matter what their skin color or religion or ethnic origin, were supposed to be treated like full-fledged Americans. America owed you the chance to be included as a first-class member of the American family. Whatever heritage or customs you brought with you were none of America's official business. They were just the salt and spice for the great stew in the melting pot. A stew whose savory aroma attracted the world, like the smell of wake-up coffee in the Folger's commercial.

We used to laugh at ourselves, but we were a country to be taken seriously. Now we take ourselves very seriously, and the results are almost laughable. The melting pot has stopped melting. The ingredients demand to be put back in their boxes. Nobody wants to be part of the recipe for the stew.

Recipes are tricky things. There's a big difference between a mushroom and a toadstool. Just like there's a big difference between diversity and division. My wistful little Bodhi Day wish is that we find the enlightenment to know the difference.

— *December 8, 1993*

## *The Anglo file*

They changed jurors again in the big trial in Los Angeles. I heard about it on public radio. "The judge has dismissed an African-American from the jury," the announcer said. "The African-American juror has been replaced by an Anglo juror."

I wasn't exactly sure what kind of juror an Anglo juror was. So I called a friend of mine who is a walking catalog of the new, politically correct ethnic categories.

"What is an Anglo?" I asked her.

"You are," she said.

"Since when?" I said.

"Well," she said, "these things happen gradually. Anglo is not that common a term yet. But there is a trend in its direction."

"Who do I see if I want to stop it?" I asked.

"I don't know if you can stop it," she said. "It's an official word. It's in the dictionary. Why? Does it offend you?"

"I don't know," I said. "I'll have to think about it."

And I have thought about it. And it does offend me. Not to the point where I'm going to lose any sleep over it, you understand. But the fact is, I don't want to be an Anglo.

She was right about it being in the dictionary. In fact, it's in two of my dictionaries. My 10-year-old dictionary says: "Anglo: English. Norman." My 3-year-old dictionary says that too. But above it, it says: "Anglo: A Caucasian inhabitant of the U.S. of non-Latin extraction."

So there you are. Somewhere between 1985 and 1992, somebody somewhere decided that people like me needed a category too, since everybody else had one. And the category I was assigned was pre-owned. It used to belong to the English.

Now, by the most amazing coincidence, on the very same day I was wriggling around inside my Anglo identity to test the fit, the phone rang and who do you suppose was calling me? Maybe I better just tell you and end the suspense.

It was a fellow named Michael Feagler, who recently came to

town from Chicago to teach Latin at Laurel School. Michael Feagler pointed out, quite rightly, that Feagler is not a common name. He was calling to see if we were related somehow. I hope we are, because being related to a Latin teacher at Laurel School would, I feel, enhance my sense of Anglo pride if I stay an Anglo long enough to need one. After all, since I've only been an Anglo for a couple of hours, my Anglo self-esteem is a wax tablet. It is my duty, if I'm stuck being an Anglo, to develop a list of Anglo role models and accomplishments.

It was instantly apparent that Michael Feagler knows more about Feaglers than I do. His research has revealed that the first Feaglers were Hessians who came over here during the Revolutionary War. To fight for the British.

That is the kind of thing I wouldn't have wanted to see in "Mary, Mary" 200 years ago. But I suppose enough time has passed that it's all right to let it out now. And it is astonishing, is it not, that on my very first day of being an Anglo, a Latin teacher telephones to point out an English connection. Only in America. Makes me glad we lost the war.

But with all of that, I still don't want to be an Anglo. And I have no intention of just sitting here and letting somebody turn me into one without my permission.

I remember a conversation I once had with the Rev. Otis Moss about the terms "black" and "African-American." African-American had entered the language, but black had not departed. Everybody wanted to do the right thing but there was some confusion, and some well-meaning liberals started using the term "Afro-American" until a merciful person of color tipped them off that an Afro was a haircut.

Rev. Moss observed to me that people ought to be called what they want to be called and it was my duty to determine what that was and call them that. That made sense to me then, and it makes sense to me now.

Usually, the way you find out what somebody wants to be called is, he tells you. I stopped using the word "Oriental" a couple of years ago when an Asian-American kindly instructed me away from it. Long before that I learned that while it is OK to call a man from France a Frenchman, it is not OK to call a man from China a Chinaman. But I didn't know until I was told.

So I wish to tell anybody who is listening that I don't want to be no Anglo. Not only that, but I would make a strong wager that if the city were polled, nobody would voluntarily elect to be called an Anglo. I'll bet my wallet on it—me, a person too cheap to buy a lottery ticket.

Once there was a time when we thought of America as a melting pot. You could taste each individual ethnic flavor, but it was the blended dish that was the gourmet adventure.

Lately we've reversed things, like the videotape of a cooking show run backward. All the ingredients have jumped back out of the stew and disdainfully shaken off the gravy. The carrots demand their carrotness, the onions their onionness. We don't know whether "diversity" means integration or segregation. It seems to depend on what day of the week it is and who's talking.

I thumb my nose at nobody's heritage. The old neighborhoods of this city taught me never to call a Slovenian a Slovak and my store of ethnic awareness has been growing ever since. But all the Hessian is out of me and I've never missed it. So leave me alone. I can't see any payoff in being an Anglo or even an Anglo-American. It's my guess that the Anglo category doesn't come with a handful of group rights to go with the monogram.

Plain old American is all I want, and the rights that go with it. I wistfully remember a time when that's all anybody wanted. I thought we were getting there. What happened?

— *March 3, 1995*

## Without a prayer

A little girl and her math teacher have decided they don't like prayers before Cleveland school board meetings. So they whistled for the ACLU, which came bounding over like Lassie, wagged its tail, and filed a lawsuit.

This was the first time the ACLU challenged a school board for opening a meeting with prayer. Naturally, there's a lot of civic pride about it.

The little girl and the teacher held a press conference to explain what they had done. "I asked the board at one meeting how they would feel if the religion being espoused was one that they didn't agree with, like devil worship," the teacher said.

I'm not on the school board, but I can answer that question. First, there ain't gonna be any devil worship prayers at the meeting, so I don't worry about it. That's the literal answer.

Second, the hypothetical answer. The only way there would ever be any devil worship prayers at the meeting would be if the ACLU won them the right to be there. "Today, let's begin our meeting in the spirit of cultural diversity and the equal value of all beliefs by asking Warlock James Mangle to offer a few words of reverence to Satan."

The math teacher looks young enough to be an old hippie. He showed up at his press conference wearing a sweat shirt with a slogan on it. So I can't blame him. He came up in a generation where anybody who shaved was considered a fascist.

And I certainly don't blame the little girl. She's 14. She's spent her whole life listening to people tell her how important rights are and how, in order to get some, all you have to do is claim you're a victim.

"Everybody in this country is not of the same religion," the little girl said at her press conference. "It offended me because of that."

Well, I wonder how deeply it offended her. My problem, I guess, is that I am not a very easily offended guy. I don't happen, for instance, to be Jewish. And yet I've gone to a zillion meetings, public and private, where rabbis have been called upon to ask a blessing. I don't remember even coming close to being offended. If I held a press conference, I've forgotten about it.

What would offend me is if somebody asked a Ku Klux Klansman to lead a Christian prayer at a public meeting. I mention that because down in Cincinnati—where they always have a nice hatred display at Christmas—the Klan won the right to display a cross near a Jewish menorah in a public park.

Naturally, the ACLU helped the Klan in that case. The ACLU is anybody's dog. Wave some rights under its nose and it licks your hand no matter who you are.

If any group in Cleveland needs the power of prayer, it's the Cleveland school board. A school superintendent shot himself and left a note blaming his misery on the board. A board member was exposed as a tax cheat and threatened with jail. Another board member went to jail for welfare fraud. Another board member mooned a motorist on a freeway. Those are just the high points.

My recollection is that no teachers or students held press conferences to complain that their right to a decent education was being violated by all this. And the ACLU stayed in its kennel. But one look at God and they send for the bouncer.

The Klan has the right to display a cross in a public park. The school board may lose the right to say a prayer at a public meeting. I pray for guidance to understand the complicated issue of rights in today's America. And God answers my prayer and whispers in my ear.

"Everybody's got 'em but you and Me," He says. Or is it I?

— *January 2, 1993*

# A *wing and a prayer*

The ACLU has taken God to court again. This time in a lawsuit aimed at closing down the chapel at Cleveland Hopkins Airport.

The lawsuit is a little startling because this isn't the God-suing season.

Usually, God is sued around Christmas time when hunting parties of lawyers fan out all over America to get the manger scenes off the city hall steps.

We've gotten kind of used to that and suing God at Christmas has become a part of the American Christmas tradition, like Bing Crosby and plum pudding.

So far, God has given no sign that He's sore about this. But why push our luck?

Now I ought to make clear that I am no enemy of the ACLU. I think we ought to have it. I think it does a lot of God. I mean good.

But it's only human and, God knows, it is subject to human faults. And one of its faults is that it puts principle ahead of common sense. It's a lot like the Boy Scout who helps old ladies across the street whether they want to go or not.

For some years now, there has been a little chapel at the Airport run by the Catholic diocese. It's tucked away in a corner. It doesn't exactly hit you in the eye like the Cathedral of Tomorrow. Or the saloon. Or the Playboys on the newsstand.

However, the City has charged the diocese far less rent than other merchants have to pay for space in the Airport. That's what sticks in the ACLU's craw. That and the fact that the ACLU doesn't believe that spirituality and government mix. A view obviously shared by government.

So the ACLU filed eviction proceedings against God. And, by the time you read this, God may have been thrown out of the Airport as if He were a Moonie.

Is this wise?

It seems to me that if there's one place you don't want to make God mad, it's in an airport.

Next to foxholes, more prayers are said in airplanes than anywhere else. Usually right at takeoff, when you're flattened back against your seat praying the plane off the ground.

Or at landings, when there's that grating little rumble you hear when they let the wheels down. If you've got any religion in you, that'll bring it out.

Now, personally, I'm not a Catholic. I'm ashamed to tell you the last time I was in church. I do watch the television preachers from time to time but only for the sex scenes.

But the chapel in the airport has never bothered me. Has it ever bothered you? Who, then, has it bothered?

I'll tell you what would bother me, though.

What would bother me would be to be flying back to Cleveland some night in a snowstorm with the crosswinds blowing and the wheels rumbling down . . .

And having the stewardess come on the intercom system and hearing her say . . .

"Ladies and Gentlemen, we are about to land at Cleveland Hopkins Airport and obviously it ain't gonna be easy.

"Local time is midnight. Local temperature is minus three degrees with a wind chill of minus 53 degrees.

"For those passengers attempting to make connections with God, please be advised that He isn't there. He's sitting over in Judge George White's courtroom up on aggravated loitering charges."

That message might do a lot for my Constitutional rights.

But it wouldn't do much for my constitution.

— *February 13, 1991*

# *Add it up*

Wow! If you've misplaced anything, call the Clinton administration. Guess how many homeless people they found on the streets of America we didn't know were there?

Aw, you'll never get it. Six million, four hundred thousand. That's right. The Republican administrations estimated there were 600,000 homeless. But Donna Shalala went out and counted and came up with 7 million.

That's the good news. At least, it's good news for a fellow named Fred Karnas, director of the National Coalition for the Homeless. He was crazy about Shalala's new math homework.

Her study, quoth he, "doesn't just talk about mental illness and substance abuse. It also talks about housing and poverty and racism. It really does say what we've been trying to say for a long time."

It also talks about money. And boldly, I might add. If I asked you how much money it would take to clear up mental illness, substance abuse, housing problems, poverty and racism, you might say you were clueless. But Donna Shalala knows. It'll cost us $40 billion a year if we do it on the cheap. I supplied the word "us." Shalala left it out. They have a habit, in Washington, of acting like money just arrives. Probably because it does.

Here's the bad news, though. Since we are a deadbeat government, the money will have to come from somewhere in particular. There is some talk about getting it by eliminating the tax deduction for interest on home mortgages. Right now it is whispered talk. Shalala probably fears, rightly, that if she said it out loud, she might find herself out on the street. Thereby raising the number of homeless to 7 million and one.

Every time I write about homelessness, I am accused of heartlessness. Clergymen send me letters advising me to soak my soul in some kind of fabric softener. Once I was taken to lunch and lectured sternly by a nun. She implied that my hope of a glorious hereafter was in serious jeopardy.

So I'll tell you what I did.

I asked a very compassionate friend of mine to find me two homeless people whose stories would turn me to mush. He hurried away, his eyes glowing with the hope of my redemption. Soon he returned with two women, taken from a homeless shelter.

The women were in their late 20s. One was white and one was black. I will call them Nancy White and Nancy Black. My compassionate friend told me that Nancy Black was not only a victim of homelessness but had, as a result of her homelessness, suffered an attempted rape. Then he left us, wearing the smug air of a man who has played an ace.

Nancy White told her story first. She had come to Cleveland from Florida where she had had a job in construction, which she had quit. The reason she had come to Cleveland was that she had met some guy from Cleveland who had told her that if she ever came to Cleveland, she could live with him.

But when she got to Cleveland, she couldn't find him. He was not at the address he had given her. Had she made any attempt before she quit her job to call him first and tell him she was coming? No. She had just quit and come up? Well, he had said she could.

Was there any place on Earth she could go and live? Well, her father would probably take her in. Where was he? He was in Tennessee. Had she told anybody in Cleveland she could go to Tennessee? No. Had anybody asked her if there was some place she could go? No.

That was Nancy White's story. I checked the rime of frost around my heart for any signs of thaw. Negative. Ah, but there was still Nancy Black to be heard from.

Nancy Black had come to Cleveland from Louisiana. Why? Well she, too, had met a guy from Cleveland who said she could come up and stay with him. But when she got here, he, too, was nowhere to be found.

Now this WAS interesting. Could it have been the same fella? No, the address was different. Could there be some kind of society of Cleveland men who sprinkled the southland with shack-up IOUs? Nancy Black didn't know.

Well, how about the attempted rape? The way that happened was that Nancy Black had gone to a bar and a couple had invited her to go home with them. And when they got home, the couple had invited Nancy Black to sleep in the same bed with them. In the middle. And in the middle of the night, the man had rolled over on top of her and Nancy Black had fled through a window.

Was there any place Nancy Black could go to find a home?

Oh yes. She had an aunt in Houston who was ill with cancer. This aunt had always liked Nancy Black and very much wanted her to come down and nurse her. Nancy Black had always liked this aunt and very much wanted to go.

Had she told anybody at the shelter about this aunt?

No.

Had anybody asked her if there was some place she could go?

No. They had just said to sit over there and fill out this form.

I thanked the Nancys and they disappeared back into the crowd of between 600,000 and 7 million homeless, depending on how you vote.

Now there are no funds in the Shalala piggy bank earmarked to address the problem of the Nancys. They were not mentally ill, they didn't abuse substances, they knew of homes they could live in. They were not victims of racism. They were poor, but then they had both quit jobs.

You might say they were hopelessly dumb. I won't. I'm in enough trouble already. Besides, it isn't true. The Nancys were not a couple of Einsteins, but they had adequate brains.

What they lacked was judgment. Any sense of cause and effect. Bad things happened to them because they lacked the ability to see that, if they behaved in a certain way, bad things would.

This is a massive problem in America and it seems to be getting worse. I would cheerfully give a portion of my mortgage-interest money to correct it. But it never makes the list of fashionable ills. There is no money in reason. There is no National Coalition for the Development of Common Sense.

Throw money at the two Nancys and it would bounce. It would probably bounce back into the coffers of bureaucratic organizations that feed on problems rather than examining them.

I would have put one Nancy on a bus for Houston and the other on a bus for Tennessee. And saved the county money in the bargain. If that be heartlessness then, clergymen, lick your stamps.

*— February 18, 1994*

# CRIME AND PUNISHMENT

*Murder gets personal*

Helen Simpson was the 196th.

Homicide. In Cleveland. This year. As compared to 170 at this time last year.

That's the way you write these things. I know because I've written a share of them in my time.

In this business, we reduce murder to a statistic. If it is a good murder, it lingers in the newsprint like a grade-B rerun of an old Perry Mason show.

Ask the guys on the police beat and they'll tell you how impersonal murder can be. Get the name spelled right, get the address right. If it's a good address, try to come up with some theory as to why a killing happened. Was it booze? Was it sex? Was it robbery? It's a mechanical skill. Every cub reporter knows it.

So Helen Simpson was the 196th. The only problem I have with that is that I knew her.

She was a chubby, adorable public relations gal from Channel 3 who tried to sell you a story occasionally and called you "poopsie."

She had a sign on her office door that said "I Hate People Who Sing in the Morning" and it had a picture of Snoopy under it.

Somebody gave her a toilet seat fashioned in the shape if a smile button and she always meant to hang it on her wall, but she never got around to it. It stayed in the clutter of her office over at the television station.

I'd see her over in Pat Joyce's on occasion, holding court, drinking a spicy Bloody Mary. She was one of the few gals that, when she bought you a drink, you felt comfortable about it.

Once, a while back, when a guy named Gilligan was just getting started in politics, some swanky Cleveland Heights family gave him a soiree and he made a very long, very dull speech. Helen got impatient and urged some of us to capture the balloons and we boycotted Gilligan and went off on a party with the car full of balloons and Helen giving war whoops from the back seat.

All of that takes a back seat now though, because she was the 196th.

Three detectives tramped up to her office in WKYC yesterday morning and cornered her associate, Ilze Kalnins, to ask about Helen's last day.

Ilze said it was just a day. Helen had two staff meetings, she had lunch at the Leather Bottel, she was writing a report, she kidded with the people on her staff. She stayed downtown to work late.

She drove home then. She didn't mind driving home alone late at night. She had told Harriet Peters of this paper that nothing could happen to her. She believed that.

Well, she was wrong. Somebody shot her at E. 121st St. at Shaker Blvd. The homicide boys are working on it and the crime lab boys are on the job, too.

And the damnedest thing about it is, at this writing, it looks like there wasn't any motive.

It appears she was killed just because she happened to be where she was, when she was, in the year of our Lord 1972 when crazy people are walking around the streets with .38-caliber pistols, shooting into car windows.

Helen wouldn't like that plot line. She knew a story when she saw it and it had to have more to it than that.

The newspaper guys who knew her were around Pat Joyce's yesterday. They were talking about bullet trajectory and angle of entry.

But they knew it wasn't much of a story. Odds are they won't catch the guy who did it. It will fade from the papers in a couple of days.

Murder is generally just a number until it happens close to you and then it becomes a very real thing for a while.

And you remember all those editorials about how the homicide rate is alarmingly high and about gun control.

And then you forget them again, because nobody can stand to look insanity in the face for very long.

Helen Simpson was, after all, only the 196th.

There has already been a 197th.

I didn't know him though.

— *August 16, 1972*

## Meeting a statistic

Words spoken on television are lighter than air.

The planet cannot contain them. As soon as they are spoken, they are launched. Through the roof of a studio, through your living room. Into space. Already discarded. Electronic lint, blowing toward Neptune.

The other night, when anchorman Leon Bibb said that the homicide rate among children in Cleveland has risen 100 percent in the last five years, those words passed over Beachwood and Bay Village and headed off to shock the stars.

Print is a little better. I know they say television is the "impact" medium because of the pictures, but I have never believed that. The pictures tend to run together, toothpaste, cleanser, tampons, shootings, stabbings, Vanna. . . . Print commands your full attention. If it can stop you. If it can sucker you in.

But news of inner-city kids dying is not a stopper anymore. When the eye, moving across the printed page, encounters a story about black children and gunfire, the eye sends an immediate message to the brain. "Whaddaya think?" the eye says to the brain.

"Skip it," the brain says to the eye. "Same old stuff. Irrelevant."

The other night, though, just as I was leaving work, news came in that a 17-year-old boy, identity unknown, had been killed by a stray bullet at 116th and Union Avenue.

And because that address is half a mile from the house where I was born. . . .And because I'd spent a month in the neighborhood last fall talking to kids at John Adams High School, my old school. . . . Because of that, the news had weight for me.

I fretted all weekend. I had a feeling, a premonition, that the dead boy was one of my kids. By that, I mean someone I had met. Someone I had talked with. Someone who was, to me, not an image of electrons or a space-bound echo but a real person. A real kid.

This is the time of year when all the suburbs of Cleveland have what they call "home days," or "heritage days."

We who live in the suburbs, most of us, once lived in Cleveland. And if we really went home to touch our heritage, we would return to the old neighborhoods we moved away from . . . fled from.

If we did that. If we went back to 116th and Union and ate hot dogs in the street and threw darts at balloons on a board and met the people who live there, we would know they are whole human beings. Not images on a screen. Not police statistics.

The boy who died, who I didn't, after all, know, was a real boy who got A's and B's on his report card that very day and was proud of it all day until he died.

The printed word told about that. But if the word could have been made flesh . . . if we could have talked to the boy. . . .

("A's and B's. Good for you. What are you going to do after high school?" . . . "I'm going to join the Army and study auto mechanics." . . . "OK son. But I was in the Army. Don't let those recruiters snow you now . . .")

A brief make-believe conversation with a youth, 17, identity unknown.

But if he was known to us. If we had met him. On streets we left, in the neighborhoods we abandoned, then the news of his death would hit us like a rock.

Then we would feel that somebody was killing OUR children in OUR neighborhood.

And we would stop it.

— *July 6, 1991*

## Eddie Watkins' cellmate

Some of the boys had a job for William Michael Rooney last night. Once it might have made his mouth water because it was in a bank. It had never quite happened to Bill Rooney this way before. He's been around a lot of safes in his time. He's sniffed the ozone of a lot of crime scenes. He's done a lot of time. A lot of cops have tapped him on the shoulder. But when Cleveland police collared Bill Rooney last night, what they wanted was a favor. They wanted him because he knew Eddie Watkins.

The green sheet on Bill Rooney is longer than an Amtrak timetable. It starts way back in 1928 when Bill was a boy gone wrong. If the crime has something to do with burglary or a con job, Rooney might have been there. But now he says he is retired. In his home town, Cleveland.

The police wanted him out of retirement last night. They wanted him for the big con. They wanted him to con Eddie Watkins out of the bank at W. 136th and Lorain.

Way back in the '60s, Bill Rooney and Eddie Watkins had celled together in the pen. The cops wanted Rooney to use a little Auld Lang Syne on Watkins.

The way it happened was, Rooney was sitting home minding his own business when he heard about the bank drama on television. He decided to amble over and take a look.

So he put his French poodle in the car and he dressed up sharp like he always does — the motif last night being plaid — and he doused himself with plenty of cologne in case a happened by and he went over to see the action.

It wasn't until he got there that he found out his old cell mate Watkins was the guy inside. Then the cops asked him to go in and try to talk Watkins out.

So Bill Rooney went into the bank. He saw a long, low row of tellers' windows. He saw a bank of extension phones with policemen attached to them. The phones hooked up with another phone in a back room where Watkins was holed up. A cop shoved Rooney a phone and told him to talk.

"Eddie," Rooney said. "Eddie, this is Bill Rooney. Eddie, I always thought you had more class than this."

Rooney was thinking fast. How do you con a con?

There had been times . . . There was the time Rooney stood next to a safe he had ripped off, its alarm ringing wildly, and watched a platoon of cops bearing down on him.

"Officers, the man you want went that way," Rooney told them. And they chased off in the direction he was pointing and he ambled away. Yes, there had been times . . .

"Eddie," Bill Rooney said into the phone. "You have too much class to hurt these people."

"Bill," Watkins told him. "Listen. The FBI has got the rest of my life to find me if they let me go. Those aren't bad odds. I swear if they don't I'll blow these people up."

Cops kept shoving notes at Rooney. They all said, "Keep him talking." He kept stuffing the notes in his pocket.

"What do you know about dynamite, Eddie?" he asked.

"I know enough, Bill," Watkins said. "I learned about it in the mines."

Bill Rooney tried. Once, during his own burglary trial, he had taken a reporter to lunch. The reporter, elated, picked up the tab. He thought Rooney was a juror.

Maybe one more time . . .

Rooney walked out of the bank into the chill night. He had no topcoat. He was worried about his poodle.

He walked up to the reporters. He likes reporters.

"They are going to have to kill him," he said.

Then he went home. He had to get up early this morning. The cops want to take a new picture of him.

— *October 30, 1975*

## Vigil for a hostage

You can see the Terminal Tower from the corner of the suite of offices in the Federal Bldg. where Marty Hacherian works.

See it good, too, because Marty's office in the Federal Civil Service Commission is on the 29th floor. Look out the corner office window and there you are—way up in the sky above most of the buildings in town. Marty can look right at the 36th floor of the Terminal Tower where her sister, Allie, works.

Marty and Allie work way up there in the sky in Cleveland and they live together in Cleveland Heights with their brother, George.

Yesterday morning, Marty and Allie drove in to work as they always do. Sometimes Marty brings Allie all the way downtown and drops her in front of the Terminal. Sometimes she drops her at the University Rapid stop and Allie takes the Rapid in. That's the way it was yesterday.

Marty got to work about 8:30 and greeted her friends in the office—her boss, Morris Berke, and Fran Pierce and Pat McQuaid, 19, a Cleveland State student who is working with Marty this summer.

If Marty had bothered to look out at the Terminal, she would have discovered it shrouded in fog and snuffled in a light drizzle. But she didn't look. Why look?

Before noon, Marty had to give a lecture to some federal employees who work with Spanish-speaking people. The purpose of the lecture was to tell these employees about federal training programs that were available. When she broke for lunch, Marty hadn't finished her lecture.

She had lunch with Morris Berke and asked him what was new. He told her he had heard something about a sniper around the Terminal Tower. In fact, the Federal Bldg. security people had requested that the blinds be pulled on the high floors facing the Tower.

"Allie," Marty thought. But only briefly. Marty went back to her lecture. She hadn't been lecturing long, though, before they came and got her.

There was a phone call from Jack Ford, Allie's boss. Jack Ford told Marty that Allie was a prisoner in the Tower, out the corner window. The fog had lifted by then, but that's when the air in between the two tall buildings filled up with fear.

"Just keep cool," Jack Ford told Marty. "Just keep cool."

Marty sat at her desk. She gave up smoking some years ago. She doesn't drink much coffee. She sat at her desk and stared at the telephone.

The others in the office were helpful, they really were. Fran Pierce scrounged a portable television set from the Army recruiting people and a portable radio from Cong. Mottl's office. Everybody clustered around Marty's desk—first listening to the radio; then trying to get something on television.

The phone kept ringing. George called. Was Marty all right? Yes, she was all right. She was with friends. Jack Ford called back to reassure Marty.

Then, at 3:29, the phone rang and it was Allie.

Marty sat up at her desk and squeezed the phone tight. "Allie . . . I know everything . . . How are you? . . . It seems like you are going to be there until 7 o'clock? . . . I'll wait here . . . Allie, what's he like?"

But Allie had hung up.

"He let her call," she said. "I think that's a good sign," she said.

Everybody agreed that it was a very good sign.

A little after five, they turn the air-conditioning off in the Federal Bldg. Marty's office grew very hot. The remarkable Fran Pierce brought in a fan he got somewhere. They plugged it in.

"I'm going to stay right here," Marty said. "Allie said maybe she could call back. George may call. I better stay here."

Once she got up to walk to the corner office. There was the Tower, glowering in the dusk. She could see Allie's floor. You see things all your life and you look right through them. Then one day, you see them and they are changed and they stay changed.

Marty went back to her office.

The television set was saying that the gunman might let everybody go if he got on national television.

The reporter suggested a pool.

"Look," he told Marty. "I just know she's going to get out of there all right. I bet 7:30 on the dot."

"That's a bad bet on Short Vincent," said Morris Berke. "You didn't ask for a time spread and I'm gonna say 7:20."

Fran Pierce took 7:40. Pat McQuaid took 8 p.m. Everybody looked at Marty as if to say, "See, nothing is going to happen. Would we be doing this otherwise?"

So Marty took 7:05 because that was close to the time Allie had said the man would let her go.

The radio was still on. A reporter on the street said, "Oh. A shot has just been fired. No. Wait. It was a backfire."

Marty put her head in her hands briefly. Then looked up.

Roger Mudd was sitting in for Walter Cronkite. He had stories about the Ford-Carter debate. And Legion Flu. Then an Ex-Lax commercial. Then the story about the gunman in the tower.

Marty saw it. Allie and the gunman saw it. And at 7 o'clock, the gunman came out of the Tower. Marty saw him come out on the Army's television set.

"Oh," she said. "Oh."

Then the phone rang and Allie was calling. She was fine. The FBI was talking to her. Pretty soon she would be through and Marty could take her home like she does every night.

"Hey, Marty," the reporter told her. He pointed to a pile of change on her desk. "You won the pool."

And then. And only then. And finally then, Marty Hacherian put her face in her hands and sobbed.

— *August 27, 1976*

## *Steele's smile*

Every time I ran into Robert Steele he was friendly. He would always smile—would always be cordial. It was that way from the very first time I met him, when I asked him to show me exactly how it had been the night his wife had been murdered.

There is a facet to the business of being a reporter that puzzles a lot of us. We talk about it sometimes. It is this:

An amazing number of people are gracious about inviting us into their tragedies.

Someone's husband dies in an auto accident. Someone's son is slain in a senseless shooting. And the next morning—while grief is still white-hot and searing—a reporter shows up on the front stoop, wanting to know if he can take a picture. Wanting to know if he can come in and sit on the couch and scribble some notes.

We know we are intruding. We know there is a chance that the door will slam in our face. And sometimes it does.

But an amazing number of times it doesn't. Still dazed—still in the shock of grief—people let us come in and pry into their agony.

Robert Steele was the friendliest of all of them. From the first he would always talk to reporters—spend as much time with them as they wanted to spend. Tell his story over and over again without hostility.

"Tell me how it was, Judge," I asked him the day I met him more than eight years ago.

"I was upstairs looking in on my boys when I heard the shot," he said. "I ran downstairs as fast as I could and the front door was slamming. I ran out of the house but I wasn't fast enough to get a good look at who it was."

"Could I ask you something a little presumptuous?" I said. "Would you mind walking through it for me? So I can get it absolutely right?"

Of course he would. He'd be happy to. So we climbed the

stairs and walked to the bedroom where his sons had been sleeping. We entered the room. There was one bed right next to the door. Then a space. Then a second bed. Then a narrow space between the second bed and the wall.

"I walked into the room," he said, showing me. He walked past the first bed, past the space between beds, past the second bed. He turned and slid into the space between the second bed and the wall. He moved all the way to the corner of the room.

"I was right here," he said. "I had just bent over to kiss my son when I heard the shot."

It didn't add up. It was the most awkward route to kiss a sleeping son I had ever seen.

But it put him as far away as possible from the front door of his house at the time he claimed the shot was fired. I thanked him. And he thanked me.

He was always thanking reporters. When we got a tip that Steele had been dating a court clerk, Barbara Swartz, they sent me out to ask her about it. She denied it angrily.

Paul Lilley went out to ask Steele about it. "I have some nasty questions to ask you," Lilley told him.

Steele invited him in. He sat on the floor at Paul's feet and told him he had always admired the stories Paul had written and that he was glad it was Paul who had come out. And then he admitted his affair. Paul Lilley had been a good newsman for a long time and had seen a lot. But Steele's behavior startled him. It was just too nice.

The years went by and occasionally I'd see Steele on the street and say hello. Once I met him briefly when he was representing some people who figured in a story I was writing.

It was always a shock to see him. There was something creepy about the fact that he was walking the streets of the town which had given him such a bad time—such a spate of lurid publicity and shame. I used to wonder why he stayed here. Why he didn't go some place where his name wasn't known and start a fresh life.

I felt sorry for him. If he had had no part in the death of his wife he had suffered horribly. And if he had had something to do with it, I would have assumed that knowledge would be driving him crazy.

But he stayed friendly to the last. He spent his last moments before the jury came in the other day swapping yarns with half a dozen reporters. Right until the last he was very good about interviews.

Even after the sentence was pronounced, he waved to his wife and winked at her. I'd like to think that maybe he felt a little peace because it was all over.

But I can't think that. I never could figure him out and I can't pretend that I can now. I don't know what kind of private hells drove him but they wore a smile.

Or something that looked like one.

— *April 13, 1977*

## A *father's hope*

Frank Papesh was watching the NBC Nightly News on television when he thought he saw his daughter.

He thought he saw her in a crowd—just for an instant. Just the back of her head, the curve of her cheek, the color of her hair, the way she held her head, the shape of her neck.

These things jolted him forward to stare at the television screen. But the camera angle changed and the girl was gone.

The announcer was talking about Cuba. The crowd in the picture was a crowd of people on the streets of Havana.

Tiffany Papesh vanished from her Maple Heights home two years ago. Police have been unable to find a single clue to her disappearance. In that time, Frank Papesh has done everything he can think of to hunt his daughter. He has issued statements praising the police. He has issued statements scolding them. He has contracted the services of an ESP expert. He has never stopped hoping.

Now here was this picture of a girl in Cuba. Could his daughter have somehow been taken to Cuba? Of course she could. She was somewhere. Frank Papesh was already moving toward the telephone.

At noon the next day, he arrived at the studios of Channel 3 News. He brought Detective Ron Arko with him. George Wolf, the news manager and Jon Halpern, producer of the 6 p.m. news, had the tape of the previous night's national newscast already racked on a viewing machine.

Neither Wolf nor Halpern believed that the girl Frank Papesh had seen was his daughter. They didn't think the picture was revealing enough for any kind of identification. Halpern and Wolf thought they would have been unable to identify their own family members from such a picture. They also knew that Frank Papesh was determined to cling to anything he could call hope—to believe in anything he could call a miracle.

They ran the tape for him. A woman wearing sunglasses

walked toward the camera. In the foreground, a girl's head appeared.

"Stop the tape," Wolf said. "Freeze it."

"That's my baby," Frank Papesh said. "Her neck, her head. That's the way her hair would look if it had grown longer. I took care of my baby's hair. I know. I'm telling you, that's Tiffany."

Wolf and Halpern conferred. They still felt that Frank Papesh couldn't possibly have identified his daughter from the picture on the viewing screen. But his reaction could not be ignored. They decided to try something that was the longest kind of long shot.

If they could figure out when the picture had been shot, who had shot it and where the tape was, there was a very slim chance that the photographer might have photographed the girl from a slightly different angle—an angle that had been eliminated when the tape was edited.

Halpern got on the phone to New York. This was the busiest part of his day. He had an hour-long newscast to prepare. He didn't think there would be any other camera angles of the girl. If there had ever been any, they probably had been thrown away. But he was determined to find out.

Halpern reasoned that tape shot in Havana probably had been processed through the NBC news bureau in Miami. He telephoned Miami while Wolf called the Nightly News offices in New York. People in both cities checked and came up dry. Somebody suggested Washington. It turned out that the tape had been shot by a camera crew from Washington. Wolf began cajoling NBC Washington to track down any excess footage.

And astonishingly . . . against all odds . . . there was another camera angle of the girl. The news operation in Washington paused in its daily frenzy long enough to find it and transmit it to Cleveland. In the Channel 3 newsroom, the transmission was recorded, the frame was found. The picture of the girl was frozen on the screen.

By now, half a dozen news people were aware of what was going on. They gathered around the screen and stared at the profile of the young girl. They were excited. They didn't know if they were looking at Tiffany Papesh but the very fact that they had located another picture of the girl seemed, somehow, a breathless and portentous thing.

"Call Frank Papesh and tell him to come back," Wolf said.

The picture hung suspended on a newsroom monitor, as Frank Papesh drove back to the station from Maple Heights. He carried another picture in his head. He carried a picture of his daughter, not as she had looked when she disappeared, but as she might look today, two years later. It was the picture that Frank Papesh knew he would forever try to match.

He arrived at 6:30. The detective came back with him. Halpern was down in the control room directing his news show. Wolf led Papesh to the television set. Papesh looked at the new picture of the girl. He looked at it the way a religious man might look at something holy . . . the way a saint might look at a possible relic. He said nothing for a few seconds. Nothing at all.

Then he spoke.

"No," he said.

— *April 23, 1982*

# A *sane solution*

John File helped Michael Levine kidnap Julie Kravitz for ransom 14 years ago. File was driving the kidnap car when Levine shot and killed Kravitz. Both File and Levine were charged with murder, but it was File's bad luck that Levine got to plead first.

"How do you plead?" the judge asked Levine.

"Your honor, I am insane," Levine said. And thanks to a good lawyer, a couple of shrinks and Ohio's nutty insanity law, Levine was found not guilty of murder. So they sent him off to self-help prison and told him he'd have to stay there until he cured himself.

Then it was File's turn to come before the court. But File had a theatrical problem. There was only one good line and Levine had used it up.

Suppose File had said:

"Your honor, I, too, am insane."

It would have bombed. Why, it would have sounded like rank plagiarism. So File pleaded not guilty. And he was convicted of murder and sent away to prison for so-called life.

OK. At that point you had Levine, who had killed Julie Kravitz, judged not guilty of killing him. And you had File, who had not killed Kravitz, judged guilty of killing him. That's act one. Now there will be a brief intermission while we go over and throw rocks at the law school.

Once he was down in self-help prison, Levine's immediate task was to get himself pronounced cured so he could get out. Given the rigors of the law and the mystery of the human mind, lawyers and psychiatrists will tell you that this is a very complicated process. I, however, will tell you that it ain't. In my untutored opinion, Levine was never insane in any absolving sense. You might be riding on the bus right now with somebody crazier. Sorry. Not a happy thought.

If you beat a murder rap on insanity, the amount of time you spend locked up usually depends on the celebrity status of your victim. Everybody who is not a lawyer or a psychiatrist knows this.

Sirhan Sirhan, who killed Robert Kennedy, could be as sane as Dr. Joyce Brothers but nobody's going to let him walk yet. The timing's not right. Same for John Hinckley, who shot Ronald Reagan. Michael Levine killed a beloved and respected man. That, not the condition of his head, is what kept him locked up for so long.

But this summer, they let him out. Instantly, he began searching for a publicist to help him "tell his story." Apparently, while impounded, he had been keeping track of the deterioration of America. In the old days, if you had a "story" like Levine's, you kept it to yourself. Or maybe you moved to a new town way across the country and whispered it to a priest.

But these days, if you are a walking atrocity, you've got a pretty good chance of being invited to appear on about six talk shows. You might even get a talk show of your own. Levine is free to make money from his "story" since, in the eyes of the law, he didn't do anything. He committed a guilt-free killing.

While Levine was strutting around, drinking beer in the Flats and giving interviews to the media on the ills of the justice system, John File was still sitting in prison for so-called life. And as he sat there, he began to feel very sorry for himself. Levine, the killer, got out, he reasoned. Why not me, the killer's little helper?

But there's a flaw in File's thinking. Not that I blame him for it. It is natural that he's confused. He's trying to make sense out of an insanity law that makes no sense. The law is, indeed, unfair. But not unfair to John File. Unfair to Julie Kravitz. And to society, which is us.

File shouldn't be comparing his situation with Levine's. He should be comparing his situation with Kravitz's.

I said that File was sent to prison for so-called life. That means he's eligible for parole next year, having served 15 years. Fifteen years may be "life" for certain of God's creatures, but not for a man. Although Gov. George V. Voinovich on Tuesday declined to commute his sentence, if File gets out next year, he'll have a lot of life left.

But Levine and File took all of Julie Kravitz's life. All of it. They never gave him a hearing, either. He didn't get to circulate a petition asking that he be allowed to live. He didn't get to ask the governor for a reduced sentence.

So, while it's true that File may envy Levine, it's a pretty sure bet that he doesn't envy Kravitz—the man he helped to kill.

I am getting weary writing about this sorry saga. The only worthwhile people in it are Julie Kravitz and his widow, Georgene. I met Julie Kravitz a couple of times and he was a hell of a nice guy. Everybody said so. His employees loved him and he did a lot for this city. But now he's been under the ground for 14 years and everybody is acting like this case is about File and Levine.

It's not. It's still about Kravitz. If File has to wait until next year to be paroled, he can spend each day thinking that, for Kravitz, there won't be any next year.

Maybe that will make the time go faster. I hope not.

— *November 19, 1993*

## Not guilty?

They're going to parole John File in time for Memorial Day. Maybe he'll pause and remember the man he helped murder.

On the other hand, why should he? The justice system shows little respect for the violently dead. The dead have no rights. Their killers steal them and put them in their own pockets.

For years now, we've been asked to worry about File's rights. File helped Michael Levine kidnap and murder supermarket executive Julie Kravitz—a nice guy who did a lot for this town.

Levine and File thought they'd become millionaires if they kidnapped Kravitz and his wife, Georgene, and held them for ransom. The plan didn't work right, so Levine decided to abandon it. He shot Julie and Georgene with a .357 magnum and threw them out of his car like trash bags. Georgene lived.

She can't forget File's eyes on her. File claims he was just a poor, unwitting dupe of Michael Levine. But Kravitz remembers the way File looked at her over a gun barrel the morning of the murder. He didn't look like Levine's caddy.

Levine came to trial first and pleaded insanity. There wasn't enough insanity available for File to order some, too. It was first come, first served. Levine got the nut role, and File had to settle for dupe.

The nut was found not guilty and sent away to be cured. The dupe was found guilty of murder and sent to prison for life (ha ha). There ought to be a rule in newspaper stylebooks that, when writing about life sentences, the tongue-in-cheek form is used.

File has served 14 years. That is considerably less than life for a man, even a duped man. Fourteen years may be life for a cocker spaniel. But it is not life for a parrot or a man or a reasonably well-kept horse. File will be 41 when he finishes his life sentence. Most of us hope our lives last longer than that. But you never know. After Julie Kravitz met File, his life was measured in hours.

Levine was released from a mental hospital last spring. The witch-doctors shook some bones at him and pronounced him cured of future tendencies to shoot helpless men with big guns. As soon as Levine got out, he proclaimed that the insanity law was just a big joke. That opinion proves he's sane, all right. Not that he ever wasn't.

Americans are beginning to demand higher standards from their homicidal maniacs. If we're going to tell a murderer he's blameless, the least he can do is foam at the mouth a little. Or babble in strange tongues. Or pick up signals from Satan through the fillings in his teeth.

It is no longer sufficient for a murderer merely to say he just couldn't help himself. That's OK to say when you eat a whole box of chocolates. But if you are going to prune your husband's twig with a butcher knife like Ms. Bobbitt or blow your parents' heads off like the Menendez boys, you ought to have a better excuse than the kind they give at Weight Watchers. Levine is right. The insanity law is nuts.

When Levine got out, File began yelling, "Hey! How about me?" What was the poor, confused justice system to do? If Levine, the shooter, was free, how could we tell File he couldn't go out to play? That wouldn't be fair, now would it? It would make File a victim. These days you get to be a victim no matter which end of the gun you're on.

So we're going to let File loose. According to his lawyer, he will visit schools and churches to talk to young people about crime and tell them what it was like to be in the penitentiary.

I am not very big on this idea. The country is full of felons who are writing books and appearing on "Oprah." We live in a land where fame, no matter how you get it, is considered the ultimate human achievement. I do not view the celebrity murderer as a deterrent to crime.

After all, what is File's story? He helped murder a man and went to prison for it. A lot of people thought that wasn't fair. While he was in prison, he got his high school diploma and a college degree in marketing. Now, at age 41, he's on the job market. His so-called "life" sentence turned out to be 14 years long. Thank you very much, and Mr. File says he'll be happy to sign a few autographs.

Personally, I prefer the story of the Three Little Pigs or Little Red Riding Hood. In those stories, the wolf gets what's coming to him. He doesn't end up on the lecture circuit with a marketing degree. And there's no confusion about who's the victim.

So if File comes to your school, keep your kid at home. Keep him away from File's story. Tell him, instead, the story of Julie Kravitz—a nice guy who did a lot for this town. Who gave money to charity and provided jobs for people who needed them. And whose life was taken away—all of it—by a couple of guys who are both looking forward to a nice summer. Because we've marked them "paid in full."

*— April 8, 1994*

# When rights are wrong

I got a letter the other day from Richard and Martha Hicks of Akron. You don't know them.

Even though you don't know them, I'm going to ask you to put yourself in their shoes for the length of this column. In Richard's shoes or Martha's shoes, depending on the gender of your footwear.

In their letter, Richard and Martha reminded me that we had met a few years ago. And so we had, on a couple of occasions.

Good, plain, salt-of-the-earth people is the way I remember them. Middle-aged. Christians, in the old-fashioned way. Work ethic. Strong feelings for the value of their privacy. Concerned about America and troubled about some of the things that go on these days that didn't used to go on.

In fact, it was their concern for issues that prompted Richard and Martha to write me. They wrote in response to my column about a killer in Florida who wants to become a songwriter and profit from the notoriety he's gained through his career in atrocity. Richard and Martha think that's wrong.

"Society continues to make heroes of criminals and families of these same criminals wealthy people," Richard wrote. Then he asked me to support an Ohio Senate bill that would stop criminals from benefiting from publicity about their crimes.

All this is perhaps mildly interesting in a kind of low-key, do-gooder way. But I'm aware that nothing I've told you so far is going to move you to put yourself in Richard and Martha's shoes.

So let me describe them this way.

Richard and Martha Hicks are the parents of Jeffrey Dahmer's first victim.

Their dead son's name, by the way, was Stephen.

If you were listening really hard the other night, you heard Stephen Hicks' name mentioned on national television. It was on NBC's "Dateline" show.

It was a big night for the folks at "Dateline." First, anchor Stone Phillips interviewed Jeffrey Dahmer and his father, Lionel. They were all up in the prison in Wisconsin where Jeffrey is locked up. Then Jane Pauley took over and interviewed Nancy Kerrigan.

Now try to put yourself in the shoes of Richard and Martha Hicks. Or better yet, put yourself on their couch in front of their television set. Imagine yourself watching Stone Phillips, his beautiful face displaying appropriate expressions of sincerity and concern as he gently and deferentially interrogates the man who slaughtered your son.

"The first one was a boy I picked up hitchhiking," Dahmer says. "I took him home and knocked him out. I almost didn't stop for him."

"That was Stephen Hicks," Stone says, displaying the fine work of the NBC research department.

Imagine you are Richard and Martha, hearing your son's name whiz by. A footnote. Part of Jeffrey Dahmer's batting average. Then you find out that Lionel Dahmer has written a book. Stone piously states that most of the book's profits will go to the families of his son's victims. And you also hear that Jeffrey Dahmer's mother is writing a book, destination of proceeds undisclosed.

The book contracts and the television interviews belong to the ghouls and their families. Nobody wants to buy a book written by the parents of a murdered boy. A boy whose circumstances render him unavailable for interviews.

What could such a book say? He was our son and, in the labor room, he was born in the midst of joyous pain. Then we tried to raise him right and made sure he learned his manners and did his homework and stayed out of trouble. Then, one day, he was hitchhiking, and a young man who almost didn't stop picked him up and took him home and killed him. The end.

"Dateline" was much harder on Nancy Kerrigan than it was on Jeffrey Dahmer and his father. Jane Pauley took the hand-off from Stone, and in no time she had Nancy Kerrigan crying about the disgrace of allegedly letting her public down. The tone and blend of the two interviews was such that it was hard to tell which was the bigger sin. Was it making smug remarks to Mickey Mouse as Nancy Kerrigan had done? Or was it killing, dismembering and eating human beings as Jeffrey Dahmer had done?

If you play by the rules of the television talk shows, it doesn't matter. A freak is a freak and, by the time the talk shows get through with you, you are some kind of freak whether you are a cannibal or an ice skater or the president of the United States. Different acts, same vaudeville.

I have heard Lionel Dahmer interviewed twice more since the "Dateline" interview. He is on his book tour now. He is a quiet, timid man who obviously has no idea why his son became a monster or what, if anything, he could have done to stop it.

So there seems no particular reason to buy the book, but people will. Because the name Dahmer is a hot-shot name. If I had put the name Dahmer in the first paragraph of this column, I could not have said, "You don't know him."

Richard and Martha Hicks are not a very good interview. There are long silences in the room when you talk to them. Like Lionel Dahmer, they have many unanswered questions. Why our son? Why that day? Why that particular time of day? Why that particular road?

They will quietly ask themselves those questions for the rest of their lives. Stone Phillips won't come calling to help them with the answers. But they, too, are worth our attention and concern. Worth, I think, at least one column. Nice people. Bad box office.

— *March 16, 1994*

## Lawyers, guns and money

I want to make it plain right off the bat that this is no slam at Cleveland Councilman James Rokakis. He's an all right guy in my book and his heart is in the right place. In his chest.

He thinks there are too many shootings and killings out on the streets, and so do I. He thinks something has to be done about it, and so do I. On goals we agree. Only on methods do we differ.

Councilman Rokakis thinks the city ought to pay 50 bucks to anybody who will come down to City Hall and turn in a gun. He thinks this will take the guns out of the hands of gangs and other people who might use them for harm. And that's where I think his logic is flawed.

The biggest shoot-'em-up gang I can think of in the history of American violence was the Al Capone gang in Chicago back in the '20s.

Now suppose the city of Chicago had offered 50 bucks for every gun turned in. Do you suppose Al Capone would have told his gang:

"Gee, youze guys. I know the illegal booze business is paying us millions, but there's nothing like a sure thing. And it says here in the paper that if we take our guns over to City Hall and turn dem in, we can make $650 cash. So what are we waiting for?"

I don't imagine that happening, do you? Because Al Capone was a crook. And a gun is to a crook what a wrench and an accountant are to a plumber. Tools of the trade.

But even non-crooks might be reluctant to cooperate with the Rokakis plan.

I can't, for instance, see the Lone Ranger showing up at City Hall and saying:

"Here are my guns. That's a hundred dollars for me and 50 dollars for Tonto, makes 150 dollars. Now about the bullets. I'm willing to leave you one bullet. So you'll know I was here. I do that.

"But I'm taking the rest of these bullets with me. Silver, you know. Worth a fortune."

No, I don't see guns coming in from non-crooks, either. Especially the kind of non-crooks who keep guns in case, somehow, they ever run into crooks.

So who does that leave?

I'm afraid the only people who would ever take a gun to City Hall would be people who never had any intention of ever shooting one. And that's not the target audience.

Not only that, what kind of guns are owned by people who have no intention of shooting guns? Usually old guns that they've inherited from somebody or found up in the rafters of old houses or something. Often such guns do not shoot.

So it seems to me that the result of the Rokakis Plan would be to rid the streets of Cleveland of guns that don't work in the hands of people who don't shoot.

Otherwise, I like it.

*— November 9, 1991*

## Stolen innocence

We are almost old now, we boys and girls. Time has played with our bodies as if they were made of modeling clay.

Anything that can sag is sagging. In school we learned that the law of gravity was about an apple falling from a tree and bonking Isaac Newton on the head. Now, in our mirrors, we see that the law of gravity can also shove our chests down to our waistlines. The hair—what's left—is white or colored from a bottle. If we have our own teeth, they are mostly gold and silver from a mine.

But Beverly Potts is still 10 years old. She looked out at us again from the front page this week, and she hasn't changed a bit.

She is still the same as she was when we first saw her in the hot summer of 1951. When she made her debut beneath bold headlines in all three Cleveland papers. Headlines that demanded to know, "Who Stole Beverly Potts?"

She was a child star that summer. She even looked a little like that other great child star, Margaret O'Brien. Our parents all thought of Margaret O'Brien as a real kid. But we didn't. Real kids didn't get into the movies. The closest a real kid got to a movie screen was during a yo-yo contest on the stage of the neighborhood movie house on Saturday afternoon.

Real kids didn't get their faces on the front page of the newspaper day after day either. In space normally reserved for President Truman or Gen. Matthew Ridgeway, who was off in Korea running a war people muttered about. That was the summer a French general named de Lattre de Tassigny visited Washington to try to drum up support for the French war in Vietnam. But nobody paid much attention to that. Beverly Potts shoved the French general to the inside pages. She, this real kid, was the real news.

She gave our mothers something new and strange to worry

about. Until Beverly Potts, our mothers felt that only two things could get us: polio and traffic.

Traffic, while dangerous, was not mysterious. Polio was the terrifying thing. Mothers grimly scrubbed fruit and yelled out the kitchen window when they thought their kids were getting overheated. August was the height of "polio season," and swimming in the lake or even a swimming pool was out. Since nobody knew what caused polio, anything could. And since anything could, our mothers didn't want us to do anything in July or August, except maybe sit in a chair and stay there.

The vanishing of Beverly Potts, like polio, was both terrifying and mysterious. Beverly Potts had been watching a Show Wagon show in Halloran Park one minute. And the next minute she had disappeared. Somebody had "stolen" Beverly Potts, and we, her kid peer group, had no idea why.

I dreamed that August about Beverly Potts. In my dream, she walked down a street to a corner. Then she turned and waved. Then she just vanished. It was like a magic trick, but it was somehow frightening.

In those days, what you knew about kids being stolen you got out of fairy tales. I owned a Bobbsey Twins book in which there was some talk about kids being stolen by gypsies. I had never seen any gypsies clumping around the Harvard-Lee area. But Beverly Potts had been stolen from W. 117th St., all the way over on the West Side, somewhere near Indiana. East Side kids had no idea what strange things might happen over there across that oil-slick of a river. Were gypsies a possibility? We didn't know.

The only other option seemed even more far-fetched. We had all read fairy stories in which children had been stolen to work as servants in the houses of wicked people—usually witches or trolls. Had Beverly Potts been stolen to wear rags and an apron and scrub floors in some hut in a forest or cave in a hill? No. We were a little too old that summer to buy that one.

Our parents were no help. When asked directly what could have happened to Beverly Potts, they were evasive. They spoke to us instead of the perils of strange men offering us candy bars from the front seats of parked cars. Which, as far as we could tell, had nothing to do with the question of who stole Beverly Potts.

There is only one good picture of her, and it's the one they always use—the Margaret O'Brien one. We, who were once her contemporaries, have seen our own photos alter as chins are added and hair departs. But Beverly Potts will always look just like her picture. Every couple of years, at random intervals, her face reappears, as it did this week. It happens when somebody thinks he has at last found the answer to the riddle. Then the answer evaporates and the riddle remains.

Time has left her alone, but it has changed us and the world around us. Polio was defeated by, of all things, a sugar cube. Fear of traffic seems wistfully tame compared with the fear of drive-by shooting. And, on second thought, we were interested in that war in Vietnam after all.

In this new world of ours, our 10-year-old children or grand-children would have no doubts as to what probably happened to Beverly Potts. They sit on the rug in the living room and watch Jeffery Dahmer interviewed about his homicidal urges and his exotic cuisine. They watch a $7 million anchorwoman debrief Charlie Manson one more time about his blood orgies. Today, at 10, they are already little sophisticates of atrocity, our chil-dren. They wouldn't need a fairy tale book to instruct them on the riddle of Beverly Potts. The 11 o'clock news will do.

But we who have made the journey from knowing too little to knowing too much can look at Beverly Potts and see ourselves and remember the innocence with which we greeted her mys-tery. And pretend, though we know better, that, at 53, she might still be alive and stolen away from our world. With gypsies never sighted, or in a forest not on any map.

Instead of just a little girl who was swallowed by a world of harshness and brutality. A world into which we all have followed her beckoning hand.

— *March 11, 1994*

# Begging the question

The news stories have stopped merely calling Anthony Mitchell homeless. They've started calling him a vagrant. This is a small step in the right direction on the long journey back to sane English.

Police say Mitchell knifed a man to death in the Flats the other night. He is accused of killing Armando Farago, 19, an Italian immigrant who was married here five days before he died.

Mitchell was in the Flats Tuesday, panhandling at Panini's Bar and Grill. He was asked to leave and wouldn't go. An argument started and he pulled a knife and stabbed three people. Farago was the least lucky. Police say he was trying to protect his new brother-in-law when a knife thrust to the chest ended his honeymoon and his life.

At last report, Mitchell had no known address. Perhaps this is a justifiable reason to call him homeless. But it is a word we use lightly. It is casually applied to anyone seen begging on the street with a Dixie cup.

I asked a Cleveland cop what he would call people who panhandle in an insistent and menacing way.

"Thieves," the cop replied promptly.

The cop I am quoting here will remain anonymous. Anonymity, in these twisted times, is often the price for truth.

"More and more of these guys are getting belligerent," the cop said. "I've seen women downtown who go out to lunch carrying a handful of change. They are scared of these guys and they don't want to get into a confrontation with them. It's easier just to throw a couple of quarters in the cup and keep walking. If I frighten you into giving me money, I'm a thief. A robber. I don't have to pull a gun to qualify."

The cop told me about a panhandler he had rousted from outside the Stadium recently.

"This guy had a great big cup," the cop said. "A lot of them have taken to using those cups you get in a Dairy Queen that hold the jumbo-sized Coke. Kind of a capital investment to accommodate increased profits.

"Anyway, some people told me this guy had been frightening them. Raising hell if they didn't give him enough money. So I went over to him and told him to move along. He said I had no right to give him orders. Said he had a right to be there. So I told him I didn't want to hear any more complaints about him."

"Then what?" I asked.

"Then I heard some more complaints about him," the cop said. "So I went back and I told him I didn't want to learn any more about his rights. I told him to move. And I pointed my finger in one direction and he started going the other way."

"And?" I said.

"And I yelled at him to stop. I said, 'I thought I told you to go that way.' And he looked at me kind of hurt and he said, 'I can't go that way. My car is parked over this way.'

In the old days, it was shameful to beg. You mainly saw beggers in news reels from India. There was an old blind man who begged in front of May Co., but he kept his eyes closed, his mouth shut and his hand out. He didn't use a giant Coke cup either. It would have been presumptuous.

In those days we separated beggars into categories. On the bottom of the list were bums. Bums needed no further definition. They were bums because they were bums. Next came the panhandlers or unfortunates. They were begging because of some physical, spiritual or addictive disability. Personal demons or inadequacies had forced them out on the street.

Then there were people who were "down on their luck." Fate had dealt them a bad hand. "There but for the grace of God go I," you could say when you heard about them. It was bad manners to call somebody who was down on his luck a bum. Only the bums were proud of what they were doing. Their lack of shame was another thing that made them bums.

Today we have compressed these categories into a single word. The word is "homeless" and it is meant to trigger automatic compassion. The desperate job-seeker wears the same label as the professional mooch whose cup runneth over. We have been trained to withhold moral judgments. The lack of them has encouraged the old-fashioned bum to cross the line into extortion.

We must wait to appraise Anthony Mitchell until all the facts are in. He is said to operate under the alias of Antonio. A man who goes to work with an alias and a knife would seem to have unpleasant career goals in mind. But that's a preliminary reading.

But he's been downgraded to vagrant in the news stories. If he's convicted, the state will give him a known address. Then he won't be homeless anymore, if he ever was. But Armando Farago's new bride will.

— *September 22, 1995*

## Right and wrong

The old man sits in the hanging cell in Jerusalem and the question continues to be, when we look at him, what do we see?

Some look at him and see ghosts. The ghosts of 6 million people—Jews, most of them but not all of them—killed so long ago, there's hardly anybody still alive to blame.

To the people who see ghosts and hear the voices of ghosts, the old man is Ivan the Terrible, butcher of the death camps. One of the last men on earth they can point to and say: "He did it!"

To them it is important and necessary that the old man be dead. He is 72 and it is a blessing from God that he has stayed alive long enough so that they can kill him.

To them, he is not merely an old man. Not merely a terrible old man. He is the symbol of the Holocaust, his every living breath an insult to the dead.

That's one way of seeing John Demjanjuk. Looking at him and through him and back 50 years.

But the court can't do that.

The court has to focus its vision and see the old man as merely a man. A man who has been charged with a crime and must be set free if there is any reasonable doubt he committed that crime.

In a court, ghosts cannot testify without being sworn. Emotion, no matter how raw or tortured, is not evidence.

There always has been a shadow of doubt that John Demjanjuk is who they say he is and that he did the things they say he did.

It was all such a long time ago. Memories have grown blurred. Old men and women have tottered up to Demjanjuk and pointed at his face and said "That's the man. I'd remember him until my dying day."

But what if they had seen him on the street, not in the dock? What if he had been having coffee at the next table in a restaurant? Would they have pointed and would they have remembered?

The question in the Demjanjuk trial has been whether the shadow of a doubt that darkened the case would grow into a reasonable doubt. And, if it did, whether evidence and the rule of law would triumph over emotion and the notion of cause.

The notion of cause has been strong in the case since the beginning. A while ago, I wrote a column expressing concerns about the reliability of the evidence against Demjanjuk. A rabbi in a Cleveland congregation responded to the column in his membership newsletter.

"Feagler has revealed himself for what he is," the rabbi wrote. "A dyed-in-the-wool anti-Semite."

A cause can become a tyranny. It happened in Germany 50 years ago. When a cause tries to become a tyranny, it speaks like that rabbi. "The hell with what's right or what's wrong," it says. "Either you are for us or you are against us. Decide!"

In Germany, the cause took over the courtroom and justice became a mockery. In Israel, that has not happened. It can't be allowed to happen.

Demjanjuk can be executed for a crime. But not for a cause. If he is depersonalized and executed to serve an emotional need, then the courtroom will have become a death camp.

— *June 12, 1992*

## The bishop and the chief

Wednesday—the day the big headline told the city he had been fired—Police Chief Eddie Kovacic warned his wife, Barbara, he'd be home late. He was going out on the town with Bishop Pilla.

Kovacic put on his uniform. The bishop took his off. The bishop put on civilian clothes and Kovacic gave him a hat with a badge on it. They went over to the 4th District and commandeered a responder car. "I appreciate this, Edward," the bishop said. Then the two of them sped off to the scene of a carjacking.

Bishop Pilla had been wanting to ride in a zone car for some time. This week, he said a special Mass for Kovacic's mother, Vera, who died in October. The chief was grateful. Things being as they are, he figured if he was going to give the bishop a zone-car ride, it better be soon. "Let's do it now," he said.

The Catholic church has demoted St. Christopher. Now it is the police who are the patron saints of travelers crazy enough to venture through the inner city or unlucky enough to live there. Our society has made the police tarnished saints. Watch the news and you'd think they don't do anything right. It is hip to heap scorn on police. Like saints, you don't believe in them until you need one. Then you become a believer fast.

The carjacking happened over at the King-Kennedy Estates. If you look up "estate" in the dictionary, you will not find a description remotely like King-Kennedy. An estate ought to be some place where the residents dress in tweeds and shoot grouse. The sound of gunfire can be heard around King-Kennedy, but it is people who are the targets there. Perhaps the estates are aptly named, considering the fate of the men they were named for.

When the bishop and St. Eddie arrived, police were already talking to the man who had been carjacked. The victim was trying to decide who he hated more—the carjacker or the cops.

Since the carjacker had left and the cops were there, he aimed his belligerence in their direction.

"How was the man dressed, sir?" an officer asked him.

"I already told you that. Why do you keep asking me that? I already told you. Raiders jacket."

"Well, there's two kinds of Raiders jackets. There's a short one and a long one. Which kind was he wearing?"

"I don't know. What difference does it make? How many times I got to answer these questions? Short one."

The bishop remarked on the victim's lack of manners, gratitude or cooperation. Kovacic shrugged. A cop doesn't expect anything except from another cop. From another cop, he expects everything. For example, he expects another cop to be willing to die for him. But a cop expects little but trouble from the rest of the world. And that includes mayors. In our town, it definitely does.

In our town, and in many large towns, mayors and police go to war with each other with some frequency. The police are a closed society and a power bloc. They like answering only to themselves. They don't think anybody outside the force knows how bad things are out there. Mayors feel they must maintain strict and obvious control of the police. So you have this power struggle. It is like the power struggle that goes on in a banana republic between the army and the head of state.

Any student of Cleveland history knows there had better be a compelling reason for a mayor to take on the police force. Strong mayors like Carl Stokes and stubborn ones like Dennis Kucinich found that, when they shook up the Police Department, it was their own teeth that rattled. Their "nationwide searches" for outside replacement chiefs ended in disaster.

Usually, such shake-ups happen for political reasons. Community activists complain about police response time or police brutality. Delegations of ministers camp on the steps of City Hall. But nothing like that has happened lately. The Pipkins case was a minefield, but a minefield apparently safely crossed.

So no one is quite certain why the mayor fired Eddie Kovacic.

Eddie Kovacic certainly isn't. On the force, they just mutter "political." Then they shrug. What can you expect? Nothing, as usual.

Kovacic will not talk about it. If he were ever going to unburden his soul, he's got a bishop right on the seat next to him. A bishop in strange vestments, but a bishop nonetheless.

But he's going to go out with class. He's got certain standards. There are a hundred ways to be a bad cop and, for 30 years, Eddie Kovacic has avoided all of them. He's not going to spoil it now.

The first cop he ever formally encountered kicked him in the rear end. He was bending over, shooting craps on the sidewalk in front of Sam's Cut-Rate Drug Store in his old neighborhood, E. 95th and St. Clair. "Get outta here!" the cop yelled. Kovacic ran down the street and, when he looked back, the cop was picking up the pennies and nickels from the sidewalk and putting them in his pocket.

Pennies and nickels! Now, out there in the night, you can grab a 16-year-old drug dealer and plaster him up against the car and find he's got a couple of thousand dollars in his pocket. If you take it and let him go, what's he going to do? Call the police?

When Kovacic joined the force, they gave him a gun and a billy club. The club was what you were supposed to use if you had to. Or maybe your fist. Guns were theoretical. There were only a couple of really bad streets in town. Now there are bad blocks, bad districts. There are guns everywhere. Guns like the Tech-9 pistol with a magazine as long as a set of piano keys that a punk can spray at you like a garden hose. The bad guys don't have to be Dead-Eye Dick. Just point it in your general direction and let go about 12.

Over this world—the Tech-9 World, the world of ingratitude, the world of temptation and thousands of dollars in the dark, the world that portrays the cops as thugs and the thugs as victims— over all this Kovacic has stainlessly presided as police chief. But politics got him. And now his police involvement is ending the way it started. With a kick in the pants.

He dropped the bishop off and was home at midnight. He was in his office by 9 yesterday morning. And yesterday, as usual, the town was better for it.

— *December 3, 1993*

# FROM THE BLEACHERS

## *Rocco's song*

"I love the National Anthem."
—Rocco Scotti.

Well, for heaven's sake, shouldn't he?

I mean, is there any battle-scarred, rainbow-chested, shaven-headed Marine colonel with any more reason to love the National Anthem than Rocco Scotti these days?

A while back, when there was a move afoot to trade in the National Anthem for an easier song, something hummable, is it any wonder that Rocco Scotti took pen in hand and pledged support to Cong. W.S. Stuckey Jr. of Georgia who wanted no rewrite of the anthem, thank you, suh.

In this town, when the National Anthem is played, they are playing Rocco Scotti's song. That other Scot—Francis Scott Key—hell, he's just the fellow who wrote it. But ask anybody on the Mall about Rocco Scotti and that person will say:

"The guy who sings the National Anthem at the ball game."

And then that person, if in a kittenish mood, will throw back his head (no woman could do this) and rumble forth in a rotten approximation of a rich baritone (to be defined later) the first five words and six notes of the song that Robert Goulet once flubbed on national TV, that Jerry Vale does not trust himself to sing live, opting to mouth the words while a recording plays safely in the background, Rocco Scotti's memorable aria—"The Star Spangled Banner."

Once he wanted to sing *Otello*.

Oh yes, back in Collinwood High School in the '40s that was. He knew then exactly what he was going to do with his life and that was to sing on the stage of the Metropolitan Opera. He was from a family of 10 and his father, Nick, had had the gift of a voice also. But Nick was a laborer who had no time for idle dreams of a singing career. Such foolishness was for boys.

So Rocco, the boy, left town and went to New York where he sang for Max Rudolph, who conducted the Met orchestra, and Max Rudolph, hearing him, was impressed and told him to find a fine teacher and study, study, study until the day he was ready and then . . . *Otello* perhaps.

Could anyone blame him if he chose not to wonder how many times such advice had been given before?

Now we will commit a literary atrocity and violently shift scenes away from this MGM saga of struggling artist and land (in violation of all sensible rules of narrative) on the Mall yesterday in the sunshine where Rocco Scotti is eating an Italian sausage sandwich and sipping Seven-Up and listening to a four-piece band play for secretaries and their voyeurs.

"Hey, Rocco," the band leader says, "how about singing the National Anthem to start things off, ha, ha."

"Ha, ha," says Rocco. "Tell you what, I'll maybe sing later on."

So the band plays "Tie a Yellow Ribbon on the Old Oak Tree," and Rocco talks about the Anthem.

"A lot of singers don't bother to study the Anthem," he says. "I have studied it. It is a very difficult song, you know. It requires great range. Well, I have a good baritone range and a good tenor range. And I end on a flourish. I end on a high G. Nobody else does that. It is the flourish ending that I think provides the impact. But I study the Anthem. I sing it a lot in the car. For practice."

"How did it start with you and the Anthem?"

"Well," says Rocco, "I started singing it at the Knights of Columbus track meet. That was the first place I sang it with my special flourish ending. And it caused quite a stir and it made the newspapers.

"So last year, I was asked to sing it at an Indians game that marked the beginning of the bicentennial celebrations. And it created such an impression that they asked me to sing it on weekends.

"Then, the last game of the season against the Yankees, George Steinbrenner was at the game and he called me over afterward and he told me he wanted to bring me to New York to sing it for a Yankee game. So the third of August I go to Shea Stadium and then the fourth is Rocco Scotti Day here at the Stadium.

"The Indians are giving me a day. I'll sing for a half hour before the Detroit-Cleveland game with a five-piece band. I think it's great of them."

He smiles warmly, appreciatively.

"You know," he says, "I don't want to get too excited. But I feel this Anthem thing is really going somewhere. I have letters from all over the country. Hardened sports writers, umpires have been impressed. I tell you these things because you ask me. I don't want it to sound like I'm blowing my own horn.

"But maybe — there's this idea — maybe this country needs an official National Anthem singer. There has never been one, you know and people have suggested it. And maybe I could be the one. Although, I don't know. I have learned to take it as it comes."

It just never happened for Rocco Scotti in New York, you saga-lovers, you romantics. Maybe he had the wrong teacher. He's thought about that. He just never felt ready for the Met. He says you know when you're ready. What he knew was, he was broke. He quit the teacher. He quit New York and got a job driving a truck. In the truck he sang arpeggios to keep his voice in range. Some people backed him and he went to Rome and made an album with the Rome Symphony. It flopped. Other Italian boys with good looks and big voices were singing big, pasta seduction songs and making money. Rocco wanted *Otello*. Maybe he was handled by the wrong people. He thinks about that. Who wants to second-guess? Anyway, what we are talking about here is the National Anthem . . .

"The day before I sing it in New York, Robert Merrill of the Met sings it," Rocco says.

"First Robert Merrill, then me. That ought to make a pretty interesting comparison, don't you think?" And he winks.

Because he isn't worried. Robert Merrill is a fine singer, true.

But he is Rocco Scotti, the guy who sings the National Anthem at the ball game.

— *July 17, 1975*

## The search for a dream

ANDERSON — William R. Anderson, age 61, dear father of Mary Carol Hick, dear brother of Arthur. Time of service later. Arrangements by THE DONALD MARTENS & SON FUNERAL HOME, 11210 DETROIT AVE.

That's the end of the story. For me it was the beginning.

I handed the clipping back to the lady who had given it to me.

The lady was not young. I knew her slightly. She had phoned from downstairs and asked if she could come up and talk to me. They don't usually do that. She walked over to my desk and handed me the death notice. I looked at it. It was just a death notice.

"Did you know this guy?" I said.

She looked around the busy city room.

"I want to talk to you somewhere in private," she said.

"Okay, Alice," I said. "But what's this all about?"

So she told me.

On the radio you would hear "Brother Can you Spare A Dime." You could also hear Father Coughlin and that was even more grim. Everything wasn't grim though. Spring was nice. If you were young in 1936, you were still young and there was a bounce to life, Depression or not.

So. It is a spring evening in 1936 and Alice has a job. She is the hostess in the dining room of the Carter Hotel. She is pretty and she is young and it is spring.

A tall young man stands at the entrance to the dining room. He is a big good-looking kid and if you saw him today you might say he had a "Kennedy look" about him. With a Boston accent to match.

"Dinner for one," he says to Alice. "The one is me."

She leads him to a table. She gives him a copy of the afternoon paper to read which is what you are supposed to do if somebody dines alone at the Carter. But he would rather talk to her. He says he is from out of town. How do you like Cleveland, she asks him. He doesn't like it. He doesn't know anybody here.

The dining room isn't very crowded and they chat for a while. And he seems like a nice boy.

"Look," says Alice. "Some of my friends are having a wiener roast tonight. If you'd like to go, you'd be welcome."

He would like that very much. So Alice excuses herself. She hurries to a pay phone and she calls her sister, Dorothy.

"Dorothy," she says. "If you've got a date tonight break it. I met this terrific boy. Take my word for it. His name is Bill Anderson. He's from Boston. And . . . Dorothy, wait until you hear this. He is going to be a pitcher for the Cleveland Indians!"

They played in League Park in those days.

Alice and Dorothy went to a lot of the games.

Dorothy was Bill's girl. Bill would come out on the field to warm up before the game and he would look for the girls in the stands. They could tell when he saw them because he would become intent and serious, pitching harder, showboating a little.

Only he never got to pitch in a game.

The Indians had paid him $3000 to come to Cleveland. They had signed him out of high school. Some colleges had also shown interest in him. But $3000 was a lot of money in 1936. And the Big Leagues were a dream. There were all the players he had read about in the sports page legends. There was a girl in the stands. The dream was almost perfect.

Except he never got to pitch in a game.

There was this other big kid.

The other big kid was also a right-hander—also a freshman. And he was good. He was very good.

The day Bill married Dorothy another piece of the dream came true. It was almost all there now. If only . . . if only Bill was good enough to impress his bosses more than this other new kid.

This kid Feller.

The Indians sent Bill to Indianapolis. He came home and told Dorothy. "They are sending us down," he said. That's what they called it and that's what it meant.

There had been a moment on the grass of League Park when Bill had thrown a fast ball—hopping and humming and smacking into a catcher's mitt. And that moment had been the very high point of the whole dream. And he hadn't known it. Because you never know it when it happens. Afterwards, when they tell you they are sending you down, you can look back and know that somewhere back there was the moment. And you can try to get back to it. You can spend the rest of your life trying to get back to it. But you can never own it again. You never really owned it in the first place.

In Indianapolis, Bill started drinking. They sent him down again. To some little town in Pennsylvania.

Sometimes, when you get down near the bottom of the bottle, it almost seems as if you've found the moment. Sometimes, an hour before closing time, when the bar is misty and you are way down inside of yourself, you feel as if you own the moment at the top of the dream. And then they turn the lights on and the glare hits your eyes and you are only drunk. And the moment is gone. And there doesn't seem to be anything else to do but come back tomorrow night and start the search all over again.

And the years begin to roll on. And for Bill Anderson they rolled downhill. The war came and he went into the Navy and in a blink of his eye war was over and so was any last, lingering hope of baseball. Bill and Dorothy were living in Connecticut then with their daughter Mary Carol. Bill came out of the Navy looking for work. What could he do? He could pitch. Well, what would he settle for?

He wouldn't settle for anything, it seemed. He faced the future looking backward. Things got bad. No money. More drinking. Finally Dorothy and Mary Carol came back to Cleveland to live with Alice.

They didn't hear from Bill. He sent no money for the support of his wife or child. He moved back with his parents. Sometime in the early '50s, Bill's father made an attempt to give his son a new hold on life. He gave him $1000 and told him to go to Cleveland and patch things up with his wife.

So Bill Anderson came back to Cleveland with a thousand

dollars and a borrowed dream this time. He got as far as the corner of Alice's street.

The phone rang in Alice's house.

"This is the bartender from up at the corner," a voice told her. "There's some guy in here giving away hundred dollar bills. Claims he was a ball player. Says he's related to you."

Alice took the phone. She had her last conversation with Bill Anderson. She told him to take what money he had left and go to the Salvation Army's shelter for drunks.

"Goodbye, Bill," she said. "Good luck."

That was almost the last anybody in this story heard of Bill Anderson. Dorothy's health failed and she moved to Florida with her daughter who married. News reached them that Bill had gone to a VA hospital suffering from TB. Dorothy finally went to a judge and got a divorce from Bill. It seemed safer than way. She didn't want any part of his troubles or obligations. She tried to forget him. But, of course, she couldn't do that.

Two weeks ago a funeral director called Bill's daughter in Florida. Bill had died in Lakewood Hospital of a liver ailment. A social worker had gone to the apartment where he had lived. He had his daughter's Florida address among his papers—she had no idea how he had gotten it. Nothing much else there. A letter from the Navy Department thanking Bill for his service and telling him he could now enter civilian life proud of himself. Nothing else special. Nothing about baseball.

Alice stopped talking. The death notice lay on the desk in front of us. We both stared at it.

"Let's go back to the library," I said. "Let's see if we have any clippings about him."

There were no clippings. But Fred, who is in charge of our file of photographs, burrowed among dusty envelopes and came up with two photos.

Alice looked at one of them and started to cry.

"I feel like the only mourner," she said.

Fred looked at her confused.

"If you'd like that picture," he said, "I could probably fix it so you could take it with you. I don't think we really need it for anything."

Alice stared at him. She took the picture.

"He looks just like he did the first time I saw him in the hotel dining room," she said.

The photo was taken June 16, 1936, by a *Press* photographer named L. Van Oeyen. It shows a young kid who might look a little like a Kennedy. He stands in a Cleveland uniform at League Park. Somewhere in the stands is his best girl. He knows she's there but he isn't looking at her.

He's looking at the camera, poised in the middle of a windup, ready to throw a fastball that will hum and hop until it explodes in a catcher's mitt.

Captured on the yellowing photograph was the Moment. He had spent his life trying to find it. And here it was—his moment at the top of the dream. I gave the picture to Alice. So now, in the end, someone finally owns the moment after all.

*— April 10, 1978*

## *The boys of summer*

Every year at this time, I remember my greatest day in baseball. When I was a kid, I read this book called *My Greatest Day in Baseball*, and in it, a bunch of old ball players talked about their greatest days. Babe Ruth talked about calling his shots, and Cy Young talked about pitching his perfect game. They all had their greatest day, and I had mine.

You have to understand that baseball was everything. It didn't seem to be about money. It seemed to be about glory, like a walk up front to see Billy Graham. Millionaires owned baseball teams but did not play on them. It was a different time, you understand that.

Early Wynn lived in a shabby brick apartment building on the corner of Scottsdale and Lee, next to the vacant lot where we played ball. He would lean out of his third-floor window wearing an undershirt just like somebody's father. "Here, ya kids," he would say and down would tumble a shower of brown baseballs brought from batting practice.

Jim Hegan lived three streets away on Glendale. I carried a new baseball to his house one day, holding it to my nose to smell the horse. Now, they make them from a cow, and they smell like Thom McAn shoes. Hegan was in his driveway raking leaves.

"Give me something to sign with," he said. All I had was a pencil. "It'll fade," he said.

When you walked down your street on a summer night, you never missed a play of the ball game. There was no air conditioning, so the windows were open and the game on the radio blew out of the houses on the cross-ventilation.

It was my dream to be a ball player. The love songs of that day talked a lot about dreams. Men were always dreaming of women they could not have. These days, the songs are about having them and singing about it in the middle of it. But in my youth, it was all right to be wistful. Then, you could dream about things you knew were not attainable.

This was before Wayne Dyer and Dr. Joyce Brothers. This was a time when there were things you couldn't have and you knew it.

My baseball career was a wistful one. There is no secret about why. You can look up any kid who knew me, and he'll tell you the truth in black and white. I was lousy.

When they put me in right field, I stood there praying that nobody would hit one to me. At least not in the air. If it came out on the ground, I could pick it up, but then I couldn't throw it. I had a sort of natural change-up. I threw change-ups from right field. When I tried to throw a man out at home, I threw so high the infielders had to call for it. My favorite time to come to bat was with two out and nobody on.

Now you can ask yourself, if you want to, why, if I was that bad, I still loved the game. Why would I love something that humiliated me? Why would I keep going back for more punishment, day after day?

Well, sometimes men in love do that. They do it with women. There is no law that says that you must only love the things that reward you. Though maybe there ought to be.

I have read that all good athletes must believe in themselves. But this does not always ensure positive results. I believed in myself. I believed I was lousy. In my whole baseball career, I only had one good day. So naturally, that day was my greatest day in baseball. Let me tell you how it was.

It was a day at the very end of my baseball career, though I didn't know it at the time. I had grown up playing lousy and gone through college playing lousy and gone into the Army. And one day in the Army, my company commander decided to schedule a baseball game with a rival company. It was a grimly serious game because the Army gets grimly serious about things like baseball games in off years when there' s no war going on and nobody to shoot at. I was picked to start in left field.

Here I was among strangers. Nobody had ever seen me play baseball. I trotted out to left field and prayed nobody would hit one to me.

The first two batters on the other team grounded out. Then

the third guy hit a vicious, slicing, sinking line drive out toward left.

I want to tell you that there was no way to catch that ball. When I started after it, I knew I'd never catch it. I ran toward it as fast as I could and then I dove at it. I dove strictly for theatrical reasons. It never occurred to me to even look for the ball. I just dove. And it hit my glove and stuck, and I rolled over and vaulted to my feet and trotted in with it in a kind of state of shock.

I was almost to the bench before anybody else on my team had even moved. They couldn't believe I'd caught the ball, and then, all of a sudden, they did believe it, and they ran over and slapped me on the back and said things like "fantastic," and "way to go."

"I didn't get a very good jump on it," I said. "My timing must be a little off." They looked at me in awe. Awe!

We got two men on base next inning, and then two guys popped out. And it was my turn to bat. I had been thinking about things and had decided that since I had made a terrific catch by merely pretending I could catch, I might be able to get a hit by pretending I could hit. So I went up there and tripled.

By the ninth inning of this game, I had tripled, doubled, played errorlessly in the field and struck out twice. The strikeouts were both on called strikes, and, instead of sneering at me, the other guys on the team yelled at the umpire. "Yer blind," they said. In my dignity, I said nothing.

This brings us to the ninth.

To be honest about it, when I sat down to write about my greatest day in baseball, I considered leaving out the ninth. But I'm going to tell about it as a kind of gift. A kind of gift to any boy who might love baseball but find that despite this love, they are always standing out there praying nobody will hit one to them.

We were ahead by one run in the bottom of the inning. They had two outs, but they had a guy on second and a guy on third. We were an out away from a victory and a hit away from a loss. And then their last batter came up and lifted a high pop fly out behind short.

I started coming in on it, and our shortstop started backing up. There was something in the way he was backing up that I recognized, and suddenly I knew—just knew—that this shortstop had had a baseball career similar to mine. That he, too, was lousy. That he was praying that he wouldn't have to catch this ball. And I knew that it was really my play and that if he heard me coming from behind him, he would veer off and let me catch it.

That ball seemed to hang up in the sky forever. I can see it yet. I can see it now and see the kid backing up toward me and see myself kind of tiptoeing in so he wouldn't hear me coming.

I knew as sure as I knew my name that that kid would drop the ball because he was made of the same athletic stuff I was made of and if there was a play that had to be made, he would muff it.

But I also knew that this was my greatest day in baseball and if there was ever a day I would be able to catch that ball, this was it.

Ah, little kids in right field—little wimps, little losers. Take it from me, life is full of these moments. You don't leave them behind when you retire from baseball. All your life, they keep hitting balls to you that are beyond your abilities to handle. All your life, you have to make a choice whether to try and maybe fail and be the goat or not to try at all and keep your shame private.

I let the kid try to catch it, and he dropped it. Two runs scored and we lost the game. That was my greatest day in baseball. Even your greatest days are rarely 100 percent great. You have to live with that and hope that someday, the bad parts fade like the pencil signature on the Jim Hegan baseball. It vanished like a summer in my youth, leaving only the memory that once it was there.

— *April 11, 1983*

## When legends were neighbors

Before the ball game the other night, we got a chance to visit with Reggie Jackson in his Park Ave. apartment.

The television camera got us in there and that's a good thing because most of us wouldn't have made it on our own. They have doormen at such joints, you know. Doormen and frosty people sitting at reception desks inside the lobby who say, "Whom did you wish to see?" Stammer and you're in the street.

But the camera got in and we were listening to Reggie talk about his decor—he had chosen, he said, earth tones—and we got a chance to look around an apartment owned by a millionaire who made his million the hard way. It is not, after all, that easy to make a million dollars if you cannot hit a high, inside fast ball.

We did not see the apartment of the wealthy Louis Pinella, who has made a bundle in the left fielder business. But we did gain some insight into how Mr. Pinella spends his leisure time when he is not at work in a game.

"Lou relaxes by checking his investments in the stock market," the announcer told us. "He knows exactly how all his holdings fare each day."

I stole a glance at my 15-year-old son who was watching this placidly. Too placidly.

"Ahem," I said. "Let me tell you about something that happened when I was a kid."

He regarded me sourly as I knew he would. But I had my grabber timed and ready.

"When I was a kid," I said, "I lived near two ball players. One of them you probably heard of. That's Early Wynn. He's in the Hall of Fame. The other one was a super catcher named Jim Hegan."

"They lived near you?" he said. "You're putting me on."

"Wynn lived in a luxurious high rise apartment at the corner

of my street," I said. "Hegan lived four blocks away in a sprawl-
ing mansion covered with earth tones."

He snorted. "I saw where you lived," he said. "There weren't
any mansions or high rises."

"Remember that five-story apartment at the corner of Scottsdale and Lee?" I said. "The one where Schultz' grocery used to
be on the bottom? The one I told you was next to the vacant lot
that used to be our ball field before they built a rib joint on it?
Well, that's where Wynn lived."

"He lived in that place?" my son said with wonder. "You got
to see him? Talk to him?"

"All the time," I said.

"What did he used to say to you?" asked my son.

"Well," I said, "let me think. When he came to the window
he used to wave and say, 'Hi!'"

"Yeah?"

"And when he threw us the balls and bats, he used to say,
'Here!'"

"That's all?" said my son.

"That was enough," I said. "It was with Hegan that I had my
truly long conversation when I went over to visit him one day.
He lived over on Glendale."

"You said he lived in a mansion," said my son.

"That was to get your attention," I said. "I figured you
expected that. Actually he lived in a bungalow. You remember
the house I lived in?"

"Yeah."

"Well, Hegan's house was smaller than mine."

"But what about the earth tones?" he said.

"Leaves," I said. "The day I went over to see Hegan, he was
raking leaves."

"What did you talk about?"

"Well," I said. "He was raking these leaves. And I had a baseball and an autograph book. So I went up to him in the driveway and I said 'Can I have your autograph?' And he said 'Sure.'

"So then he asked me for a pen. But I was so excited at coming to see him I had forgotten to bring a pen. All I had was a Laddie pencil. So then . . ."

"What kind of pencil?" asked my son.

"It's not important," I said. "I had this piece of pencil so I gave it to him and he signed the book and the ball. And then he said something I still remember."

"What did he say?"

"He said, 'It's hard to write on a ball with a Laddie pencil, you ought to get yourself a pen, this will fade,'" I said.

"That was all he said?" asked my son.

"Baseball players didn't say as much in those days as they do now," I said.

"What happened to the ball?"

"Well," I said. "Hegan was right. It faded away—his name. And I waited until it was absolutely all gone and then I took it up to the vacant lot next to Wynn's place and we played ball with it until the cover came off and then I wrapped it in friction tape, I guess, and played with it some more until it probably went down a sewer. That's where most of them ended up."

"What about Wynn and Hegan?"

"Oh," I said. "They moved away. But you know the important thing was that we had them for a while. They were there right in the middle of us. On our streets. We'd walk past Hegan's house on the way to school and we'd actually be quiet because we wanted him to get his sleep after a night game. I mean, in a way he was ours."

"Well," said my son, "if they had paid them as much money as they pay Jackson, they would have lived in fancy apartments too."

"Listen," I said, sore at him, "any bum can live on Park Avenue as long as he's got a million dollars."

"I don't know what you mean," he said.

"Skip it," I said. Because I wasn't sure myself. All I knew was that whatever I meant seemed very obsolete.

— *October 19, 1977*

# A *quiet pleasure*

Baseball was a quiet game for my grandmother. She could not hear well enough to pick out the crack of the bat or the smack of a fastball into the catcher's mitt. The roar of the crowd after a home run was audible to her, but only as a sigh of wind through trees.

We would board the Ladies' Day special bus before noon on Saturday and ride downtown past the red brick Carling's brewery and Bartuneks and down Broadway and past the steel mills where the tongue of fire shot out of the pipe.

We didn't have much to say to each other on these rides. I had to practically yell to make her hear me. So we did not chat much, my grandmother and I. We just sat and thought, or she looked out of the window and I read a comic book.

In front of the Stadium, she marched stolidly past the "Getcher scoreCARD! LineUP!" sellers and the sidewalk photographer who snapped his black camera as fast as a machine gun. He tried to hand you a little buff-colored claim check you could mail in for the picture, but most people threw them away, so the ground was covered with them and you walked on them like leaves.

I wish I had a picture of us now. I am 12 and she holds me firmly by the hand. In her other hand, she carries a picnic basket full of delicious, cold, breaded pork chops and a thermos of iced tea. She would eat a hot dog only if the butcher was a relative or somebody whose character met with her approval. High up in the right-field stands, in our 50-cent Ladies' Day and kid seats, we dine royally, having arrived early enough to watch both teams take batting practice. Her deafness lends her face a very slight and totally misleading scowl. But she is happy. Especially if we are playing the St. Louis Browns or the Washington Senators, whose maladroitness will probably make the bus ride home a victory parade.

She never talked about her deafness. Never. And it was only

after she was dead that I got the full story from my mother. My grandmother caught scarlet fever when she was 14. A doctor was summoned, but some kind of infection ran its course and she became a little girl who couldn't hear.

At school, her teacher put her in the front row. But the next year she got a new teacher and she was assigned a seat near the back of the classroom. She did her best. Then, one day, when she didn't respond to a question, this teacher gripped her by the shoulders and gave her a shake.

"You go home and tell your mother to wash out your ears!" the teacher said.

After that, my grandmother would not go back to school. She got a job in a factory that punched paper doilies with machinery so loud that most people quit after a week. She met my grandfather there and they married and had two daughters who learned, as I did, to speak loudly when they wanted her to hear them. We are a loud-speaking family, and that is why.

In the early '50s, a hearing-aid salesman rang the doorbell one day. He brought a box as big as a transistor radio, with an earpiece that he fitted into my grandmother's ear. All winter long she fed the birds, but on this day on her back porch, she heard them sing to her.

The hearing aid cost so much down and so much a month. My grandmother sent my mother and my aunt upstairs to get her purse. They couldn't find it.

"Where did she say it was?" my aunt asked my mother. And from downstairs my grandmother called: "I told you girls, it is on my dresser." They hugged each other and cried, these two grown women. It was the first time their mother had ever overheard them.

Well, the hearing aid was a mixed success. Much more noise had come into the world since my grandmother was 14, and there was much she didn't care to hear. Traffic sounds bothered her. So did the loud noises of a roomful of people talking. If she didn't like what she heard, she reached into her bosom and turned the volume down. She knew what she liked, my grandmother did.

I am ashamed to tell you how old I was when it occurred to me to wonder why she liked baseball so much. It kind of stuck out, baseball did, from her usual solitary pastimes of gardening, baking and canning.

And then I thought: What do you do with a little kid of 12 who is your grandson when you can't really hear him? When you can't hear well enough to answer his endless 12-year-old questions, or talk about his day in school, or have long conversations about what to do when life unfairly grabs you by the shoulders and shakes you?

There is the ballgame, which he loves. Which you can watch together and be together and share a common joy. There is that.

The other night, the baseball broadcaster remarked to his partner that the deeper the Indians pushed into this winning season, the more noise the fans made. "Jacobs Field is getting to be a loud place," he said.

And that's good. But quiet can be nice, too.

— *June 26, 1995*

## *The name rings a Belle*

It begins and ends with this: Joey Belle and Albert Belle are the same fella. Everywhere Albert Belle goes, Joey will go with him.

That isn't nice but it's true. And, if you're Joey-Albert Belle, looking for a star to steer your life by, true is better than nice.

I smelled trouble coming when Joey Belle got out of alcoholism treatment and announced that he wasn't Joey Belle anymore. He was now, he told the sportswriters firmly, Albert Belle. Joey Belle was gone. Expelled. Exorcised. Sent off with a one-way ticket to the land of Doesn't Count.

The sportswriters played along. They traditionally allow athletes great latitude when it comes to publishing utterances below the wisdom curve. And, in this age, when drug abuse has been dragged out into the open so we all can misunderstand it, they probably felt they were being appropriately and commendably sensitive.

But even the sportswriters should have known better. They go to movies in the off-season. The story Joey Belle told them was one they must have heard before.

After all, it is the stuff of science fiction. Of Stephen King. One man comes to live in another man's body. For a while, all goes well. Then the former occupant—often an ax-murderer—begins to struggle to take over the new tenant's soul.

The ex-drunks who sit around at AA meetings in church basements have a saying that covers this phenomenon very nicely.

"The man I was will drink again," they say.

They know he's still in there, that drunk. And he wants out. You can leave town, move to Albania and change your name to John Paul II and he'll greet you like the Welcome Wagon and say, "Hello there, Joey. Didn't think you could get rid of me that easily did you?"

So it was that, in the seventh inning of the ball game last Saturday, Joey Belle went in to play left field in place of Albert

Belle. Albert Belle was temporarily tired of being Albert Belle. Albert is still young and weak and Joey is a lot older.

And it was Joey who threw the baseball at the smart guy in the stands who brayed at him about being a drunk.

Now, of course, the issue is surrounded by crap as most such issues are. The league suspended Belle. Belle appealed. The smart guy, we hear, is thinking of suing. Some people are on the smart guy's side. Some people are on Belle's side.

I am on Belle's side. But I'm talking about the real Belle. Joey-Albert Belle. I am on his side and that's why I think he ought to be suspended, fined and maybe even sued.

Joey-Albert, the ex-drunk, has to learn a trick. It's a very important trick—as important as learning how to hit a curve ball. If he doesn't learn it, he'll go back to the minors. And worse, maybe the saloons.

He has to learn who he is. He has to learn that he's Joey-Albert, not just Albert. He has to learn that Joey is never going to go completely away. Not ever. He's on the roster for life. And, if that isn't fair, what's fair? Life is full of curve balls.

There are people who say that what Joey Belle needs now are cheers. Cheers to drown out the insult hurled by the smart guy.

These are well-meaning people. And there's nothing wrong with what they say, as far as it goes.

But if you filled the Stadium to capacity and if the well-meaning cheered for five straight minutes, that wouldn't muffle the voice that's taunting Joey-Albert Belle.

It wasn't the voice of the fan in the stands that caused him to lose it last Saturday.

It was Joey's voice—still inside him. It was Joey's voice, hissing, "Hey, Albert. Did you hear what that SOB said?"

— *May 17, 1991*

## *This year is different*

As the week began, there was a hint of spring in the air. Not yet the kind of spring that poets write about. But the dingy, preliminary signs were unmistakable.

The calendar said it was spring. Rain began to melt the snowdrifts, turning what was left of them into mounds of dirty crushed ice. The temperature pushed up toward 60. And the baseball reporters were down at spring training.

For decades, spring training for the Indians has been an empty and pointless affair — like a baby shower for a false pregnancy. But this year, there was hope that things might be different. That this year was a special year.

There was a new, young team that seemed to be starting to jell. A new spring training facility. History, we battered baseball fans hoped, was turning a page. It would be the last year in the old Stadium and a new one was under construction right under our fascinated noses.

So it seemed that, this spring, Clevelanders could share in the warmth of the old hope that is kindled every spring in meadows of grass and Astroturf. That this year, the Indians would be a team people would be talking about. . . .

I have never been a sports fan but I have always been a baseball fan. In the Cleveland of my youth, baseball was the big game. Three things changed that. The team got worse. People got television sets. And the attention span of the nation dwindled.

Baseball is not a television game. The dimensions of its action are too vast for the eye of the camera to follow or the living room to contain. There is no way the camera can show us a runner, trying to score from second base while — 320 feet from home plate — an outfielder is chasing down a ball, whirling and launching it on a trajectory meant to intercept the runner 8 inches short of his goal.

You have to be there. Or, if you've once been there, you can listen to the play on the radio and let your mind's eye supply the picture. But television, which has become our substitute for being there, can't do it. Television prefers the photogenic dimensions of football or basketball. And television's tastes have become America's tastes.

For the MTV generation, used to a different and violent image every three seconds, baseball is quaintly slow. Boring, they'd say. About 50 percent of the game is spent watching 10 men on the field doing nothing but wait. Waiting—even waiting for pleasure—is scorned in our society. That's why everybody has three credit cards and no savings account.

But despite all of this, there are many of us (including myself) who believe that baseball is the game closest to America's soul. America's soul was shaped by wide, open spaces and sky over head and farm boys throwing rocks at the barn and running and hitting things with sticks. The history of baseball is the longest vital history of any American sport. So Cleveland, after 40 years of frustration and apparent indifference, had never really given up. And this year, we hoped, might be different.

And it is.

At first the tragedy seemed to be overcovered. Overreported. Exploited by the media. But then it became obvious that there was a real and vast echoing grief in the city over the horrible thing that had happened in Florida on a lake with a name like a banjo song.

It was a real tragedy for the families of two young men, Steve Olin and Tim Crews, who will contribute no new pictures to the family album. A sports tragedy for two young athletes who will contribute no new numbers to the record books. And a tragedy for the fans who can only express sympathy and sorrow from the grandstand.

The tragedy of the fatal boating accident Monday night will not stop the spring. The spring will get better and summer will follow. And it will be a special year. The players will be closer to each other and the town will be closer to them.

We all leave the game. But the game goes on.

— *March 28, 1993*

# Names that start with zzzzz

I've never liked to mention this before, but when I was a kid, I used to be a little ashamed of the names we gave things in Cleveland. They seemed so dull.

Public Square. It's such a generic name—like the cans of peaches in the Army that were labeled Peaches, Can. Compared to, say, Times Square, Public Square is cold meat.

Terminal Tower. It's so obvious, it's too obvious. I've had visitors from out of town with IQs above 100 ask:

"Terminal Tower? Why do they call it that? It's such a strange name."

"It's called that because it's a tower and the train terminal used to be in the bottom of it," I tell them.

"Oh," they often say. "Oh, yes. That makes sense then. I was thinking of 'terminal' as in 'the end,' you know. Like 'terminally ill.' So Terminal Tower sounded like a kind of high-rise hospice, ha, ha."

Not funny.

Then there's Public Hall. Not far from Public Square. It all sounds a little socialist-state somehow, doesn't it? And of course Municipal Stadium. Maybe the worst name of all.

No native ever calls it Municipal Stadium. To us, it's always just the Stadium. Out-of-town sports announcers frequently call it Lakefront Stadium. And on big Browns nights, when the urinals overflowed and people started relieving themselves in sinks, it could have been called Public Latrine.

Now we are going to have a new baseball park called Gateway. Finally a name with at least some life to it. But don't get used to it. The Gateway people are a little short of money (what's new?) so they are offering to name the ballpark after anybody who gives them 20 million bucks.

I figured there would be plenty of takers, but so far there haven't been. That's probably because millionaires have learned how to nurse a nickel and not throw their money away on things that don't pay off.

Years ago famous stadiums named after people included Briggs Stadium, Griffith Stadium and Ebbets Field. But people who knew those names had no idea who Briggs or Griffith or Ebbets were. The Cleveland phone book has a column and a half of Griffiths. If one of them gave 20 million bucks to Gateway, nobody would remember which Griffith it was. Why, Fred could claim the stadium was named after him. If he were that kind of guy, which he isn't.

Business people don't lust after fame in a name. I remember when the Clark's Restaurant chain was sold, a tycoon bought the one over near 55th and Euclid. He didn't want to buy a new sign, so he just filled in the C in Clark's and added a little mark. So the name of his restaurant was O'Larks. That was probably carrying things too far. It's like changing your name to Hilton because that's what all your bath towels say.

Maybe the best candidate as namesake for the stadium is Joel Hyatt. He hopes to win his father-in-law's seat in the Senate and naming the stadium after himself might be helpful in his campaign.

He's going to take a lot of shots anyway for hoping to inherit the Senate seat as if he were part of a royal family. So he could pay his 20 million and call the stadium the Hyatt Regency. It's probably the only way we'll ever get one here.

And that's better than going back to the taxpayers for more money. I'm one of them and you have my word on it.

*— September 5, 1993*

## The peace pipe

Gateway has bitten the nicotine-stained hand that feeds it.

We smokers, whose cigarette taxes helped build the ball park, are not welcome there. If we want to smoke, we are going to have to get out of our expensive seats and go stand in a corridor somewhere.

Naturally this is no surprise. The more government asks us smokers to cough up for its whims and whimsies, the shabbier we are treated. It is worse than taxation without representation. It is taxation with condemnation. They dumped tea in Boston harbor for less.

Do I expect to get much sympathy for this position? Of course not.

The non-smoking public is constantly bombarded with terrifying statistics about the death and calamity we smokers cause. Compared to us, Typhoid Mary looks country-fresh enough to put in a kissing booth at the county fair.

Almost every day you pick up the paper and read a story that goes something like this:

"A new study released today shows that the number of smoking-related deaths last year exceeded the total population of the nation.

"Furthermore, the study says, the number of illnesses and deaths attributed to secondary smoke rose to a figure twice the population of the planet. Smoking cost the national economy a sum so astronomical that it nearly equals the combined annual salaries of Diane Sawyer and Barbara Walters, a figure beyond which no calculator can compute."

I don't know where these numbers come from, and neither do the people who publish them. Maybe there is a cave somewhere in Montana stuffed full of imaginative number-crunchers who hang from the ceiling like bats clutching little Casio calculating machines. They have a direct pipeline to USA Today, which they rely upon to rush their every figment into print on the front page of the "Life" section.

So every other week we read that booze is good for our hearts. That coffee is bad for our sex lives. That eggs are harmful. That eggs aren't harmful. That oat bran is the secret to eternal life. That it isn't after all. And so on and so forth. The information highway is so cluttered with shady statistics, nobody knows anything for sure anymore.

All this is not to defend smoking. I don't know a smoker who defends smoking. Smokers are good citizens. We pay more taxes than other citizens in our income bracket. We allow ourselves to be pushed around like the untouchables society has made us.

"Don't breathe on me!" we are told. And we don't. "Go stand in the doorway in the snow!" we are told. And we go and stand there. At a time when all imaginable categories of human being are coming out of the closet to celebrate themselves, we smokers are not allowed an empty closet to smoke in.

And now the Indians have announced that we can't even smoke in the open air stadium we have helped to create. If my 84-year-old father, who has been smoking Camels damn near since Lawrence of Arabia was riding one, should go to the ball park he has grudgingly built—very grudgingly, I might add—he will have to leave his seat and stand on hard concrete in order to smoke the very cigarette that has made the ball park possible. This is not justice.

Here's what would be justice. Here's an idea so reasonable and feasible and right that it probably stands no chance of acceptance. But I'm going to propose it anyway.

The Indians have 81 home dates this season. They ought to take a mere six of them and designate them as "Smokers Appreciation Nights."

On those nights, smokers will be allowed to visit Gateway and smoke in the seats they've paid for. Without anybody coming along and calling them names.

We smokers believe in the Golden Rule. So we will not insist that attendance on Smokers Appreciation Night be limited to smokers only. Non-smokers are free to attend and sit among us. But the first one of them who wrinkles his nose and waves his hand in front of his face, will be smacked with a fungo bat by Tonya Harding's bodyguard. And not necessarily in the knee either. The puss will do.

This is a good idea. It is a fair idea. There is absolutely nothing wrong with it. Its only enemy is political correctness. And you wouldn't expect too much political correctness from an organization that insists on using a team name and logo that offend many Native Americans.

If it wasn't for tobacco there would be no Gateway. If it wasn't for Native Americans, there would be no tobacco. Tobacco is sacred to Indians and smokers alike.

So if Gateway isn't careful, it might be letting itself in for an 81-day rain dance. We smokers wouldn't mind. They've got us standing out in the rain already.

Let them put that in their pipe and smoke it. And not in a hallway, either. Who's got a light?

*— March 18, 1994*

# Opening Day

People are going to save tomorrow's newspaper.

That one will not go lightly beneath the parakeet. Or under the dog. Or around a fish. You'll think twice before you dump the coffee grounds on it. Or wrap the china in it for a move across town.

They say that nothing is as dead as yesterday's newspaper. Most days that's true. But there are a few days every decade when a newspaper becomes a candidate for second-class immortality. It escapes the trash compactor or the garbage can. It finds salvation in a cupboard drawer or on a closet shelf. It yellows and becomes brittle. Maybe we rarely look at it. But we want it anyway. We want to take it with us into tomorrow.

The papers we save are witnesses to very special days in our lives. That handful of days when big public news was also big personal news. Days that mark a turning point of some kind. Usually a turn for the worse.

"JFK Shot in Dallas" is yellowing on many closet shelves. It testifies to the shock and bleakness of a day which seems to have changed all the days since. And "Japs Bomb Pearl Harbor" is still in a few attics. All crumbly and politically incorrect.

But all the news we choose to take with us isn't bad news. There's more to life than calamity. "Man Lands on Moon" was a keeper. So was "War Ends in Europe," the prelude to "It's Over! V-J Day." And on a local level, "Indians are World Series Champs" has survived moves to the suburbs and basement floodings to remind some of us of the baseball glory of 1948.

(The baseball glory of 1954 turned so suddenly sour that, in our house, "Indians Drop Series in Four" ended up on the basement floor, a contribution to the personal hygiene of my wire-haired terrier, Prince, who, though paper-trained, never read them.)

I don't know how they'll word the headline on tomorrow morning's *Plain Dealer*. You can be sure they'll take a little extra care with it. The poor, much-maligned folks on the copy desk know this is their shot at posterity. The pressure's on them. They have to capture it all in fewer words than you find on the scrap of paper in a fortune cookie.

And it's been a long time since our town awoke to a headline that announced that things here would never be quite the same.

Back in the '60s we built a whole city out of ink and newsprint. It was a fictitious town that existed only in the fantasy of planners. There was maybe going to be an airport in the lake. There was maybe going to be a bridge to Canada at the foot of E. 9th St. There was maybe going to be something called a "people-mover"—a contraption that would propel pedestrians past the grimy second-floor windows on Euclid Ave. So you could window-shop the offices of podiatrists and the parlors of tea-leaf readers.

While we were building a fantasy Downtown with headlines, the real one was mouldering in decay. Forsaken, desolate, dirty. And finally in default. A deadbeat city.

We became the joke on Johnny Carson. A dull comic could coax a cheap laugh from a bored audience by merely mentioning our name. They rewrote the old Philadelphia jokes and made them Cleveland jokes. First prize, a week in Cleveland. Second prize, two weeks in Cleveland.

Maybe tomorrow's headline ought to be "Ha, Ha. The Joke's On You." But no. That's too mean-spirited.

When the town actually began to come back, who believed it? We had been stung too many times by smoke blown from pipedreams. But little by little, it really appeared. First Playhouse Square. Then the Flats. The Warehouse District. Tower City. More Flats. More Playhouse Square. The jokes began to dry up.

Gateway was a bloody battle. People complained, with logic and undeniable justification about the sweetheart deals and the sin tax. Other cities figured the Indians were packing. In St. Petersburg, they built a stadium, a field of dreams, and waited for the Gateway proposal to be defeated. The night of the vote, the Tampa area movers and shakers installed a phone line in the home of an Indians executive. When we lost the team, they wanted to pop the champagne right away.

I supported Gateway. To this day my own father thinks I'm nuts. But one night, I went for a walk over to Lakewood park and watched a group of kids playing ball. A foul came rolling toward me and I picked it up. "Here, kid," I said to a youngster in an Indians cap. "Catch."

Then I walked home thinking that this city, which had once been great, didn't get that way by accident. As a kid I'd been handed a vibrant, marvelous town. I'd been there for "Indians Are World Series Champs." Somebody's vision and sacrifice had worked for my benefit. What kind of town would this generation pass along?

The answer will be on tomorrow's front page. We still have all the problems America has. And we don't have solutions for them. But we brought Downtown back from the dead anyway. We did that. We did it for ourselves, not Dick Jacobs. And we did it for the kids who will save that paper until it gets brittle and yellow. I don't know what the headline will say, but I know what it might say:

It might say, "Here, Kid. Catch!"

*— April 4, 1994*

## Summer fling

By week's end, our summer romance with baseball might be over. I don't know what you plan to do, but I plan to throw a tantrum. If I can learn how.

It is my intention to take advantage of the cultural exchange program going on between the sexes. Women are doing many of the things once done only by men. They are pumping iron and enrolling in military school and growing ulcers in middle-management jobs. Men, however, have been slower to explore territory once considered the exclusive domain of the female.

If the ballplayers and the team owners jilt us, after trifling all summer with our affections, we should look to the sisterhood for instruction. Women know how to react when scorned. Men are terrible at it.

When a man is dumped, he either blubbers or turns mean. There is an old saying that nothing is so deadly as a woman scorned, but that isn't true. Probably a man invented it. O.J., if not deadly, was certainly dangerous. Scorned men become bullies and predators more often than society cares to think.

The other kind of scorned man reacts with wet self-pity. He bores his buddies in saloons. "How could she do this to me?" he weeps into his Bud Lite. "You're better off without her," his friends say. But the scorned man doesn't want to hear that. He wants to wallow in his pain.

A tantrum is best, and men are bad at them. A scorned woman is capable of smashing her best china and flushing her earrings down the toilet. She finds release in that which mystifies a man. A man will not break his possessions. He'll go after hers.

If we are jilted Friday, I suppose we could break the stadium. After all, it's ours. We built it, especially us smokers. But that's a bad idea. Vandalism would only land us in prison and we'd be sorry, even though they let you smoke there.

Some kind of tantrum is definitely called for. Indians fans

have given their hearts to this team. We have been led to the altar of a pennant race and now, with the church a sellout, we learn the groom is just a gold digger. Next year, fans should demand a prenuptial agreement.

A good baseball season sprouts tender shoots of emotion where you least expect them. Some weeks ago, you and I got involved in a long discussion about whether Cleveland fans should adopt the Chicago custom of throwing a home run ball hit by an opposing player back on the field.

This caused an amazing amount of mail and calls. Many of you thought catching a home run ball was the thrill of a lifetime and you vowed that if you caught one, you'd keep it. Others thought throwing it back was the proper gesture of team loyalty.

You were conflicted. You were caring. It was touching to hear you struggle to do the right thing. Most touching of all was a call from an ex-Cleveland cop. I will call him Joe, since his story has a little harmless graft in it.

"All my life since I'm a little kid I've been going to Indians games," Joe said. "I never got close to a ball, fair or foul.

"Then I got on the police force and I started pulling security duty down at the Stadium. I got to stand right down on the field. Foul balls started coming my way and I caught a lot of them.

"But I was in uniform. And every time I caught a foul ball, the fans would yell at me.

"'Give it to the kids!' they'd yell. 'Give it to the kids!'

"Well, what could I do? As much as I wanted that baseball, I had to turn around and throw it to the kids in the stands and put a great big smile on my face while I did it.

"Finally I retired from the force. But I knew all the ushers, so I could wangle my way into a game for free. And they usually gave me a good seat, right down front.

"So one day I'm sitting there in civilian clothes and here comes a foul ball. I can see it's heading right for me. I tense up, you know. I tell myself 'Don't miss. Don't miss.' And I catch the ball.

"Well, the fans are all yelling at me. I figure they're congratulating me for making the catch. But then it sinks in what they are yelling. And what they are yelling is, 'Give it to the nuns! Give it to the nuns!'

"So I turn around and sitting behind me are three of the oldest nuns I've ever see. Two of them don't even look awake and the third one doesn't look like she's sure where she is. But by now the fans are really on me. 'Go-wan, give it to the nuns!' they're yelling.

"So I take this one old sister's hand and I put my baseball in it. It could'a been a glass of beer for all she knew. And then I put the smile back on my face.

"But I was crying inside. It was one of the worst days of my life. And if I ever catch another ball at the stadium, I'm taking it and running out of there and straight home as fast as I can. Ain't baseball special?"

Yes, Joe. It is special. And, like a lot of special things, it can break your heart in a great many ways.

We like to think that part of the game belongs to the fans. To fans like Joe the cop. But this is the week we discover we've been living a lie. Joe doesn't sit in the meetings between the millionaires and the billionaires. He's stuck in the kind of stinkin' relationship you read about in Ann Landers. He's been faithful. He's given baseball the best years of his life. And now baseball is going to walk out on him. Cast him aside like an old shoe.

If this isn't tantrum time, what is? If the players jilt us, who can blame Joe for throwing a plate? Or a nun for throwing a slider at Chief Wahoo's chin? He's got it coming, Sister.

— *August 8, 1994*

## Throw it back

The other night during the ball game, somebody on the other team hit a home run, and the Indians' fans began chanting something that sounded on TV like "Hackensack" or "bric-a-brac." My Miracle Ear wasn't working, so I couldn't tell.

"They're yelling, 'Throw it back,' my viewing companion said. "It's becoming a custom now that if an opposing player hits a home run, the guy in the stands who gets it throws it back as a gesture of disdain."

Disdain? For a major league baseball caught during a major league game? Look where our valueless society has brought us. Is there no room for sentiment anymore?

Suppose the ball belonged to a little kid? Think how much it would mean to him. Think how bullied he'd feel if he couldn't keep it. In the old days, we had an appreciation of such things.

I remember a tender moment in father-son bonding when I caught a ball at the Stadium. Principle compels me to admit, I got it on the carom after a Boston Red Sock fouled it straight back, and it bounced off the press box window. Maybe it wasn't an all-star play. But my small son was with me, so it meant a lot.

It is a proud feeling for a father to catch a ball and present it to his small son. When I think back on the event, it fills me with warm nostalgia, especially if I slightly blur the truth.

"Here," I said. "A baseball. A real Major League baseball off the bat of a real Major League player. And it's all yours to keep." And I handed it to him.

"Thanks, Dad," my son said.

"Let me have it back a minute," I said, taking it from him. I held it up to my nose and inhaled, like Juan Valdez sniffing a coffee bean. My son observed this without comment.

"When I was your age, these were made of horsehide," I said. "There was nothing as good as the smell of a brand-new horsehide baseball right out of the box. It made English Leather smell like a pair of sneakers. But this one doesn't have the smell. Well, here it is. Enjoy."

"Thanks, Dad," my son said.

We watched the game for a while.

"What are you going to do with it?" I asked him.

"I don't know," he said. "Play with it?"

"Oh, no," I said. "You don't want to play with it. You want to save it. Give it back to me a minute."

He handed it back.

"Look," I said. "Right here on the side of it we'll write the date and the player's name who hit it."

"I never heard of the guy," my son said.

"That's not a very good attitude to have," I said. "I never heard of him either, but he's a Major Leaguer. And Yaz is in the lineup. You can say you caught a foul ball hit by a guy who batted eighth after Yaz."

"You caught it," he said.

"Yes," I said. "But it's yours. Here."

"Thanks, Dad," he said.

We turned our attention back to the game, but I watched him out of the corner of my eye. He shook the ball and made throwing motions with it. Then he actually tossed it in the air about six inches and caught it.

"You better not do that," I said.

"Do what?" he said.

"You better not wave it around like that," I said. "What if it slips out of your hand and falls back on the field? We might not be able to get it back."

"What should I do with it, then?" he said.

"Well," I said, "I've got an idea. Why don't you kind of sit on it? That way, nothing will happen to it."

So he sat on it. But pretty soon he complained that sitting on it was uncomfortable. So I took it back from him and held it during the game. Naturally, I gave it back to him when we got into the car.

"Thanks, Dad," he said.

But he started fooling around with it in the car again, and it was a hot day, and the window was down. And since my technique of raising kids was based on a well-founded belief in anticipating the worst, I figured I better get it back again. For his own good.

"Better let me have your ball until we get home," I said.

That was a long time ago, and by some quirk of coincidence or oversight, I seem to have it yet. The ink I wrote on it with is all faded now, and I can't remember the name of the ball player who hit it, who batted eighth after Yaz. But I've still got my son's ball—his any time he wants it. Unless he's forgotten it's his. In which case, maybe I'll remind him. One of these days.

That's what catching a ball at the ballpark used to mean to a kid. And that's why the idea of the crowd yelling "throw it back" at some kid whose father has just handed him a home-run baseball seems like child abuse.

If not abuse of the child next to the father, abuse of the child inside the father. That kid has feelings, too, you know.

— *July 7, 1994*

## Morons in the stands

About a month ago, a fellow named Louis Lerer sent me a copy of a letter he had written to Art Modell.

Lerer, a Vietnam vet, was suffering post-traumatic shock syndrome. But not from the war. From the previous day's Browns game.

"I was stunned as I went into the men's room in the first quarter and saw two men selling cocaine as if they had a souvenir stand," Lerer wrote. "As I walked out, I had to wade through a flood of beer. A vendor had an attack of some kind and was lying in this filth as people just walked around him. What a beginning!"

What a beginning indeed. Lerer's account gets a lot better too:

"Garbage was constantly being thrown through the air and landing on the spectators. Pot was being smoked everywhere. The foul language and insults offended even me—and I've heard it all in the jungles of Nam . . . .

"Fight after fight began to break out in our section. I began to feel as if I was a hostage in Beirut. My friend and I wanted to leave with about eight minutes left. We were sitting in Row 56, Section E, and for the next 30 minutes there was a constant barrage of fighting in the stairs going down for about 20 rows. There was no way out. There was fear in the eyes of the spectators not involved in the fighting."

I thought Lerer's letter was terrific, so I saved it. As I say, he wrote it a month ago, but you can see that it isn't out of date. There were more atrocities in the stands last weekend, and the Browns have announced a new "get-tough" policy on drunken morons.

And that worries me.

Speaking as a baseball fan, it is my opinion that football is a game that was made for drunken morons. The reason football has become more popular than baseball is because we live in an age that is kind to morons, drunk or sober.

When the moron is sitting at home, watching a football game on television, he can be kept reasonably tranquilized. The television camera gives him a close-up view of the grunting, groaning, mindless mayhem that he regards as sport. All you have to do to keep him quiet is give him 12 cans of a brand of beer he thinks cowboys drink and he will remain civilized as a baboon.

But at the stadium it is a different matter. Most of the time it is impossible to tell exactly what is happening on the field. And, since the average football fan has the attention span of a fly on a clean sink, his mind, such as it is, will wander.

Since we live in an age that pampers morons, most morons are under the dim-witted impression that they are interesting people. They think they are cute. They think they have talent. They think they are gifted.

And so they begin banging on their neighbors and spilling beer around and yelling foul language and waiting for some talent scout to discover them and put them in a movie opposite Madonna.

It has always been a big relief to me to know, on a given Sunday afternoon, that Art Modell is babysitting 60,000 of these cretins down there on the Lakefront. It gives the rest of us a shot at using the parks. So I am naturally dismayed to hear that he is thinking about kicking them out.

That's why I didn't tell you about Lerer's letter before this. Lerer obviously wants the morons kicked out. I want them to stay there. Kick them out of football games and they'll start going to baseball games. Some of them already have. That's why we have the wave and designated hitters.

But now that the cat's out of the bag and Modell is going to do something, what he ought to do is what I'm told they do in other cities. Give the drunken morons their own section across the field from a section for normal people.

If that works, maybe we can give them their own state. But it will have to be one of the big ones.

— *October 22, 1986*

## Farewell to Art

So long, Art, if that's your attitude.

You understand how business works. You bought the football team for a song. You made a better deal than the guy who bought Manhattan Island from the Indians. Excuse me for mentioning Indians. I know it's a sensitive word for you.

I figure that's what this is about. Hurt feelings. It can't be about business. That's impossible. Because you're asking the taxpayers of Cuyahoga County to make a business deal you'd never make.

You're asking us to pony up $154 million to fix up a stadium you won't promise to play in. Naturally, the Cuyahoga County commissioners have finally made up their minds to put the issue of extending the sin tax on the ballot for voters to decide. How could they do anything else? You've given them nothing to work with. You painted them into a corner. You've kept your mouth clamped shut—except to issue a statement through a spokesman that $154 million might not be enough.

That's no way to do business, and you know it. That's why I don't think this is about business at all. Most people are calling you arrogant. But I don't think it's arrogance. I think you're sulking.

You and I have only met a couple of times, but they have been very pleasant times for me. You've been nothing like the Art Modell I hear people knock on the sports talk shows. I found you and your lovely wife charming. You've got a good sense of humor, and you tell a good story. And you've fiercely supported your players when they've had the kind of personal problems that run rampant in professional sports.

My armchair analysis of you isn't worth the price of a cup of coffee. But I think you feel abused. And I've got some sympathy for you.

I'm no football fan. But during all those bleak years when the Indians were playing the kind of baseball that would embarrass a sandlot team in Latvia, you were the only thing that kept sports alive in Cleveland. If it hadn't been for you, sports fans would have had to turn to canasta tournaments for excitement.

Then, all of a sudden, out of the blue came Dick Jacobs. We didn't even know he was in town. Next thing you knew, the voters built him a state-of-the-art ballpark and threw in an arena for the basketball team. The price tag the voters got didn't include cost overruns, and the architects of the scheme probably knew that. But it happened.

So now there's a sold-out Jacobs Field and a Gund Arena. And you—who ran the only game in town for so many years—all you've got is a crummy old silo with plumbing like a Calcutta sewer. And you can't even put your name on it. Not that you'd want to.

If I were you, my feelings would be hurt, too. It's a reality of the human condition. People with small egos do not play in your league. But there are other realities.

Your timing couldn't be worse. The town's gone crazy over the Indians, and football suddenly seems like a remote sideshow.

And now there is this Rock and Roll Hall of Fame thing that the media and the town hypesters are saying will make this city a Deadhead Mecca. The words you hear on the street are "play-offs" and "World Series." Money men in fancy suits who think a Bon Jovi is something salty that comes on a pizza are praising the virtues of rock music and carrying copies of *Rolling Stone* to work inside their *Wall Street Journals*.

The public is fickle, and today, you are yesterday. So it's a bad time to ask for money with no guarantees. Especially since certain people are already a little squirmy about putting all this public dough into pleasure palaces when the public schools are falling in on the heads of the city's children.

If there was ever a time for good public relations, this is it. And yet, for some reason, Art, people think you just don't care. My hunch is you care a lot. I don't think these are happy days for you. But it will take a minor miracle to get the voters to give you that $154 million. So it would help if you asked nicely. It would help if we were on speaking terms.

If the voters speak first, my guess is they'll say, "So long."

*— September 1, 1995*

# We'll live

This is for the sports fan, unhinged by rage and grief.

Calm down. Breathe deeply. We'll live.

What do the dons of the sports Cosa Nostra have to do to convince you that this is only about greed? Wasn't it enough for you that the baseball teams walked off the public-financed grass last year and sabotaged a pennant race that two world wars could not extinguish? Why do you still speak of loyalty, and wail and curse like a jilted lover?

You, with your pennant and your painted face and your adoration, are a vulnerable child in the hands of men who want your money and scorn your love. A diversionary game is played on the field and it is designed to thin your wallets and liberate your kindergarten emotions. But the real game is played behind closed doors by men who keep score with adding machines and are coached by tax accountants. Why not just accept that? Accept it and things will be instantly easier.

You offer your heart but it's your assets they want. They get a bite of every hot dog you buy and a piece of every sweatshirt with a logo on it. They are waiting for you at the turnstiles, where soaring ticket prices spoil family outings like rain at a picnic. If you decline voluntary contributions, they send a tax collector around to frisk you. They have turned spectator sport into a rich man's game, like horse polo. The poor only get close enough to smell the manure.

You call me on the phone and want my opinion and you often say you know I'm not a sports fan. What has that got to do with anything? Where are the sports fans this week? Are they holding news conferences in Baltimore or Dallas? Is there a seat at the table in the NFL bunker for the so-called "12th man?" You couldn't get in there if you were room service.

What I'm not, is an extortion fan. What I'm not, is a sucker. A wise man doesn't fall in love with hookers. I've outgrown saloon infatuation. Many startling and painful lessons are learned

when they turn the lights up at closing time. The glare of reality
sends phony romance scuttling away like a cockroach.

When I want to see people playing for the love of sport, I go
to the park and watch girls' softball. What goes on in the Stadium is Wall Street with face guards. If you accept that, you're
on your way back toward sanity. So stop sniffling.

Dry your eyes and reason with me, sports fan. What have we
learned this week? That they have the teams and we have the
money and the only question is, how much do we want to spend
to lease the teams. Forget about heritage and tradition and team
names. You're dealing with flint-hearted hucksters who laugh at
that stuff.

The Houston Oilers may go to Tennessee, where the biggest
deposit of oil was on Elvis's hair. Men calling themselves Cardi-
nals now disport in Arizona, where the true native birds live in
holes in the ground and go "meep-meep!" The Baltimore
Browns is a travesty, but, in case you haven't noticed, nobody
cares about travesty but you.

So blow your nose and think calmly. Ask yourself if it makes
sense to dump $175 million into that old crypt on the lakefront.
It happens to be sitting on the best piece of development real
estate in the comeback city. If we are smart, a Hyatt Hotel might
someday grow out of the rubble of that all-purpose, no-purpose
relic. Baltimore claims it can build a new park for $200 million.
It's a bad deal for us to waste land with a view so people can get
drunk and bark and look at the ground.

At least let's make no more mistakes about the rules of the
scam. It hasn't been long since everybody was saying, "If Art
wants a stadium, let Art build it." In today's climate of naked,
unprincipled capitalism, that's baby talk. You either pay the
blackmail or you don't. Don't waste your breath quaintly moral-
izing about it.

I agree it would be nice to figure out a way to stick it to the
NFL. We're dealing with serial killers here and they're not going
to stop knocking off cities of their own accord. Protests are great,
and boycotts would be wonderful. A woman seeking therapy on
one of the talk shows suggested that nobody show up for the next

Browns game until the second quarter. That won't bring us a team, but it's a great way to give organized crime the finger on national television.

Finally, this. We need a breath of air from all this sports obsession. We've spent two years thinking mainly of sports and rock music. Sometimes I feel like I'm stuck in a remedial school where everybody is majoring in gym and recess.

We've got school problems and crime problems and two other sports facilities to pay for. The loss of the Browns leaves a hole in our lives, but so did the loss of John Adams and West Tech and Higbee's and Richman's and Hough Bakery. We can find a new team with a coach as good as Belichick, but where is the pastry chef to make a chocolate cake like Hough made?

You wanted my opinion and that's it. I could have just reprinted a column written a couple of months ago while Modell was secretly betraying us. It was called "So long, Art." All I would have had to add was, "Don't let the door hit you in the tush on the way out." But it already has, don't you think?

— *November 8, 1995*

# MILESTONES

## *Special delivery*

My good friend Tom Skoch wrote a story this week pointing out that there is a growing demand among women to have their babies in their own homes.

Tom's story indicated that having a baby in a homey setting is a restful and rewarding experience. Well, there is another side to that.

The reason I know is, 39 years ago today I was born in the front bedroom of my grandmother's house on Anderson Ave. And the circumstances of that occasion are enough to make ladies think twice about having babies at home — or even having babies at all.

My father was away from the house when things began to get serious. He was far on the Southeast Side, supervising the construction of a new house for us. My mother was left in the custody of my grandmother, who was quite hard of hearing. Along about noon, it became obvious that help was needed. My father couldn't be reached by telephone. So my grandmother dispatched my aunt to fetch him in an auto. Then she telephoned Dr. Saltzman, who soon arrived with his nurse, a starched, no-nonsense woman who ran a birth like George Szell ran his fiddle section.

And so I was born. In a restful, homey atmosphere. Without, as they say, complications. The complications occurred about 10 minutes later.

My grandmother was in the kitchen making coffee. Dr. Saltzman was in the bathroom washing his hands. The nurse was in the bedroom keeping a drill sergeant's eye on my mother.

And outside, weaving up the front walk, listing first to port, then to starboard, came my cousin Edward—back from South America.

Cousin Edward was somewhat of an adventurer. Most of his adventures were inspired by sips of stimulant.

He crashed through the screen door.

"Who's home?" he called. My grandmother did not hear him.

"Edward's home, that's who's home," he answered himself.

He climbed the stairs, seeking someone to welcome him. There was no one in the upstairs hall. He walked into the front bedroom.

The nurse glanced up, spotted him and sniffed. She had never met my father, but she was used to the way of brand-new papas. Here was one, she figured, who had been celebrating the birth of his son. She forced a smile. "It's a boy," she told Edward.

"That's a baby!" said Edward. He was delighted. This was even a better homecoming than he had bargained for. He picked the baby up and began waltzing around the room with it.

My mother, still woozy from her experience, became aware of the commotion. She focused her eyes and there was Edward.

"Put him down!" she shrieked. "Put him down!"

Downstairs, my father had just arrived from the new house. He was covered with mud. He heard my mother's shrieks and raced upstairs. The nurse didn't know who he was but she knew he was unsanitary.

"Stay out!" she barked. "Stay out!"

"Let me in there!" my father yelled. "Let me at him."

Dr. Saltzman rushed in from the bathroom. Edward waltzed past him blissfully.

"Who is that man?" the doctor thundered.

"That's the father," shouted the nurse.

"Put him down," shrieked my mother.

"Let me in there," yelled my father. "Let me at him."

"I'm back!" Edward announced.

In the kitchen, my grandmother became dimly aware of a commotion above. She hurried upstairs, armed with a broom.

The doctor grabbed the baby and my grandmother grabbed Edward, turned him about-face and swatted him down the stairs, down the walk and, presumably, back in the direction of South America. He has been there—or somewhere—ever since. His name still comes up.

Having babies at home went out of style soon after that. Now Tom Skoch tells us it's coming back into fashion. But it's not the thing a person ought to rush into. Having a baby at home may be more of an experience than you bargain for.

I know I haven't been the same since.

— *July 29, 1977*

## Christmas at Aunt Ida's

On Christmas night when I was a kid, we all went over to my Aunt Ida's house—an old house in the old neighborhood . . .

What did you think I was going to do today? Talk about the president's sex life? Or Michael Jackson's? Or the Trump Wedding?

It's Christmas Eve, my friend. Let us rest our wearied brains. Let us consider matters more vitally important than the headlines. Let us turn our back on earthbound "stars" and *People* magazine celebrities and media "personalities." Let us visit some people whose names only get into the newspaper when they die. And even then, just in the tiny type of the "Death Notices."

Let's go to my Aunt Ida's house. Come on. It'll only take a couple of minutes. You'll be home in time for "A Current Affair," I promise you.

The house wasn't far from the steel mills, and the fallout from the mills made the dirt in Aunt Ida's yard black and rich. When the wind was wrong, the air in the neighborhood smelled like a chem lab. Breathing it might have been bad, but nobody knew that then. My Aunt Ida had great luck with flowers.

On Christmas night we'd all be there. The old folks, the young folks and the kids. The young folks were the men just back from the War and their wives. The old folks could remember World War I. The kids, like me, weren't old enough to remember much. We were busy collecting memories, and this is one of them.

There was no TV. The only one among us who had a TV was my cousin Stanley, who sold them. He hasn't sold one to any of the rest of the family but he keeps trying. He knows it's only a matter of time. After all, what isn't?

"I have a 10-inch screen," he says, a cigar in the corner of his mouth, a big brown beer bottle at his elbow. He's sitting at the dining room table with the rest of the young men playing pinochle. They have all, just for a minute, assumed the present tense. A Christmas present tense.

"They are never going to be able to make a screen bigger than 10 inches that will give you a decent picture," Cousin Stanley says, importantly. "According to the laws of electronics, 10 inches is as big as you can go."

The Army Air Corps gave Cousin Stanley a job fixing radios. That's where he got his electronic knowledge. So my Uncle Ziggy, who flushed out snipers on Okinawa, and my Cousin Melvin, who knocked out tanks in Italy, are listening to him with respect. Stanley—the trumpeter of the dawn of the age of television.

(By now, the tiny type has recorded Stanley's name. And Ziggy's. Melvin's too. And my Aunt Ida's. Time killed them. The tanks couldn't do it and the snipers couldn't do it. But Time? It does it every time. Time is an eraser but it does not erase cleanly. If you look hard enough, you can still see traces of them all, faintly. And if you look even harder, they are right here.)

But where are the women? They are all in the living room, talking about babies and recipes and operations. Nylons that have come back again, so you can throw the leg makeup away. Electric stoves that practically cook your meal for you. Jobs that they can quit now—are expected to quit now—because the men have come back from the war.

It is talk to make a feminist despair. They talk of "female trouble" and permanent waves. And the Christmas crowds at Halle's and Taylor's and Bailey's. And the big Sterling, Lindner tree that looked a little bigger this year. And Hough bake shop cookies. And trolley cars that turn on Public Square, showering the safety zones with sparks.

Jay Leno isn't here. I told you, there is no television set, except the one Stanley is describing, sketching it in the air with his cigar. Nobody has bothered to turn the radio on. There is just talk. Endless, trivial, sometimes mysterious. Sometimes, if a kid comes into the room, the talk suddenly stops. "Ix-nay," one of the aunts will say. There are things, in this time, that a kid is not supposed to hear about. If, for some unfathomable reason, anybody said the word "condom," it would take the room an hour to recover its equilibrium.

Where are the kids? Would you mind, my friend, if I went looking for myself? It won't take long. I know just where to look.

I am with my cousins in the unheated bedroom at the back of the old house. We are burrowing under the piles of coats that have been dumped on the bed. Moutons, mostly, with a few Persian lambs, for animals do not yet have rights. Just a glimpse of myself is all I want. I don't want to look too hard. For this trip is a wistful mirror.

The door opens and Aunt Ida is standing in a rectangle of light.

"You kids go into the living room now," she says. "Santa Claus is coming soon."

We go. And as soon as we leave, Aunt Ida opens a bureau drawer and reaches under some flannel sheets and pulls out a moth-eaten Santa Claus suit and a scraggly beard. The pants of this suit have long since disintegrated. So my Aunt Ida hikes up her dress and pulls on a pair of my Uncle Billy's blue serge pants. Over these she pulls galoshes.

She takes a pillow from the bed and yanks off the pillow case. She stuffs the pillow under the Santa jacket for a tummy. She fills the pillowcase with toys from Woolworth's, Kresge's and Grant's. She puts on the beard, the cap. She tiptoes out into the hall. Out the back door into the night—air so cold it makes her nose sting, sky lit with a faint glow from the mills.

Around the house she goes and up on the side porch. She pauses and looks in the window.

She sees what we see now. Me at 7. My young, handsome father and pretty mother. The old folks, the young folks and the kids. Moving, though they can't feel it, down a river of time.

They can't see her. She is on the other side of the dark windowpane. The adults know she's out there. We kids aren't sure. It's a moment of suspense for us. We are not yet old enough to understand that life is predictable. That there are only a handful of plots, endlessly repeated.

I promised I'd get you back. But let me take a last look into that room. Most of the people you see there are gone now. But they haven't gone far and, on Christmas, they are very close. They are just the other side of the windowpane.

We can't see out through the windowpane. But they are out there, those simple people who loved us and took care of us. And left us blessings we rarely count. But, if we let them, they come back at Christmas. With gifts of everlasting life.

*— December 24, 1993*

## Longest day of the year

The longest day of the year makes a very nice day to celebrate. It is a neglected holiday.

The longest day of the year has, after all, certain unique characteristics. It cannot, for example, be moved to a Monday the way the Fourth of July and Washington's Birthday have been moved to Mondays.

No, there is only one day on the calendar that can be the longest day of the year. And this year it was a Wednesday.

And so, after supper Wednesday, I looked for somebody in my house to celebrate with. Everyone claimed to be busy, but I drafted my smallest son, who is still small enough to pay attention when I tell him that certain things are important and must be done.

The one correct way to celebrate the longest day of the year is to go out in the street in front of your house and hit fly balls until the light has faded to the point you can't see them anymore.

My smallest son didn't know that. In his experience, the proper way to hit fly balls is on a playground in a Little League uniform. He suffers from the over-specialization of his era.

So I told him that the way it used to be was that you would go into the street after supper with a league ball wrapped in friction tape because the cover had been hit off it.

You would begin in full sunlight but soon the light would dim and the shadows around the houses would grow purple.

By then it became hard to see the ground balls and the low line drives. Your friend would smack the ball and you would hear the crack and there would be a moment of terror when you would wonder if the ball was coming straight at your nose.

Only the very high ones could still be seen clearly—falling black dots against a sky that was turning gray.

I told my smallest son all this, and then we went out and did it. We used a tennis ball (because I am older and play it safer now).

He hit and I caught until the shadows lengthened and the lights came on. Then I hit and he caught—because even on the longest day of the year I cannot see the ball as long as I used to. Though I don't know why.

Eventually, I really got under one and put it way up in the air so that it disappeared for me into the final light of sunset. My smallest son saw it though and tracked it back, back, back . . . and patted his glove and captured it.

He captured the absolutely last ball it was possible to catch on the longest day of the year.

Then we walked proudly toward the house. It was a very satisfying celebration, and now the days would be shorter for both of us.

But I saw no reason to mention that to my smallest son.

*— June 23, 1978*

## A *razor's edge*

My son, R. Jr., who is going on 15, has developed a substance beneath his nose.

I noticed it a couple of weeks ago and figured at first that it was grime. But, of course, I knew better. I knew it wasn't grime at all. And the other night, I caught him in a strong light and confirmed what I already knew but had been avoiding.

It is whiskers.

Or, to be more accurate about it, it is fleece. It will not be whiskers until it is cut. One of these days, my son is going to have to shave. And when that momentous event happens, I am going to have to host it.

I could tell you my planned involvement in my son's first shave is motivated by safety reasons. I could claim that I can't send him alone into the bathroom with a razor for fear he would cut his throat and a tourniquet would have to be applied to his neck.

But of course that would be a lie. A son's first shave is the only initiation rite his father can participate in without embarrassment. It is much more awesome than teaching him to hit a curve ball. It is much less awkward than trying to explain sex (something most fathers of my generation haven't figured out for themselves yet).

When I was 16, my father caught me one day and led me squirming to the bathroom where the implements of the rite were already arranged. They were—as I recall it now—a new Gillette safety razor loaded with a sharp new Blue Blade. A tube of Mennen brushless shave cream. And a styptic pencil, parked like an ambulance on the side of the washbowl for emergencies. He sat on the logical thing to sit on and talked me through the process—how to get a blade out of the wax-paper envelope without slicing your finger off. How wet to get your face. How to shave against the grain without skinning yourself.

Blood is part of the ceremony and I shed some—a satisfactory but not critical amount. When it was all over—after the stinging slap of Aqua Velva—he showed me a device that I have never seen elsewhere. It was built on the order of a pencil sharpener and you put your blade in it and turned the handle and a couple of belts stropped the blade. That was before they were making blades from space metal.

His father had been initiated with a mother-of-pearl handled straight-razor, sharpened with a strop that hung on the back of the bathroom door. There was something fine and permanent about a good razor—something time-honored and moving about the ceremony of a father giving a razor to his son. The father is giving him more than a razor. He is giving him a milestone which says "You have taken a step you cannot retrace."

I stopped in the drug store last night to look at razors.

"Here's something new," the lady behind the counter said. "A disposable razor. They come two to a card for 49 cents. You use them until they get dull and throw them away."

"Why would you want to do that?" I asked, really wondering.

"For convenience sake, I suppose," she said.

I don't understand that. But then I have never understood the growing romance our nation has with disposable things.

When the time comes for me to capture my son (and I am not hurrying that time, for his milestone is my own also) I will present him with a hefty metal razor that will last for years and gather a handsome coat of verdigris as it ages.

It will not be a disposable moment for either of us. It will be something in the nature of an adventure and the equipment will be right.

I know it's a small thing. But every year, the small things grow bigger and the big things become less important. A man gets to know that about the time his son develops a substance beneath his nose.

— *November 5, 1976*

## Play that funky music

My twin daughters have something going with someone named Skip O'Brien. I do not approve but I'm powerless in the face of their grand passion.

Skip O'Brien plays records on a radio station which is called G-98. That means that he is responsible for certain bursts of obscene and discordant music that waft down from my daughters' bedroom and are about as soothing as reveille on Judgment Day blown by a Gabriel gone mad.

My daughters, who are 15, sit up there amidst their menagerie of stuffed, fluffy animals and rock back and forth in time to selections Skip O'Brien chooses for them. Selections like:

"Play that funky music, white boy. Play that funky mu-oo-sic, white boy."

This white boy was horrified the first time that came down from upstairs. My horror came from the fact that I misunderstood what kind of music was being requested. I mistook the funky for something else. Partly because I did not grow up with the word funky and additionally because, the way it is sung, you are supposed to mistake it for something else. It's enough to bring a blush to a stuffed bunny.

You gather, I assume, that Skip O'Brien and I differ on questions of musical taste.

Now, I am a tolerant person and it would be okay with me just to let Skip O'Brien go his way while I go mine. I am quite willing to leave him to his funky music and let him leave me to my "Fiddler on the Roof." In a town this size, it should be possible for Skip O'Brien and me to live our separate lives and stay out of each other's hair.

But that isn't the way it is working out.

First there is the matter of the radios. I go away from home for a couple of hours and return to find every radio in the house tuned to G-98 and set at full volume. My daughters, it seems, can't bear to switch rooms unless Skip O'Brien follows them. He is waiting to get me every time I turn a radio switch. I never know when the clock is apt to jerk me into the world in the morning by shrieking:

"PLAY THAT FUNKY MUSIC, WHITE BOY. PLAY THAT FUNKY MU-OO-SIC, WHITE BOY!!!" at me. It's like waking up next to an angry George Forbes.

Then there is the matter of the telephone. For weeks now, my daughters have spent hours at a time on the telephone. Well, I can live with that. I know that is normal. Except that once, when I picked up an extension, I found that there was no one on the other end of the line. All I could hear was the steady ringing of a telephone somewhere.

"We're trying to call Skip O'Brien," my daughters explained to me. "It takes hours and hours to get in. But if he answers, you get on the radio. And he asks you what your favorite station is and you say G-98."

"And?" I said.

"And you've really talked to Skip O'Brien on the radio."

"For this I pay a phone bill?"

"Sometimes," said my daughter, Linda, "if he feels like it, he gives you a record album." And she said it with the wistfulness of a fallen spinster who has heard of heaven but doesn't think she has enough points to get there.

This then is something of life with Skip O'Brien. Except the other night something happened which pulled Skip and me together and now, Lord help me, I need him.

I came home from work and the girls weren't around.

"They are upstairs calling Skip O'Brien," my wife said.

"This kind of persistence could have brought a B in math," I said.

Suddenly one of the twins, Cathy, galloped into the kitchen. She snapped on the radio and turned it up full. Skip O'Brien's voice boomed through the house.

"Where do you live, Linda?" purred Skip. "Aurora," she said.

"Well, Linda," Skip said, "you've just won the new Beatles Rock 'n' Roll album. What's your favorite radio station?"

"G-98," she screamed. Then she slammed down the phone and raced downstairs and ran into the kitchen and jumped up and down and said:

"Did you hear that? Do you believe it? I got through. That was me. I talked to Skip O'Brien. I was on the radio. He talked to me and I talked to him. I won a record. From Skip O'Brien. I don't believe it. I don't believe it."

Nobody said anything. Then I said:

"But, Linda. You didn't tell him your last name. Or your address. He doesn't know who you are."

Hitting her would have been more merciful.

For all I know, she is still trying to get back to Skip. But she doesn't expect to. One miracle is all you expect when you are 15.

Look, Skip, it's like this. I gotta use the phone sometimes, see? Now that Linda from Aurora was my Linda from Aurora. You can take my word for that, though I'd rather you didn't spread it around.

If she gets her album, I promise I'll stop calling you what I've been calling you. I won't make them turn you off. I'll play that funky music. Once in a while.

I'll do better than that. I'll tell my daughters I think you're the best thing since Major Bowes.

For that, though, you got to promise not to send the album. That'll be our secret.

*— August 9, 1976*

## *It won't be April foal*

Dobbin? Whirlaway? Silver? . . . Trigger? Tony? Champion?
. . .

Pardon me, but I've got a lot on my mind. Any minute now, my telephone will ring. When I pick it up, a breathless voice will say, "It's a boy." Or, "It's a girl." I have to be ready.

My horse is having a horse.

When a guy's horse is having a horse, it's time for that guy to take stock. To be alone and think about the events leading up to this awesome occasion.

As a child, I had little to do with horses or they with me. In my neighborhood, two horses came around.

There was a dissipated theatrical pony. Once a year he was led down the street by his agent, a hollow-cheeked man who carried a suitcase. The key to the suitcase was a five dollar bill. When somebody's mother handed the agent a five dollar bill, he opened his suitcase and produced a moth-eaten pair of fuzzy chaps, a bandanna, a cowboy hat and a camera.

Then he hoisted some kid on the weary pony's back. By now, the neighbors were outside watching. A picture was taken. A pattering of applause followed. It was as close as anybody on my block got to the Pecos except for the Wilsons who once went to St. Louis.

There was a bony horse who shuffled down the street with his head bent low as if he were looking for dimes. He pulled the wagon that belonged to the pepparex man.

"Peppa-REX!" this old man shouted over the creaking of the wagon. "Peppa-REX!" he implored. I was 27 years old before I figured out he wanted our paper and rags. By that time, he and his horse had long since rounded the corner of E. 161st St. and clattered and caterwauled into oblivion . . .

Citation? Scout? Fury? . . .

I grew up and had twin daughters and moved them to the sylvan suburbs. No peddlers in their life style. No scissor grinder, no umbrella man. Theirs is a poorer world of fresh air, water and parental chauffeur service.

From some mysterious tendril of their roots, my daughters grew a fascination—an obsession with horses. I didn't understand it but I tolerated it on the theory that horses were safer and less grabby than boys.

"I read somewhere it's a sexual thing," my wife said.

"I don't want to hear about it," I said, shocked.

We bought them a horse. We got it cheap because it was pregnant. It was a complicated deal consummated (you should forgive me) by my wife. We would buy the horse cheap, feed it while it was eating for two, and surrender the foal to the guy we bought the momma from.

That was 10 months ago. The horse, who is gray, has broadened in those 10 months until its back resembles the flight deck of the Saratoga. I drive my daughters to the horse farm and I drive them back. I do not otherwise involve myself.

"We helped breed mares today," my little girl said once. "It's hard to hold them still enough."

"I don't want to hear about it," I said, shocked.

Now I sit here, waiting for the birth announcement. They are all at the farm—my girls, my wife, my horse. All my women. I am left out. This is the day.

I feel I should contribute something. So I search my mind for a suitable name for the foal. It should be, I feel, a name that hints of some proud heritage. A name that speaks to me of some great nag of my past. A name that sounds good with Whoa and Giddy-up!

What you do you think about Rex? You know, Rex. As in peppa.

— *March 2, 1977*

# A *summer storm*

I have always liked summer storms and I can't tell you why. I had a great-grandfather who was a Baptist preacher and my grandmother told me he would walk in his garden in the midst of a horrible thunderstorm and look heavenward—certain that God had nothing against him. If I inherited his love of storms, I did not inherit his certainty.

We had a summer storm at our place the other night—a storm that arrived a season early along with the summer weather. It nearly caught me in the open as I was taking an evening walk.

The sky, which had been a hazy blue all day, grew discolored, bruised by the coming storm. The noise of the thunder rolled from the southwest as if Hudson were being bombed to rubble. The air grew still with waiting.

My smallest son, Bruce, is going to camp next week. He has never been away from home, more or less on his own before. What he has seen of life, he has seen in company with us . . .

A faint breath of breeze moved out of the storm and the trees, feeling it, turned their leaves inward so the underside showed, palms up. And I walked faster.

When I was 12—my smallest son's age—I went to a Boy Scout camp in the South Chagrin Reservation. The snores of the other boys sounded strange in the cabin at night. There were no sheets and the blankets were rough against my skin. One night, five of us hiked miles away from the cabin. A storm moved suddenly out of the west. Rain-soaked, we raced back, unsure of the way. Lightning flashed around us and our faces were fright-white in its glare and our shouts were carried away on the wind . . .

Once they go away on their own, they never really come back—not all the way. Once they go away on their own you will never totally possess them again. It is a mistake to try and every parent makes that mistake.

I beat the rain home by five minutes. My wife was doing laundry. My older son had gone off with a friend in a car. His mother had asked him when he'd be home and he had mumbled an answer—incomprehensible so that nothing was on the record that could be used against him later.

"Let's go out on the porch and watch the storm," I said to my smallest son.

The porch is large and screened. At the end of the lot, the lake stretches for two miles. The storm came at us over the lake. Lightning pierced the water close enough so the thunder was torn out of the sky with a ripping sound . . .

The reason you don't want them to leave is because you know you have failed with them. What you wanted to do when they were born was make them invincible. You knew something about living. You knew that life could turn on you with a cold fury. Could find your smallest weakness and strike at it and split you as a bolt of lightning can split a tree—striking from a sudden storm, seeking the smallest weakness in the trunk.

You don't want them to leave before you can make them perfect—before you can fix it so they will be forever safe. But you never can. You never can . . .

An atomic flash of light and we blinked. A blue ball of fire hung in the air over the woods to the left. There was a clicking sound and the thunder clashed down on us, shaking the shingles. The lights went out. We sat stunned a moment, then hunted for candles.

"That was close," my smallest son said.

"But no cigar," I said. "God has nothing against you."

And I lit him to bed by candlelight so he could dream heroic dreams.

*— May 25, 1977*

## "Peppa-Rex!"

A reader sent me a clipping of an obit. No note came with it. The reader figured I wouldn't need one.

The headline above the obit gave the dead man's name. Then the word "dies." On most newspapers, death is an active verb. As in "John Smith Dies, Was Avid Bowler."

A writer of obits sorts through the meager facts available to fish out one short phrase to pin on the funeral wreath. The clipping I got said the departed "Was Peppa-Rex Man." With that resume, the deceased was sent to meet his maker.

The obit writer labors under a barrage of kidding from his colleagues. But management never laughs at him. His is one of the most important jobs on the newspaper. The mini-biographies he writes will be read by the critical and tear-scalded eyes of a family in pain. His work will be cut out and placed, not on the refrigerator under a magnet, but in the family Bible. His clippings are saved in shoe boxes and bureau drawers. His spare prose achieves a literal life after death denied to the fellow on, say, the sewer beat.

At the old *Press*, young reporters were urged to write obits with the care of any other human interest story. The triumphs and tragedies of the departed's existence should be included. Then the fact of his demise should be wedged in somewhere, subtly, so it hardly showed. A good obit, we were told, should have a beginning and middle as well as the obvious end.

I was eager to make a good impression on the city editor. My first morning on obits, I drew the name of a Murray Hill shoemaker who had passed away in the night. I telephoned his widow and asked her how she would like to see her newly ex-ed husband chronicled for posterity.

She told me, in broken and heavily accented English, that his life had been hell. That he had worked his fingers to the bone without appreciation. That the children he had striven for had turned their ungrateful backs on him. That the last years of his life had been spent in deep and often alcoholic depression.

All these facts I dutifully put into the obit. To add further drama, I quoted the widow's lamentations. One did not usually see quotes in small, local obits. I felt that hers, couched as they were in halting English, added realism and pathos to the story. The headline, I envisioned, would have gone something like "Tony Maroni Dies, Widow Says Life Had Become 'Bitter Joke.'"

Pleased with my effort, I placed it in the city editor's "in" basket. Then I returned to my desk and peeked at him from the corner of my eye. Eventually, he put my obit in front of him and stared at it for a considerable length of time. At one point he lifted his copy pencil and then slowly put it back on his desk. I interpreted this as a sign that he could think of no way to improve my narrative. Which, in a manner of speaking, was true.

Finally he looked over at me. His face seemed pained, which I took as a tribute to the moving quality of my prose. He beckoned me over with a finger. I approached him modestly. In low tones, he told me that he admired what I had done. That he had never seen any obit quite like it. I blushed with pleasure.

He said, however, that he wished I would rewrite it. He explained that, after her initial grief passed, the widow might regret having spoken so candidly to me. He added that a good thing to keep in mind when writing obits is that they should seek to provide pleasant memories.

The reader who sent the clipping about the death of the "peppa-rex" man knew it would stir such memories in my soul. There aren't many peppa-rex men left. Someday the last one will die, and when he goes he ought to go on Page One, like the last World War I veteran will. But this is unlikely. Nobody keeps paperwork on peppa-rex men. Certainly not peppa-rex men themselves, who, if they had such paperwork, would sell it.

The first warm breezes of summer brought a parade of commerce to the streets of the East Side in the old days. The waffle man trundled his apparatus along the sidewalk. The scissors grinder, who also fixed umbrellas, passed by ringing a bicycle bell. He would sharpen your knives at your front stoop.

You could signal the baker's van by putting a card in your window. Either Star or Spang, depending on your bakery of choice. When the driver saw the card he would stop and skip down off his truck carrying an oversized basket full of bread and doughnuts.

The peddler came down the street in a rickety wagon drawn by a mangy horse. The wagon was mounded with fruits and vegetables. The peddler's boy, in his teens, ran ahead of the wagon and knocked on doors to alert housewives, ironing to the drama of "Helen Trent," that the peddler was passing by.

In spring, just about now, a traveling photographer led a shaggy pony down the street. He carried a cowboy hat, a pair of chaps and a bandanna. He would decorate a kid in these items and sit him on the pony's back and snap a picture that would arrive in the mail a month later for display on the piano or the spacious top of the brand-new television set.

But the worst horse you ever saw was the horse that pulled the wagon driven by the peppa-rex man. It was a horse that looked to be in the final hours of a remarkable life span. "Pep-A-Rex!" the peppa-rex man shouted. "Pep-A-Rex!" And housewives, who had been saving their newspapers and old rags for weeks, lugged them to the curb and sold them for pocket change.

The reader who sent me the peppa-rex man's obit, hoped, without asking, that I would remember those long-ago springs. And find a place for the memory between sermons on crime and violence and sex scandals.

So call this an obit for a spring long gone. Old Spring Dies, Leaves Pleasant Memories. There is sorrow, too. For a gentler springtime that is irretrievable and fading, even in memory. But I'll leave the sorrow out. That was the lesson of the shoemaker's wife.

— *May 16, 1994*

## Labor Day

The first time I joined a union was when I had a job unloading trucks at the old Eaton Heater Plant on E. 55th and Central. It was labor in the literal sense and I think about it often on Labor Day.

My aunt, who worked in payroll, got me the job to earn money to help pay for my college. I worked with four other truck unloaders, two from Tennessee and two from West Virginia. None of them had finished high school. So I decided to keep my mouth shut about going to college. But one of the guys from Tennessee found out anyway.

He raised the matter one day while we were all eating stuffed cabbage and mashed potatoes in the company cafeteria. In those days, companies had real cafeterias where old ethnic ladies wearing hair nets scooped great dollops of simple food on thick white crockery. None of this putting two dollars' worth of change into a machine that either swallows it and gives you nothing or pitches you a microwaveable sandwich that tastes like cardboard and paste.

"They say you're in college," the Tennessean said.

"Oh. Yeah. Sort of. I guess I am," I said.

"What are ya larnin'?" he wanted to know.

"I'm majoring in English," I told him.

"Anglish!" he said. "What kind of thang is that to be studyin'? If I had money to go to college, I'd have larned dentistry or somethin' useful. Waste of money to study Anglish. Seems like you know it already."

"Maybe I'll switch," I said. I wanted to be as agreeable as possible. I feared that my colleagues might treat me with derision when they found out about my secret life as a college boy. But the opposite thing happened. When they learned I was so stupid as to major in something everybody already knew, they adopted a protective attitude toward me and treated me like a dimwitted younger brother.

They showed me nooks and crannies in the mountainous stacks of cardboard cartons where I could hide for a little snooze and not be discovered by the foreman. They instructed me on how to lift things without getting a hernia. They showed me how to pace myself so I could last all day when it was 80 degrees outside, 90 degrees in the plant and 100 inside the sweltering box of a fully loaded truck.

The nicest of them was a West Virginian named Bill. He was a skinny little fellow, prematurely bald, but he worked like a demon. The others treated him with a sort of tenderness and one of the Tennesseans explained why. Bill had a little daughter with polio. He was trying to get her to walk again. The therapy was costly. Bill very much wanted his job.

The company knew of his problem. One day the foreman called him aside. He told Bill there was a job opening as a checker. It paid 40 cents an hour more than Bill was earning. He would no longer have to wrestle heavy pallets from the tropical recesses of trucks. All he would have to do was keep a count of the cargo as it was unloaded. Then, when he had assured himself that the shipment had arrived intact, he would sign off for it.

We were all very happy for Bill. We knew he needed the extra money. We knew his frame wasn't up to the heavy work. The next day, when we punched in, Bill was there ahead of us with a clipboard and a pencil in his hand. But he looked nervous.

The first shipment of the day pulled in and we unloaded it. It was paint. We always liked paint because we had to haul it over to the paint shop and this gave us a chance to take a little trip through the plant. It broke the monotony, like a Sunday drive.

When we got back from the paint shop, Bill was in an argument with the truck driver. This was strange because Bill never got into arguments with anybody.

"Come on, pal," the truck driver was saying. "Sign the form, will you. I have to get out of here."

But Bill hesitated. He licked the pencil. He was sweating a little bit, even though this new job was supposed to put his sweating days behind him. Finally, he scribbled on the form and the truck driver spat on the floor and left.

The next day Bill was back with us unloading trucks again. When we asked him why, he said he had quit the checker job. He said he hadn't liked all the responsibility.

"But what about your daught—?" I started to ask.

My Tennessee friend elbowed me in the ribs. A couple of minutes later, he pulled me aside. He made sure that Bill was out of earshot.

"It was them forms was what it was," he said. "I don't think Bill ever learned to read English so good."

That plant is long gone—moved South where labor is cheaper. Polio is not a worry for a working father anymore. But there are other worries.

Back in that long ago summer, people like Bill were able to earn enough pay with their sweat to raise a family. All over this smoky and noisy town, men spent their days bending and lifting. Grunting and straining. You could make a decent living doing that and, at night, your wife would fill up the bathtub with hot water and bring you a shot of Kesslers to sip on while your muscles untied.

But on this Labor Day, it takes more than labor to make it. Yet the high schools are still sending people like Bill out into the job jungle. Too many Bills and not enough room for them. More every year and a lot of talk about it, but not enough done about it. For the lucky ones who get jobs, today isn't just Labor Day. It's Thanksgiving too.

Sometimes I wonder what ever happened to Bill's daughter. I'll never know, but I'll tell you what I'd like to think. I'd like to think she's a dentist. And that he's proud of her. And that he learned to read. He sure knew how to work.

*— September 5, 1994*

# Memories of a price war

When I was a kid we bought most of our groceries at Schultz' Grocery store a block away from the house.

The way we did this was, my mother would sit down at the kitchen table and take the back of a used envelope and make a list with a pencil. Then she would give me the list and a couple of bucks and walk to the front door and watch me cross the street so I wouldn't be struck dead on my way to get a box of oatmeal.

It was a block down and a block over to Schultz'. If you got there on a Friday, there would be a sign in the window that said: FR LAKE ERIE BLUE PIKE, which we always bought on Friday out of patriotism to our lake.

There were two employees in the store—Schultz and Mrs. Schultz. She usually stayed up front by the cash drawer and adding machine. He usually was on station at the meat block in the back.

And when you came in they would both greet you. Schultz would amble up the aisle, affable in a blood-flecked apron. He would take the envelope from your hand. He would reach behind the counter and get his big stick with an artificial hand on the end of it. This was for reaching up to high shelves.

He would walk around his store, expertly filling your order— bringing each item back to the front counter where Mrs. Schultz punched it up on her adding machine. "Howze your momma and pappa?" he would say. "Howze about a piece of candy?" he would offer.

Sometimes an old lady would be in the store and this old lady I would regard with awe because she was a shoplifter.

Oldness, I knew, had done something to her head. She would come in with a market basket and go around the shelves putting canned goods in her basket. Schultz would follow her around taking the things out again and putting them back. If he didn't she would leave without paying for them and he would have to call her son. Such a call was embarrassing for everybody. As shoplifters go, she was not adept, but she didn't really know she was a shoplifter, Schultz told me one day. An accident of fate had made her one.

At first, when the supermarket opened up the street, life at Schultz' stayed pretty much the same. I still went there a couple of times a week. Except now the lists on the back of the envelope were shorter.

Every Saturday morning now, my father would get out the Chevy and we would ride to the supermarket. You could save two cents on this, three cents on that. A high school boy would put your bag of groceries in the trunk of your car. Schultz got the business his customers had forgotten to give the supermarket on Saturday morning.

He would still say "Howze your momma and poppa?" He would still give you candy. But when you went into the store now, there would be no other customers. Even the shoplifting lady seemed to have transferred her business to the supermarket.

Then, one day, the Schultzes were gone. Overnight, it seemed to me. I didn't understand this because, when you are as old as I was, you expect that everything will always stay exactly the way it is.

What killed the Schultzes was two cents less on a can of Carnation milk. They were casualties of a price war.

But not the kind of price war we have been reading about all week. The supermarket took Schultz like Hitler took Czechoslovakia. Blitz. And he got no headlines.

When this current price war ends, I have the feeling that nobody will bleed. I think that's about as legitimate a conflict as the Ali-Wepner fight. Everybody gets a purse.

Schultz' war was different. He fought it in silence. I haven't seen one of those window sticks since he went out of business. And I've gotten damn little free candy either.

— *June 20, 1977*

# 40-year-old meets himself

The alarm clock went off a half-hour early. The fellow who this is about swatted at it with his hand until it shut up. Then he lay there for a while. "The hell with it," he said. "I won't get up." Then he got up.

On a chair next to the bed was a brand new pair of tennis sneakers. A new pair of white cotton socks. An old pair of tennis shorts. An old sweat shirt.

The fool who is the subject of this column put on these clothes. The shoes felt nice and springy the way new tennis shoes always feel. He walked softly from the bedroom. The dog, lying on the bedroom floor, opened one eye.

Outside, the grass was dewy. The air was cool and morning clean. The street was quiet. The middle-aged man who is the hero of this piece walked down his driveway and stepped into the street. "Right face," he said. "Double-time, march!" And he began to trot.

The night before, he had driven past his house and on down the road, keeping one eye on his odometer. The pavement changed to dirt but he drove on until five-tenths of a mile from his house. Then he stopped the car and looked for a small land-mark to mark the place. He saw that a channel of the lake cut close to the road at this spot. Satisfied, he drove home.

Now he trotted past his neighbor's house in the direction he had driven the night before. To the channel and back was a mile. He hoped his neighbor had already gone to work.

"I wonder if . . . I'll really do . . . this every day . . ." he thought as he ran rather awkwardly, his thoughts in cadence with his feet. "I know I won't . . . If I think about . . . it too much."

By the time the pavement changed to dirt, he was breathing heavily and there was no style in his running. "Damn fool . . . to think . . . make mile . . . first day," he thought.

Yet this, he knew, was the way he had always been. Full of expectations that were not grounded in reality. There was a part of him that believed he would never die, would write immortal books at least, could drink anything and eat anything, could raise perfect children and build a perfect marriage, spiced with perfect almost righteous love affairs. There was a part of him that believed he could do anything he wanted to and it had been quite a shock to him to realize one day . . . one year . . . that that part of him could kill him. He had, after all, been so proud of it.

He could see the lake now and, beyond it, the place where the channel nudged the road. His halfway point.

"Forty is half . . . of 80 will . . . I make 80 probably . . . not will I . . . make 70 . . . with a little . . . luck I will . . ." he thought as he trotted on."

He wondered how many men, on the day they were 40 and startled, vowed sensible programs of regular exercise. Millions, he guessed. Cheap vows, made with a gun to their heads. There are things you can't do if you talk about them and then there are things you can't talk about if you do them. He knew that. That was one thing he had learned. The subtle things are the hardest to learn.

"But I . . . know some . . . of them, anyway," he thought. And then the channel was ahead of him.

And now he knew he would never be able to run all the way back. Part of him was embarrassed by this knowledge. But it was the part he didn't trust anymore. The part of him that hadn't learned anything in 40 years and never would. He addressed that part of himself, smiling wickedly.

"I hope . . . you die . . . first," he said.

And then he stopped running and stood at the channel. And asked himself permission to walk back home. And granted it. And turned and stepped lightly into the rest of his life.

— *August 2, 1978*

# A *midwinter's tale*

The resort community of Lakeside, on the Marblehead peninsula near Port Clinton, is napping lightly, calmed by the sleeping pill of midwinter.

Next summer, every cottage will be rented. Real estate agents will beg residents to let out their spare rooms. The old hotel, its guest book bearing the signature "Rutherford B. Hayes and wife," will bustle with guests. Its front porch will creak under the weighty rhythm of 30 rocking chairs. The shuffleboard courts will clack and whizz. Small children will sail tiny sailboats under the nervous eyes of their parents sunburning on the shore.

But all of that is months away. The atmosphere now is one of shallow hibernation. Most of the cottages are empty and shuttered, water turned off, antifreeze in the toilet bowls, soft rubber rafts on the tarp-covered porches slowly exhaling last summer's air.

There are, though, many year-round residents. Most of them are retired folks who will maintain their cottages until the day comes when they move on, with grace and resignation, to assisted living. During the long Lakeside winters, they manufacture diversions. Some of the men play darts in the basement of the Methodist church. Women have their study clubs, where they investigate subjects like "Mexico" and "The Great Lakes."

At Christmas, there is a program of carols sung by a youth choir. Because of the age of the year-round residents, youth is a scarce commodity in winter. So young carolers are borrowed from the Catholic church in Marblehead or imported from the high school in Port Clinton. The meal for the Christmas program is catered, but most communal suppers during a Lakeside winter are pot-luck, and on Saturday night, Lakeside women can often be seen gingerly carrying covered dishes down icy driveways to cars pre-heated by their husbands.

Last Saturday night, there was a break in the social routine of dart-tossing and living room book reviews. The Heidelberg Concert Choir, of Heidelberg College in Tiffin, came in by bus to perform a concert in the church. The choir is on its way to a tour of the South, and its stop in Lakeside was a kind of warmup for this venture.

So, at about 6, a big road bus—the kind used by symphony orchestras and rock bands—snorted and hissed its way along the main street, its windows frosted with the breath of young people peering out at this strange and winter-bleak town of shacks and cottages.

Their hosts were the members of the Lakeside Methodist Church choir, which is composed of a number of fine musicians, many of them retired music teachers. They offer in church on Sunday the musical skills gained through half a century of acquisition. They ring bells in ensembles and play recorders. String solos are often heard. The credentials of these musicians are impeccable. But age sometimes takes its irremediable toll on their execution. No one minds this. The aging audience is in the same boat. Let him without a creaky voice or joint attempt to cast the first stone. This is the spirit of the congregation.

Still, by 7:30 last Saturday night, the church was filled with residents who had come to hear the young voices sing. Even the small balcony was crowded, which gave some of the church members who sat there their first close-up look at the rose window (the repair of which was a major item in the church's winter budget.)

Conversations were held in a whisper—some whispers louder than others when the whispered-to happened to be slightly hard of hearing. Then the group of young singers came down the aisle in a processional. The boys wore black tuxedos, the girls wore red dresses. They turned and faced the congregation and sang the Cantate Domino, which was older than anything and anybody there because it had been written a century before Bach.

The fullest chords of the sweetest harmony filled the church hall. The young people singing to the older people mostly hailed from, the program revealed, the small towns and suburbs that dot Ohio. Some were from out of state. They sang their centuries-old music, bridging an age gap of two generations.

Surely when they put their tuxedos and red dresses away, they are the kids we see in malls on Saturday afternoon, clustered in chattering groups, listening to rock on a Walkman. Dressed in whatever is cool this year. In that environment, there always seems to be an insurmountable and distasteful gap between the old and the young. It is easy for the old to feel that the young people who are pushing them toward a far corner of life are unworthy of the privilege of succession.

But in the small Lakeside Church Saturday night, at the end of the program, the members of the church choir were asked to stand and sing with the young people. And if you closed your eyes, there were no young and old. The strong young voices helped the old voices along. The ageless harmony of the parting hymn erased any age distinctions.

You will see on the news and you will read in the newspaper horrible stories involving the young. It is enough to make you shake your head and wonder what the world is coming to. But it is always only the bad stuff you see.

It is good to remember that the world, by and large, will be in the hands of these young singers. Who, after expressions of mutual thanks, got back into their bus, which snorted and sighed away. Leaving the year-round residents of Lakeside to reluctantly go their separate ways home through a frosty night, under old stars which gleamed so bright and new it almost seemed as if they had been polished by a cloth.

*— February 22, 1995*

## Shall we dance?

While America was deep in gloom last week, Virginia Katherine McMath from Independence, Mo. left us. She never seemed weighted by gravity like the rest of us, and last Tuesday she broke the last of her earthly bonds.

We knew her as Ginger Rogers, and we knew her in black and white. She danced with Fred Astaire through a dance card of '30s musicals that kept America's mind off the Depression. Light as a feather in Astaire's arms on screen, she was cool to him off. She felt he got too much credit for their combined grace. Ronald Reagan agreed and once said of her: "She did everything that Astaire did and she did it in high heels and backward."

Like all the great ones, they made it look easy. Sooner or later, we all grow up and find out that such spectacular talent is out of our reach. Would-be center fielders become firemen, and tenors become shoe clerks. They surrender with good humor to the impossible.

But I have sporadically tortured myself for 50 years with the delusion that I will someday learn to dance. Not dance like Astaire. Just dance good enough for one dance with Ginger. Just once around the floor.

Other people can do it. Klutzes and stevedores and six-pack Charlies can do it. But I can't do it and I've never been able to do it and I don't know why. It isn't that I have two left feet. It's worse. I don't even seem to have one left foot.

I can sing passably well in a big group. I can play "Moonglow" on the piano by ear and bang out a rhythm with my left hand that *you* could dance to. In the Army, I was a very good marcher. I was even a very good cadence-counter.

When I belted out unprintable couplets that began with "I don't know but I've been told . . .," whole ranks of dusty men were transformed into a perfectly synchronized platoon of steel-potted Tommy Tunes. But put me on the dance floor and within

30 seconds my partner will be asking if they are still serving punch.

I began my horrible dancing career with high hopes back in the sixth grade at Gracemont Elementary School. The gym teacher, Mrs. Wallace, included something called "social dancing" in with the rubber-smelling curriculum of rope-climbing and vaulting over the dreaded buck.

One day, Mrs. Wallace brought in a portable record player and put on a scratchy, generic fox-trot record. She organized the boys and girls in parallel lines and started us moving across the gym floor. "Step . . . step . . . step-close-step," she called in her gym teacher voice, beating time with a couple of those clacking sticks that gym teachers of that era took everywhere with them except, perhaps, to funerals.

I picked it up right away. Why, there was nothing to it. Before I had trodden and slithered 30 feet, I could picture Ginger right there with me. Doing everything I was doing except in high heels and backward and about 2 feet up in altitude.

Even when Mrs. Wallace paired the boys with the little girls, it wasn't so bad. We pressed our moist palms together and avoided eye contact and concentrated on the heavy-footed task at hand.

Dancing with a girl, I decided, wasn't a lot more difficult than pushing a wheelbarrow around. All you had to do was get your signals straight before you took the dance floor. This could be accomplished with the briefest of conversations, such as, "I'm going to do step-close-step, OK?" No doubt Fred and Ginger held such caucuses off-camera before starting one of their numbers.

Having thus mastered the art of social dancing, I stored it away in my bag of tricks until such time as I would have need of it. That time came about four years later, at a high school dance.

Confidently, I took my place on the dance floor with a crinoline-skirted girl named Flora. We began our *pas de deux* with some difficulty, since Flora's costume was like a chicken-wire barrier between us. But I sensed no serious difficulty until Flora spoke: "What are you DO-ing?" she asked. "Why are you dragging your feet like that? Are you trying to be Boris Karloff?"

Startled, I looked around me. There was considerable merit in her criticism. The other dancers seemed to have progressed far beyond the step-close-step style of dancing. They were whirling in circles and dipping and twirling while Flora and I plowed through them like an ore boat cutting through a yacht race.

I realized that, schooled as I was in the art of going forward and backward, I had never learned to turn. So I drove Flora into a wall and left her there and set out on a lifelong, fruitless attempt to learn to dance.

I will spare you the details, except to say that they included some lessons at a dance studio whose instructors programmed me to do one meager jitterbug. I did it one day in 1987 over at the Statler in front of Henry Hershey's orchestra. For three minutes, I had it. Then it left me and it hasn't come back since.

Now, it wouldn't matter. This is the "me" generation, and kids hop and writhe on America's dance floors as if the floors were beds of coals. They ignore their partners and anything they do they are free to call dancing.

I've tried that, but I find no triumph in it. I missed my chance and now I've missed Ginger. She has disappeared into the wings, taking a measure of class from a dwindling store.

It would be nice to think that, somewhere, there's a ballroom where she's saving a dance for me. I'll arrive carrying my burden of failure, hesitant to even try. "Come on," she'll say, "you can do it." And she'll be right. I'll be as light as a feather. Well, why not?

— *May 1, 1995*

# STOP THE PRESSES

## *Stuck*

This is about a cat, stuck in an oak tree (about three flights up) in a yard on Clifton Blvd. in Lakewood.

It is also about how the world has changed. Maybe that's mainly what it's about.

Years ago, newspapers devoted a lot of energy to getting stuck cats out of trees. This newspaper was especially good at it.

In those days, the city editor of this newspaper was a gentleman named Louis Clifford. He was a man of vast and multifarious experience. He lunched with prosecutors and racketeers. Murderers walked in and surrendered to him. He ran exposes which uncovered municipal scandals and piloted investigations which sent men to prison.

Yet he would postpone any of these grim enterprises on those frequent occasions when readers (usually women) telephoned to report anxiously that some cat or other was stuck up some tree or other.

At such times, Clifford would look around the city room for one of that category of reporters who might not be trusted to remove an errant politician from office, but who could be trusted to remove a stuck cat from a tree. Frequently, his gaze fell upon me.

I do not know, because I never dared to ask him, if Clifford liked cats. I didn't like cats and don't. If I had to guess, I would guess he either disliked them or had an utter lack of opinion about them one way or the other.

But he knew and taught me that an astonishing number of people do like cats. An astonishing number of readers liked cats. And so, since Clifford felt that a newspaper, in addition to everything else it was, was a good neighbor to its readers, he was willing to rescue cats. Or order them rescued.

In those days, this took one phone call to the Fire Department. The Fire Department would send a man out to rescue the cat and we would send a photographer out to capture the moment. It took an hour. It was an act that benefited everyone involved. There used to be such acts.

Louis Clifford is long dead but I still miss him. This column is a flower on his grave.

A lady named Elizabeth McClelland looked out of her bedroom window last week and saw a cat crouched on the branch of an oak tree. It was a small cat—a sort of semi-kitten. It was gray, had stripes and was afraid.

Ms. McClelland telephoned an animal warden, Mary Riordan, who came out at once and demonstrated concern.

Ms. Riordan vowed to do what she could. But the next day, she reported somber news.

"The Fire Department says it hasn't rescued a cat from a tree in 10 years," she told Ms. McClelland. "Its insurance does not allow it to go up trees after cats."

The police could not help either. Neither could the APL. "A cat has never died from being stuck in a tree," an APL person told Ms. McClelland, an opinion she heard repeated by a variety of people over the next several days.

Ms. McClelland opened her bedroom window and spoke to the cat daily. The cat mewed back. In these conversations, Ms. McClelland urged the cat to summon the courage to retreat from its perch, pointing out that risks must be taken in life or the spirit shrivels and dies.

The cat seemed intensely interested but did not move.

Ms. McClelland tried to lure it with a fish.

She asked a telephone lineman working in the area to climb up and get it, but his ladder was too short.

Ms. Riordan visited frequently. Last night, the two women tried to maneuver a plank from Ms. McClelland's window to the cat's branch. But this was unsuccessful.

Ms. McClelland spoke with the *Press*. She spoke calmly but

severely. To her, it seemed that society's failure to remove the stuck cat from the tree demonstrated a breakdown of proper concern. Was there any institution left, she wondered, that had time for stuck cats? The answer is yes.

If that cat isn't out of that tree by tomorrow, somebody will get it out.

I will get it out.

I will do it for Louis Clifford and his idea of what a newspaper ought to do. I can't do anything about El Salvador or the economy or the schools situation, but I can get a cat out of a tree.

Clifford told me to do that kind of thing and he died without telling me to stop. He thought it made the world turn. I'm not ready to say he was wrong. I'm as stuck as the cat.

*— March 3, 1982*

## Nuts discover television

We have entered a new era of show business and it's frightening.

It's the era of the celebrity nut. The nut who gets on television. The crazy man with a misguided philosophy of life and a cheap pistol who is able to walk out of his insanity and on to the public stage and hold the nation in his grip until he cracks.

Corey Moore is today's man with a message and a medium. There was a time, back in the good old days last year, when a man with a message rented a hall or a bullhorn and stood in a park somewhere and shouted his message to anyone walking by.

In the good old days—a couple of months ago—you could ignore the nut's message. But not anymore. Now—like the salesman and the politician—the nut has found a better way to advertise. The nut has discovered television and none of us may ever be the same again.

All day yesterday, I stood in the Warrensville Heights Police Station with my fellow reporters and watched Corey Moore use the media to his best advantage.

He was very good at using the medium—was Corey Moore.

Maybe he took lessons from Eddie Watkins or Ashby Leach. Maybe he took lessons from Kojak or Starsky and Hutch. Whomever he took his lessons from Corey Moore got to be very good at using television—so good at it that he scared the hell out of all the reporters on the scene.

Because, however the drama ends in Warrensville Heights, there can be no denying that Corey Moore knew exactly what he was doing. He decided to take his ravings on the public stage and that meant television. This is the era of televised everything else and now we have crossed a new threshold. Now it is the era of televised insanity.

Look at Ashby Leach—he was a pioneer in this new field of nut public relations. Ashby Leach carried his shotgun into the Terminal Tower with one thought in mind. He wanted to get on television. And he did. The television people who covered him suddenly found they were not covering a story but were, in fact, in the story.

Ashby Leach wanted good ratings and he got them.

So when Corey Moore walked into the Warrensville Heights police station the first thing he did was to ask for a roster of all the television people on the scene. And when he got it he chose the cast of performers who were to be the road company for his nutty philosophy.

And the television reporters approved his casting. Bill Jacocks, of Channel 5, became Moore's television star.

And when he did, Jacocks was no longer a reporter—now he was a member of a cast in Moore's psychodrama. Channel 5, uncertain how to respond to this, sent Jim Lowe, its public relations man, out to cover Jacocks. Corey Moore had made Jacocks a star and the station wanted to cash in on this stardom.

But where does it all end? As Corey Moore gets his own television show today, what nut in Des Moines will try the same thing next week? The nuts have found a good thing here and they will use it.

The frightening thing about the Corey Moore story is really that while it's over, nothing is ended.

And what has begun is something that nobody wants—even people who watch too much television.

— *March 9, 1977*

## The ghosts with me

Ghosts surround me. I hope they're smiling.

They lounge in the shadows beyond the lamplight and the blue glow of the word processor. The small, skinny one in the corner—who looks like an elf with his spectacles on the end of his nose and the white handkerchief spilling from the breast pocket of his suitcoat—that's L.B.S. Louis B. Seltzer, legendary editor of the *Cleveland Press*.

He was a figure of awe, and they said he picked the mayors, and they called him Mr. Cleveland. But in the city room, he was a mischievous uncle who punched us in the belly and threw firecrackers at us. We locked him in the men's room stall and sometimes dumped him in one of the big wastebaskets. It was a rare place, the *Press*.

Louie had faith in people and in this city, but his long, sweet marriage was his religion. When his wife lay dying of cancer and we had to get an obit ready for her, we hid the type among salami sandwiches in the refrigerator in the composing room. We didn't want him to wander back and find it and be hurt. We knew we liked him, but we didn't call it love until after he was gone, which is often the case.

Now he's back. I swear. Watching me write a column for the *Plain Dealer*.

And that's the other Louie with him. Louie Clifford, the *Press* city editor. There. The one who looks like James Cagney. It's got to be him. Sitting on his foot on a swivel chair. Cigarette stuck to the corner of his mouth. Brown copy pencil in his hand. Watching me write a column for the competition. I can't see his face, but if it looks wooden, I'm in trouble. In a fury, Clifford's face went expressionless, like the face of a hired killer.

This, I hadn't counted on. I wasn't expecting company.

Thirty years ago, shy six weeks, I walked down Ninth St. in my father's suit to report for work. But not the Ninth St. you see today.

It was a Ninth St. of flea bag hotels and red brick buildings with fire escapes sneaking down them. Jean's Fun House, where kids went to buy dirty books when they played hooky from school. Kornman's Restaurant, run by Billy Weinberger with the great Runyonesque mural by Bill Roberts behind the bar. Two Pat Joyce saloons side by side run by Iggy McIntyre, who figured if you were going to go pub crawling, you might as well crawl between two of his cash registers.

There was the Roxy Burlesque, where every week we'd go to take a picture of a stripper for the Friday magazine and the photographer would ask for "one for the boys in the darkroom" and she'd drop a couple of straps. Once Blaze Starr bumped her revealed assets into my nose and Bernie Noble shot it and blew it up poster size. I took it home and hid it in my rec room but I had to get rid of it when I found out my kid was charging his friends admission to see it.

Bernie's dead now.

So is Jerry Horton, who covered D-Day with a camera and taught me how to knock on a door. ("Don't just go 'tap-tap-tap.' Use your fist and bang it and bang it and keep it up and it'll drive them crazy and they'll come to the door and I'll flash them.")

Photographers are among the ghosts around me, even though there's no photo here but mine. Come to jeer at me for going over to the competition.

At the foot of Ninth St., where Canada's wind bit you on the face, was the *Press*. And the big city room. And the city desk, Louie Clifford reigning.

"Here I am," I said on that first day.

"That's evident without your announcing it," he said. "Sit down and I'll find you something to do."

Which he did. He found me a war to cover and an assassination and fires and stickups and con men and bank robberies and lots of murders (we were supposed to nominate the suspects back then).

And hit-skips and protest marches and a life that, for good or bad, has defined me. Louie, as you may have read, had a heart attack and died under my frantic, useless hands on Ninth St. He died in time for the final edition, but I didn't have to write it. I could have, but I didn't have to. I don't even like to tell it.

My orders in those days were simple. Beat the *Plain Dealer*. Cream the *PD*. Humble the competition.

And now look!

No wonder they are haunting me. I can't see their faces. I can't see if they are smiling at the irony or frowning at the treason.

They never leave me, those good people who taught me what I know. Who never went to college but knew this is no profession for Ph.D.'s but a working-class craft. They carved their stories into copy paper with typewriter keys and sent the paper back in a tube to be turned into hot metal type. Words poured from presses and were bundled and tossed out into this good, plain, no-nonsense city of craftsmen who want an honest story honestly told.

So, I've accepted the *PD*'s generous offer, but the ghosts are going with me.

Whether they like it or not, here I am.

— *October 18, 1993*

# Newspapers before Watergate

We've heard a lot this week about Watergate and what it did to the country. There hasn't been much talk, though, about what Watergate did to journalism, which was ruin it.

Before Watergate, none of us called ourselves "investigative reporters." It would have been considered pretentious, like a garbage man calling himself a "sanitation engineer."

A reporter was just a reporter and that was enough. If he presumed to call himself a "journalist," he got a fishy look from some of the old men on the staff. It meant he had probably gone to "journalism school," which was four years of money wasted on bad habits that had to be unlearned.

Newsrooms then were full of frustrated novelists, frustrated cops and working-class kids who had heard it was a clean job. Women were shoved over in the society section and told not to report to work until they owned a pair of long white gloves to wear to teas. An exception was Doris O'Donnell, who still works for this newspaper and who could cover a murder with anybody. She could turn heads, too, but we called her a newspaperman and pretended she was sexless. It was considered a compliment.

The copy desk was a good haven for persons of radically sour disposition. They worked alone, under green eyeshades, happily muttering curses at the illiteracy and pretension of the frustrated novelists. Assistant city editors, trapped between the tyranny of their bosses and the rebellion of the reporters, sucked Rolaids and wished they were back on the police beat with the frustrated cops.

Chronic drunks flourished, especially on afternoon papers, where the first deadline was 8 a.m. That gave them six hours after the bars closed to make the typewriter keys work. A famous drama critic in town, writing a review in the wee hours, felt an urgent call of nature. When he stood up, he found he could not walk. He could, however, crawl.

He unfolded a newspaper and laid the sheets ahead of him.

Then he crept along, constructing a path of newspapers to the men's room. This kept his trousers clean. He had the gentleman's habit of concern for his clothing and accessories. On his sixth martini, he was known to conduct long and friendly conversations with his cane at the bar in the Hickory Grill.

At Christmas, copy boys wheeled in shopping carts of booze sent over by people wishing to see their names in print. The obit writer got more bottles than anybody else. He had the power to select noteworthy deceased to write about each day. The funeral directors lobbied him to pick their customers. Elected judges sent liquor to the court reporter. If it wasn't top shelf, he would call them and bawl them out.

We spent a lot of time on damp, dark mornings beating on doors to awaken new widows. We talked our way into their houses and left with armloads of photos of their husbands who had been killed by traffic or gunfire. The goal was not to leave any pictures for the guy from the other paper. It was a young man's job. It helped to be amoral as a puppy.

From time to time we exposed corruption. But we put on no phony airs about it. We did not confuse ourselves with a constitutionally ordained branch of government. We ignored philandering and dipsomania on the part of public officials. For a politician's "character" to become an issue, he had to be a certifiable lunatic. Who were we to cast stones?

Watergate was a cheap burglary and it was handed to a couple of police reporters. The arrogance of the Nixon White House kept the plot alive. They lied too much and denied too much. Television got into the act. Hearings were held and people tuned in and the Democratic pols were delighted. Soon the press had toppled a president. This was heady stuff.

Suddenly journalists were celebrities. College assembly lines turned them out on a war footing. Miss Ohios and male models lined up to get their crack at a president. If you looked sincere and had nice face bones, you could make a million dollars on the network. Then 5 million.

Television reporters were seen in their own limousines. They opined together in gaggles on incestuous talk shows. They threw open other "gates" that led nowhere much. Koreagate, Pizza-gate. Searching for the next golden door.

They inspected politicians' bed linen like house detectives. They awarded themselves the moral ascendancy of mothers superior. Making presidents look bad became their job. The once-raffish news business turned glum and self-righteous. Its practitioners conducted themselves like people who had taken holy orders.

The press became unrecognizable for what it really is: a private business run for profit. Whose members are elected by no one, confirmed by no one and answerable only to each other. But beneath it all is the old imperative of the headline.

The Whitewater business shows how skewed it has all become. The press is the "media" now, a word that the dictionary says is plural. In practice it's singular, like the word "pack." The pack smells a scandal in Whitewater. But the new rules of scandal are that you don't even have to explain what anybody did wrong. The coverage is the story. The media are the message.

I liked it better in the old days, when we were just one of the boys. When we wore cheaper suits and owned no cloaks of questionable nobility. When we held up a mirror so society could see itself. Now we hog the mirror and primp in it. We think we look mah-velous.

"Are you running for something, Mr. Rather?" an angry Richard Nixon once asked.

"No, Mr. President, are you?" Dan Rather answered.

One of them was fibbing.

— *April 29, 1994*

# Stop the presses (for the very last time)

*(This story was published in the August 1982 edition of* Cleveland
Magazine. *An adaptation was published by Reader's Digest in December 1982.)*

The *Press* was proud of the way it handled obituaries. When
I went to work for it in 1963, it was proud of the way it did everything. Proud of the fact that it paid the estimable Maxwell Riddle to spend his full time as a practicing expert on dogs. Proud
of its brand new building at the end of Ninth Street (a site chosen by Louie Seltzer who was confident that the city would
move in his direction which, obediently, it did.) Proud of the
fact that Theodore Andrica, who spoke a babel of languages, was
sent yearly on a trip to the old country where he would look up
relatives of Cleveland's ethnic citizens and deliver greetings
from the New World. Proud, indeed, that Cleveland's large
Hungarian population was due in part to the fact that Andrica
and Louis Clifford (perhaps the greatest city editor in the nation
in the fifties and sixties) had traveled to the Hungarian border
during the 1956 revolution and greeted and wrung the hands of
fleeing refugees.

The *Press* was proud that it had convicted Samuel Sheppard
of the murder of his wife, for the *Press* saw itself as a righteous
instrument of the Almighty's will which could function where
the courts might fail. The *Press* was proud of the rumors of the
tunnel from City Hall into its editor's office through which
mayors elected by the *Press* could slip unnoticed to receive
instructions. The *Press* was proud of the fact that it paid the bills
for other newspapers in the Scripps-Howard chain . . . proud of
the fact that it scorned those other newspapers . . . proud of the
fact that it paid its own journeymen reporters so much more
than union scale that they had forgotten what union scale was
(something most *PD* reporters could learn by merely glancing at
their paychecks). The *Press* was proud of its power, proud of its

skill, proud of its staff, proud of the fact that hundreds of people in town including scores of unendorsed and chastised politicians referred to the paper and its editor as "that goddam Louie Seltzer and that goddam *Cleveland Press*." The *Press* was a proud place and it was proud of its obituaries.

"We write them like little human interest stories," an assistant city editor explained the third day I worked there. "For some people, it's the only time they get a write-up in the newspaper. So write your obit like a story . . . they're all different because people are different. Except, of course, they all end the same way."

I was still on probation and determined to prove myself. The stiff I drew to eulogize was an old tailor who had lived (until the previous day) on Murray Hill. I telephoned his wife.

"Tell me something about your late husband, Madam," I said.

"I'm a tella you, all right," she said. "All hisa life he's a work his fingers to da bone. An what he's a got to show for it? Two no-good kids so rotten they never bother to come anna see him. He's a live his life for nutting. Nutting!"

I scribbled this all down and typed it into the death notice. Then I carried it through the clean, new city room and set it down softly next to Louie Clifford. Then I went back to my desk and peeked at Clifford. In about five minutes, he casually picked up the obituary and read it. His expression did not change (it rarely did, I was to learn) but he stiffened slightly. He peered over at me, crooked a finger and beckoned me to him.

"The thing is," he said, not unkindly, "that I believe this lady said this all right. I believe this is the way she feels now. But what people do with these obituaries is, they cut them out and save them. It isn't how this lady feels now that is important. It's how she is going to want to feel next month and next year. An obit is for memories and memories should be the way you want them to be."

My memories of the *Cleveland Press* are going to be the way I want them to be. The last look I got at the *Press*, I will not save. It was Monday of the week after the paper announced its close. I went back to the office to get my clips—walking up the back stairs past the cop that had been hired to make sure that none of us tried to steal "significant" company property like a printing press.

The shabby city room was almost empty. Taped on the glass partitions around the editors' cubicles were typewritten notes telling of available jobs:

"The *San Juan* (Puerto Rico) *Star* is looking for two general assignment reporters. Must speak Spanish and English."

Inside one of the cubicles, Dan Sabol, the managing editor, was hunched in his chair looking at his phone.

"I've been on this thing for two days trying to see what I could line up for people," he said.

"What do you think you're going to do, Dan?"

"I don't know," he said. "There's something in Austin, Texas. My wife says if we got to move, what's the difference if we move to Pittsburgh or Texas?"

(On my first week on the job, nearly 20 years ago, I had gone to lunch with Sabol in one of the Ninth Street restaurants that had been chased out when the office buildings began marching toward Louie Seltzer's *Press*. "I go in and ask for a raise every six months," Sabol had told me then. "Gee," I said. "Do you get one?" Sabol had smiled, "Usually," he said.)

Out in the city room, kids I didn't know—recent hirees—were getting their things out of their desks. They looked sad—they had lost jobs in a business where jobs are hard to get. But their faces did not reflect the stun and shock visible in the faces of the older staff members. The paper had been dying for years, but dying is not dead. A hundred-year-old oak tree in your back-yard can be dying . . . but it still stands like a tree and looks like a tree and you know that it stood there before your house did . . . long before you were born. Then one morning there is a crash and the tree is refuse . . . messy trash strewn around the yard. It is a mangled corpse of a tree and the *Press*, on the last day I saw it, was a mangled corpse of a newspaper. I put my clips in a box and walked out, past the cop. "You wanna see in here?" I said. "Naw," he said, half embarrassed.

And I went home to shape my memories.

Which are . . .

Learning how to get interviews at the first light of dawn from women who hours before had discovered they were widows; their husbands having been shot or stabbed or killed in auto accidents.

My teacher for this: Bus Bergen, winner of a carton of "Pall Mall Awards" on the old radio program "Big Story."

It was a Bergen technique, standing on the stoop, to apologize for intruding on the widow's grief, then pause, stare at her and say:

"Pardon me, but what was your maiden name?"

"Kmetz," the woman might say.

"Kmetz," Bergen would say. "You look awfully familiar to me. Where did you grow up?"

"Lee-Harvard," the widow might say, or "Miles and 131st" or "St. Clair and 105th."

To any of these responses, Bergen would reply, "Why, so did I. I thought you looked familiar." And curiosity (an emotion more powerful in women than in men) would take over and Bergen would be in the door.

To this technique, I added a refinement of my own. If a new widow offers you coffee or tea, always take it. If she doesn't offer, ask her for some. Get her doing something for you and the interview will go easier.

Memories of . . .

Winsor French, society columnist, who knew everyone in the world worth knowing. "Cleveland is absolutely desolate," French would write, "entirely everybody is in Europe this month." And Bill Rice, feature writer and rewrite man would read this and growl, "Goddammit, French. Everybody isn't in Europe! I'm not in Europe!"

Crippled by disease, French tooled around the office in a wheelchair to the arm of which was affixed a bicycle horn. He and the chair arrived at work each day in French's Rolls-Royce, piloted by a liveried chauffeur named Sam. When French died, we heard Sam got the Rolls. We didn't check it because we wanted it to be true. Memories are what you want them to be.

Memories of . . .

Julian Krawcheck who while writing his graceful column would munch copy paper. He was the only man I ever knew who literally ate the stuff and he only ate the cheap kind because the expensive kind had carbon paper in it which, I presume, spoils the taste. . . Jerry Horton, photographer, who taught me how to ring a doorbell. "Nobody home," I said to Horton one day as we stood on the stoop hoping for an interview. "The sonuvabitch doesn't want to talk to us," Horton said. "We'll just keep ringing it. Watch. We'll ring it for half a minute and stop. Now we'll ring it a couple seconds and stop. Now another half minute. Then a full minute. Then a second. Then two minutes. Then ten seconds. It'll drive him nuts and he'll give up and come to the door." He did.

Memories of . . .

Louie Clifford and Louie Clifford and Louie Clifford. Who taught me all the journalism I will ever need to know. Who gave me my first byline. Who assigned me my first series . . . a series on closed-chest heart massage. Whom I feared and loved. Who, after a little boy had been killed in a suburb, sent me day after day to talk with a certain neighbor woman he suspected had done the killing.

"What do I talk to her about?" I asked Clifford.

"Just talk to her," Clifford said.

So I talked to her. Every morning. About the weather. About the proper care of her front lawn. About the other children in the neighborhood . . .

Saturday I worked. Clifford didn't. I was hoping for a day of reprieve. There was a note in my typewriter. "Go see your lady. Clf."

We talked about the family of the dead boy. About the police. About all the questions the police had asked. And finally, one morning, she asked me if I thought she should tell police about the bullet hole in her kitchen.

"No," I said. And ran to tell Clifford.

He arranged to have her picked up that day but it was two more days before she confessed. The police were sweating her in an upper room of the police station and our final edition deadline was minutes away.

"You better have something to phone in to Clifford," said Doris O'Donnell, a crack *PD* reporter.

I set myself like a sprinter and dashed up the stairs and burst through the door of the interrogation room. Startled faces looked up at me. "Get him the f— out of here," a cop yelled. They hustled me down the stairs. At the bottom, I ran into Norman Mlachak. "Call Clifford," he said. I did.

"I can't find out anything," I said.

"Just listen," Clifford said. "Don't say anything. She confessed 20 minutes ago. We have it in the final." He had telephoned the interrogation room and talked to a cop who owed him a favor. He had scooped me from 10 miles away.

Louie Clifford. He called me into the paper's conference room and shut the door. "How would you like to go to Vietnam?" he asked. "I think I would," I said. "I know you would," he said. "I'd give my left nut to go."

That was in 1967. Fifteen years have passed and yet, since the *Press* died, I have found my memory changing tenses (as memories will) so that the past has the freshness of the present and the present seems as hard and stale as a bad roll at a dull banquet. I can see the city room of the *Press* on a summer day in the mid-sixties and in my mind's eye men now dead are resurrected and men now retired are hard at work.

Bob Stafford sits scowling at the rewrite desk, rolling a handmade cigarette and preparing to take a story from Bergen, Stafford settling in because he knows that Bergen will dictate the story with the length and dramatic flair of an episode of the "Hallmark Hall of Fame."

"Listen to this, Bob, " Bergen begins. "You've never heard a story like this in your life. There's this West Side father and son, see—Elmer Monroe, 45, of 677 West 67th Street, and son Dabney, 19—that's D-dog—A—B, boy—N, nellie—E, echo . . . "

On the copy desk, one of the copy editors is humming a tuneless song, which he will continue to hum during his entire shift. Another copy editor is asleep sitting up. He will nap on the rim for weeks until one Saturday a traitorous or perhaps envious colleague will detonate a firecracker beneath his chair and he will awaken to news he is fired.

"... Now get this, Kid. Elmer and Dabney rent a house from a landlord named Henry McCrea. I'm getting the address and spelling. Now they haven't paid their rent so McCrea has the lock changed on the front door while they are away. They come home and they can't get in so they get sore. So they go to this cousin's house and they get a couple of shotguns ... "

In the darkroom, a pinochle game is in progress. It has been in progress since the day the building opened and is only interrupted, and then grudgingly, when elderly couples are led into the studio to be photographed for the Golden Wedding column.

"... They go back to shoot the lock off but McCrea is inside the house with a .45-caliber pistol and he starts banging away at them. Well, they got their 1958 gray Chevrolet station wagon parked across the street and they crouch down, using it for cover, and begin to return the fire. Both of them are pretty good shots because they are experienced hunters, see?"

"How do you know that?" says Stafford, always suspicious of reporters.

"Hell, kid," says Bergen. "They're from West Virginia. That's all they do down there ... "

Ted Schneider, photographer, comes out of the darkroom and waves. Schneider and I recently shared an interesting adventure which, had Bergen been there to report it, would have become an epic saga.

We had been sent to Mannington, West Virginia, to cover a mining disaster and the city desk had telephoned requesting a photograph that would capture the tragic effect of the deaths on the small town. Schneider decided to climb to a cemetery overlooking the village and shoot his picture—with the little hamlet in the background and a tombstone in the foreground. He soon found the perfect spot but there was no tombstone nearby.

"Doggone," Schneider said.

"Let's move one," I said.

We searched until we found a medium-sized tombstone—

about the size of an attic shutter. Schneider got on one side and I on the other.

"Lift," I said. And, grunting, we began to move the stone toward the spot he had picked. "Jesus," Schneider said. "Here comes a guy with a gun."

A man was walking up the slope carrying a rifle.

"Put it down," I commanded. "Walk around the front of it, put your head down and mourn like hell."

We stood, heads bowed, expressing a sorrow that was totally genuine. The rifleman passed 40 yards away.

"Rabbit hunting," Schneider said. "Let's get this over with."

". . . Anyhow, kid," Bergen says. "Old Elmer and son Dabney are peppering away at the house. And inside the house, old McCrea is trying to get a shot at them, only he can't see around the station wagon. Bullets are flying back and forth across 67th Street. And then, that's when Dabney . . . after all, he's just a kid . . . he panics . . ."

"Hurry up," says Stafford. He has an eye on the clock because in these days the *Press* prints five different editions each day and Stafford is hoping to make the late home edition with this story.

"Boy!" he yells. And a young woman hurries over to take the first part of the Bergen story to the city desk so that it can be edited, a fresh page at a time, and hustled into print. Copy aides regardless of sex are called "boy" and will be for another year or so. What will end the practice will be protests, not from women but from blacks.

The copy girl drops the Bergen story on the city desk and scoops up a batch of edited copy and carries that to the horse-shoe-shaped copy desk where a group of copy editors sit around the rim looking like sour-faced Apostles who have been given a bad table at the Last Supper.

A second glance at one of the men sitting there is necessary. Even in this newsroom of nonconformists, he seems out of place. He is and he isn't. His name is Bob and he is a resident of a local mental hospital. For years . . . at least three days each week . . . he has reported to work at the *Press* as if he were on the payroll and sat with the copy editors (where it must be admitted he blends best) reading the newspaper. No one has ever asked Bob to leave. Patience wore thin during a period when he was conducting a romance with one of the women patients and would bring her with him from home . . . her dress buttons askew and her hair unkempt . . . to sit with him on his glorious perch. But the bloom of romance faded and now he comes alone. "You got to get away from that place where I live," he explained to Bill Dvorak one horribly stormy day when the two entered the *Press* building together. "You stay in that place where I live it will drive you crazy."

(I must break the mood of my summer days here and tell you that Bob kept coming to the paper until the day it folded. Now, like the rest of us, he has lost his shelter. Now, like the rest of us, he must look for another place that will have him. Now, like the rest of us, he must be starting to realize the difficulties of the quest.)

". . . OK," *Bergen tells Stafford. "You got the scene. McCrea shooting at the Monroes, father and son. Then the kid panics. He cracks under battlefield conditions. He jumps into the station wagon, starts the motor, and pulls away leaving Daddy standing in the middle of the street except not for long because McCrea picks him off so in a second he's lying there. "*

"Where is he now?" asks Stafford.

*"At the Morgue, " says Bergen. "Isn't that the greatest story you ever heard? Listen, kid, I think it's worth about a lead and three pages. "*

"Yeah," says Stafford and writes it in seven paragraphs and sends it over to Louie Clifford who is waiting with his copy pencil and who trims it to five.

Louie Clifford. He was the newspaper's field marshal. Louie Seltzer and Norman Shaw were the policy makers but it was Clifford who was in charge of changing policy into type. If the *Press* decided to make a certain man mayor of the city of Cleveland, Clifford would supervise stories that were calculated to make the voters lust for the candidate's leadership. He did this well but he was at his best with the BIG story. Or that story his instincts told him could be pumped up into the BIG Story. His editorial judgements on copy were as unquestioned as Moses' editorial judgement on the Ten Commandments. Clifford, though, would have trimmed them to seven. And led with the one about murder.

To some reporters, and I am one, he was an entire university. I studied under Clifford the way some composers studied under Beethoven. To a few unlucky reporters, young and not so young, he was a menace to career and self-esteem. One night, on my way out, I passed a newsman whose desk had been positioned far from Clifford's city desk.

"He doesn't like me," the reporter, a man of about 45, said. He was nearly in tears. "I don't know why," he said. "He won't even talk to me." In a few months, the man quit, never knowing just what sin he had committed. None of us knew.

But if, for reasons equally unfathomable, Clifford liked you, then life was a lark—filled with choice assignments and page one bylines. If you loved newspapering, the chances were that Clifford would be on your side. It was his life. "I hear the guild wants to increase the retirement benefits," he told me one day. "A GOOD newspaperman doesn't live long enough to retire."

Louie Clifford. He was on his way to Indiana on a vacation one Saturday morning and he stopped in the office. Five minutes after he left, the operator paged me.

"You're on my list as knowing heart massage," she said. "There's somebody out on Ninth Street who just passed out. I don't know who."

He was on his back sprawled across the seat of his car. The seat was too soft. I pulled him out on the pavement and pumped on his chest, trying to use what I had learned researching the series he had assigned me to write. "One chimpanzee, two chimpanzee," I recited, struggling to get the rhythm right. But I was crying too hard to say it. At the hospital I took the watch from his wrist and gave it to his wife. I got to him too late. He beat me to another deadline.

Years later I told it all to Mike Roberts. "You ought to write it," he said.

"I can't write it," I said. "It's a family story."

But the family is broken up now.

Some of them are dead, except they don't seem dead when you write about them. Clifford, Horton, Dick Maher, the politics writer, who would hold court every election night in the back room of Marie Schrieber's old Tavern Chop House on Chester. Other reporters would be staked out at campaign headquarters hoping to talk to the candidates. When Maher, after dining graciously, visited the headquarters, the candidates wanted to talk to HIM. In Chicago, in the summer of '68, Maher covered the politics in the convention hall; I covered the riots in the street. We would meet in a Loop restaurant after midnight to compare notes. I was a kid and he was a dean but he treated me as an equal. Dead now.

Herman Seid, photographer unflappable. One dawn he went out with Wally Guenther to interview a fracas victim. They got in the door, but the victim appeared at the top of the stairs—a white apparition wrapped in bandages. "Get out, get out, you bastards," he screamed, then tripped and tumbled down the stairs and landed in a heap at Seid's feet. "Does this mean I can't take a picture?" Seid asked. Herman is dead.

Paul Lilley, Forrest Allen, Jack Ballantine, Hilbert Black (who manned the city desk with a sweet disposition, a sour stomach and a package of Rolaids). These were men who were so good . . . so very good . . . that they could afford to have graces. Associate with them and you would learn about class while you were learning the peculiarities of your trade.

They were knights and Louie Seltzer was King Arthur. They called him "Mr. Cleveland." We didn't. They did. They, the mayors, the governor, the President. To us, he was Louie. He did not strut the office in regal splendor. He popped in and threw a string of firecrackers on the floor of the city room. He hit reporters in the belly. He bought our children presents at Christmas. He sat on the city desk and answered the phone (to the terror of young reporters calling in from fires who were hoping not to get Clifford, let alone Seltzer.)

He had two loves. His wife and his paper. When his wife was

dying, it was necessary to prepare a "10th ad"—a story about her life and accomplishments that would be set in type and ready to run when we had learned she had died. Late one Thanksgiving eve, Ray DeCrane, an assistant city editor, approached me. "Take a crack at Marian Seltzer's obit, will you?" he said. "Four guys have worked on it and we don't think it's right yet."

"Can I see a proof?" I said.

"I got one locked in my desk," DeCrane said. "We don't want Louie to see it. We're keeping the type stashed in the refrigerator where the printers keep their lunches." I didn't have to ask him why. I knew it wasn't because Seltzer was feared. It was because he was loved.

I am coming to the end of this story and I see that it is loaded with death. It is a story about the death of a paper, but in telling it, without meaning to, I have written mainly about men who have died and about our preoccupation with the coverage of death.

The wonderful people I worked with who have survived the paper—Bill Tanner, Bernie Noble, Paul Tepley, Milt Widder, Tony Tomsic, Bob August, scores of others—I have barely mentioned. They can speak for themselves. I have tried to speak for persons and a paper who lie mute.

I notice, too, to my dismay, that the truth of the *Cleveland Press*—all of it—is not captured in this obit. What is captured here, in part—in small part—is my truth. All of us have our own truth and those of us who are left will carry our own versions of the feel and history of the newspaper with us to our own graves. Each one of us will call his version the truth but none of us will have it all because you don't get it all. In journalism or in life.

The one common denominator for all of us is love. I understand something now that I never understood before. I have read that when a loved one dies, one of the many feelings the survivor feels is resentment. This always seemed strange to me before but now I understand why it is so.

I don't resent Joe Cole or the people who, at the last minute after it was too late, tried to save the *Press*. I am glad they tried, but the *Press* I loved is not the *Press* they ran. The *Press* I loved gave me adventure, identity, travel, pay, swagger, education, friendship, some measure of fame and fulfillment.

The resentment comes (as it must I now know in the death of anything truly loved) because of what it took from me.

It took nothing by force. It took nothing I would not have voluntarily given, if I had realized I was giving. It took a kind of love that I can never give to another paper because it's all used up. It took the resources of my youth including that willingness to sacrifice personal dignity for ambition and professional zeal. Any decent man can only offer that once and then he shouldn't.

And finally, it took a dream. My dream of working for . . . of belonging to such a company of heroes. It took my dream and gave it substance—gave it an address and a certain span of years and never warned me that when the address changed and the years were over, the dream would die with the paper.

Dream and paper both will now sink through the depths of the past until they finally come to rest to lie at the bottom of my soul—a vision of wavering outline, there but not there, real but unreal, visible but unreachable. Dead but haunting me.

# POSTSCRIPT

## A *bicentennial letter to Moses Cleaveland*

*This letter was published in the July 1996 issue of* Cleveland Magazine.

Gen. Moses Cleaveland Esq.
Attorney at law
c/o Canterbury Graveyard
Canterbury, Conn.

Dear Mose,

This is an awkward letter to write. But there's no sense beating around the bush. Where the hell are you?

You got off the boat at the foot of St. Clair on July 22, 1796. You shoved off again on Oct. 18. Since then, not even a postcard. This fall it will be 200 years since you left. Some of us are beginning to think you're not coming back. There's even talk that you were just in it for the money.

We've seen a copy of remarks you made at a stockholders' meeting of the Connecticut Land Company. I have to be honest and tell you that your speech didn't go over very well here. According to what we heard, this is what you said:

"While I was in New Connecticut I laid out a town on the bank of Lake Erie which was called by my name and I believe the child is now born who will live to see that place as large as Old Windham."

No wonder a lot of those pompous snobs on the East Coast still think we're a one-horse town. If you're going to go around comparing us to someplace else, couldn't you do better than

that? Has Old Windham got one of Elvis' second-hand suits in
a glass case for all the world to see? Was Old Windham in the
World Series last year? We grow more orange barrels here in six
blocks than all of Old Windham sprouts dandelions. This is
what comes from being out of touch. You better write or phone.
Enclosed find a Growth Association brochure for your assis-
tance in future invidious comparisons.

Besides, if you remember, the name Cleveland wasn't your
idea. You wanted to call the town Cuyahoga. We convinced you
that nobody would be able to pronounce it. The natives all say
"Cuya-HOG-a." Transplants and nomadic TV anchormen say
"Cuya-HO-ga." People in Old Windham and Baltimore and
other provincial places say "Cuy-YOU-ga." We persuaded you to
name the town Cleaveland, a name everybody can pronounce.
But, unfortunately, not everybody can spell.

Our mistake was letting Amos Spafford draw the map. Amos
dropped the first "a" from your name. He felt awful about it
afterward but the damage was done. Something good came of it
though. We give English proficiency tests here now. Most students still spell like Amos but at least we don't take spelling for
granted anymore.

Some people thought the reason you never came back was
because you were in a snit about the spelling of your name. So
we put a sin tax on snuff and chaw and set up a statue of you on
Public Square with your name spelled right on it. Still not a
word from you. Lately some of the boys have been talking about
raffling off naming rights to the city to pay for loges for the new
football stadium. You could probably nip that in the bud with a
visit. Even an e-mail message would help.

Speaking of stadiums, I have to tell you that we had some
trouble with the Indians but we survived it. Remember how, on
the way to founding us, you stopped off in Buffalo to make a deal
with the Mohawks? You promised them $500-a-year if they'd
agree to live-and-let-live and you threw in two beef cattle and a
hundred gallons of whiskey. Well, those Mohawks were honor-
able people and they kept their word. So that was all right.

But not long ago, a tribe of baseball Indians held us up for a ransom in tax money for a new ballpark. I ought to explain that playing games is a big business here now and we tax the rich and poor to pay for it. We built a stadium for people who play with little round balls and an arena for people who play with big round balls. This hurt the feelings of the people who like to kick warped, oval-shaped balls around and they mutinied and took off for Baltimore. We're all busy raising money to bring warped ball back. We'll even throw in a big chunk of lakefront land. I know this sounds nutty and a little confusing but I've explained it the best way I can. I figure maybe you'll get it since you went to Yale and became a lawyer which makes you an expert on confusion and money. And balls.

The trouble is that you've been gone so long it's pretty hard to bring you up to date on everything that's happened here. So let me mention something that I know you're interested in. Let me tell you about the thing that drew you here in the first place. Let me tell you about the River.

Remember how, on July Fourth, you stopped in Conneaut? That was the day you found the old, stone boundary marker for the Pennsylvania line and you walked west into the thick, dark forests of the Western Reserve. And when the birds were complaining against the darkness, you and the 50 men and women with you stopped and built a campfire and fired 15 musket shots in honor of America and one more in honor of New Connecticut. Then you broke open the whiskey and drank toasts to everyone you could think of and finally everybody drank a toast to you.

It was up to you to find the right place for a capital for New Connecticut. And, on an old map, farther down the lake shore, there was a river. Not much of a river. But, in those days, when there were no roads, a river didn't have to be much to impress people.

So you pushed along the lake looking for it. When you found it, your plan was to build a sawmill and a gristmill on its banks. That was your idea of big-deal industry back then. A sawmill to plane trees into lumber and a gristmill to grind flour for bread that would feed the men who felled the trees. And the river would be the conveyor belt. Whatever men could dream up to make with their hands and sell, the river would carry to the lake. And the lake would carry to the world.

George Washington knew about the river. Benjamin Franklin, they say, once pointed at a map of the Western Reserve and predicted the future site of a great American enterprise. The river was your quarry, your prize, your Grail.

But when you found it, it was a twisted, crook-backed little river, arthritic and linearly-challenged. That other Moses knew the Promised Land when he saw it. You saw a sandbar blocking the mouth of a contortion. And you weren't sure. The money of your investors was riding on your decision plus $32,600 of your own. "It is impossible to determine upon the place for a capital," you said, in a black hour of doubt. You pleaded for more time to explore. And then you drew a breath and let it out and said, "We'll do it here."

Why did you never come back? Because it wasn't love at first sight? We are used to that reaction here. This city has to grow on you. Did you leave still doubting your wisdom, cautiously daring only to dream an Old Windham-sized dream? Let me tell you what happened along the banks of that ugly little river.

After the gristmill and the sawmill came giant mills you can't imagine. Men clawed the earth and pulled up rocks and turned them to steel. Ships that made your boat look like a canoe groped their way down the crazy corridor of your river. They carried what we made here all over the world.

So the world got to know about us. And men and women from Europe and Russia said goodbye to their families forever and left all they had ever known and rode in the sunless, rolling cellars of great ocean ships to get here. They brought new languages, new music and new menus. They built churches and started newspapers. The air grew foul with factory smoke but to them it was the smell of freedom. The souvenirs of their youth were their old country songs and dances, coaxed to life on Saturday nights by an accordion or a fiddle. Their kids came home from school and taught them English. A great and savory stew of them poured down your river and climbed its banks and spread beyond the lines on the little map that Amos Spafford drew. Your river irrigated a delta of humanity 50 miles wide and still spreading. From the South, black people who broke their chains but couldn't break their poverty heard the faint hum of the factories and followed the sound, lured by rumors of an equality found in grime and sweat. Generations of newcomers choked your little river with prosperity and blighted it with greed and almost killed it. But just in time, they revived it again. And now its banks are a playground for the children of the children of the children of the people who followed you here. And when they climb the bluff like you did and walk into the Public Square, there you are—a statue of you on a round pedestal with your name spelled right. You're up there looking at it all, Mose, and what you see doesn't look much like New Connecticut. The town called by your name is changing still and we celebrate its past and wrestle with its present. But we can't see its future any better than you could. Old Windham! Ha!

When you didn't come back, we went looking for you.

Some people named Mr. and Mrs. Elroy Avery found you. They were Clevelanders who went on vacation to Canterbury, Conn., in 1899. They followed indifferent directions across a cornfield. They climbed a rough stone wall to reach an old burial ground. They followed a path through some weeds to a stone marker, its graven lettering obliterated by mud and slime. When they scraped the stone slab, they read this inscription:

"Gen. Moses Cleaveland. Died Nov. 16, 1806. Aged 52."

Ah, Mose, if you'd stayed here we'd have done better by you than that. We would have planted you in style. A president rests here in splendor. Oil millionaires, diplomats, inventors, politicians all sleep in well-tended graves. Seven years after your lonely stone was found, a delegation of Clevelanders paid for a proper memorial. The inscription in front of the Canterbury graveyard said:

"In this cemetery rests the remains of Moses Cleaveland, founder of the City of Cleveland. He was born in Canterbury January 29, 1754, and died there November 16, 1806. He was a lawyer, a soldier, a legislator and a leader of men."

There isn't much left in the earth beneath that stone now. This city is your remains. And in its Bicentennial Year, your restless spirit surely won't stay in Connecticut. Wherever you are, Mose, you're somewhere around here. Down in the Flats, maybe, lost in the crowd on the riverbank. Looking around 'til your eyes ache. Looking at what you started. Looking pleased with yourself.

Respectfully,

Dick Feagler
Writer